The Flux of History
and the Flux of Science

The Flux of History and the Flux of Science

Joseph Margolis

UNIVERSITY OF CALIFORNIA PRESS
Berkeley · Los Angeles · London

University of California Press
Berkeley and Los Angeles, California

University of California Press
London, England

Library of Congress Cataloging-in-Publication Data

Margolis, Joseph, 1924–
    The flux of history and the flux of science / Joseph Margolis.
       p.   cm.
    Includes bibliographical references (p.) and index.
    ISBN 0-520-08319-9 (alk. paper)
    1. Historicism.   2. Historiography.   I. Title.
D16.9.M276   1993
907′.2—dc20   93-4134
                                                                        CIP

Printed in the United States of America
1   2   3   4   5   6   7   8   9

nothing beyond humanity,
nothing but the scruple of its best part

Contents

Preface

This book is one of a pair: this one, on the theory of history; the other, on the theory of interpretation. Generously conceived, they represent between them a unified effort to redefine the conceptual foundations of the human sciences under three conditions: (1) the denial that reality is necessarily invariant; (2) the affirmation that thinking is inherently historicized; and (3) the admission that human selves are socially constituted. In my view, these three doctrines have become increasingly salient in our time and bid fair to be the dominant philosophical themes of the new century. They are hardly universally endorsed. On the contrary, their coherence, taken singly or as a triad, is very much in doubt. The first is the most ancient: it appears already among the Sophists and was explicitly resisted by Aristotle. The second belongs to the turn of thought anticipating and reflecting on the events of the French Revolution. The third is in a way the progeny of the union of the other two, possibly the most ubiquitous conceptual puzzle of the end of the century.

The conviction that these are indeed the most important and challenging themes of our time is itself widely contested and, intriguingly, even more widely ignored. Certainly, no one has as yet addressed them in a frontal way so as to demonstrate the viability of the human sciences systematically reinterpreted in their terms. I confess I've been hostage to the project for a long time. I am only now beginning to appreciate the plausibility and full power of the idea. What I have tried to do here is show how the theory of history has, ineluctably, come to favor the themes of the triad and what may be entailed in admitting its coherence and distinctive rigor. I have put the argument partly in terms of a chronicle of the history of the philosophy of science and partly as a chronicle of the history of the philosophy of history. But I believe that the argument could be easily matched by a similar review of any of the larger empirical disciplines one could name; and, in the companion volume mentioned, I attempt to do something of the sort for the theory of interpretation in the arts and history. The point is: the practices of history and interpretation have been relatively neglected in theorizing about the natural and human sciences—even where they are broached. I try to show why they cannot now be ignored and how they effect the meaning of objectivity in any would-be science. My own conviction will be entirely obvious. But, more than that, if I am right about the importance of the triad being featured, it would be fair to say that philosophy has taken a fateful turn. I see that turn as a golden dawn, but I'll say no more about it.

I cannot hope to thank all those with whom I've explored the issues of this study. But I must thank particularly the Greater Philadelphia Philosophy Consortium and Michael Krausz, its first director and my good friend, for having invited me to conduct a small institute during the summer of 1992, at Haverford College, on the topic "Realism and Social Constructivism"; I must thank, as well, the collaboration of other friends, Richard Shusterman, Tom Rockmore, Laurent Stern, and Peter McCormick, together with Michael Krausz, once again supported by the Consortium (and its current director, Brice Wachterhauser) and Temple University, for a day-long symposium on my work on the topic "Relativism and Interpretation," held at Temple during the Fall 1992. The participants in both of these events have helped me enormously, during the final editing of the history manuscript, to give the argument its best edge. Also, I count all the participants dear friends of mine.

I must single out the special labors of Raeshon Sykes, without whose patience and skill the manuscript might never have come together, and the encouragement of Ed Dimendberg of the University of California Press, a most admirable editor.

Prologue: Change and Invariance

I

Occasionally we step back from the ordinary flow of engaged life to consider what we mean by this or that notion. For instance, what, we ask, is history *really*? Surely history is distinctive of human affairs. Stop there! Does that signify that natural events such as the eruption of a volcano cannot rightly be said to have a history?

We are already in conceptually troubled waters. Is the fertilization of a human ovum or the biological growth of an embryo of *Homo sapiens sapiens* precluded from having (or being) a history? Is there an important question here, or is it more a matter of whether *we* take a narrative interest in the temporal span of particular events and processes no matter what they are? There's an inkling of the single most strategic option concerning the nature of history. Keep it in mind: it will haunt this account.

Certainly, human and natural affairs change, take place in time (as we so effortlessly say). But is mere change history? Or the mere record of change? And is the time of natural change the same as the time of human history? Or, if they are different, how can they be different, seeing that whatever has a history must undergo change, must persist through time, in the same sense in which time fits all natural events? We are tempted by the intuition that, whatever we now mean by history, things cannot have changed all that much since the ancient beginnings of philosophical reflection to justify or require a conception of history distinctly opposed to whatever may have been meant by history in the past. But that would be a great mistake. It is undoubtedly true that the ancients speculated about history and change and time, but they did so in accord with conceptual convictions quite unlike our own.[1] In fact, such differences may be a function of our changing history. Our theory of history may have to acknowledge that the theory of history—and history itself—have histories. The complications are beginning to swarm.

II

The pre-Socratic Greeks were distinctly fascinated by the problem of change. "All things come from water," says Thales at the beginning of our official record of Western philosophy. Parmenides, however, in the sternest of pronouncements, says, of What Is, you can only say that It Is; and of What Is Not, that It Is Not—meaning thereby, apparently, to deny the reality of change (since, as the jargon has it, change implicates "What Is Not," "Nonbeing")—that is, what is unsuited to discourse. Yet, the fragments that remain of his great poem confirm that Parmenides ventures a good deal about what (on the thesis) is not real at all—namely, change. And Heraclitus, possibly the most prophetic of the pre-Socratics in the way of anticipating the general line of thought that leads eventually to Aristotle's extraordinary vision of science, plainly compromises with those who insist on the reality of change (Thales, read metonymically) and with those who insist that reality is changeless (Parmenides, for a certainty).

Heraclitus holds that the changeable world (the one we perceive and act in) must be inherently subject to a changeless law of order (the *Logos* or the lesson of the *logos*), which is unaffected by change itself. On that view, we may suppose (thinking in a looser way than Parmenides), change is real enough, since it embodies or is governed by the changeless structures of What Is. We cannot be sure that that is Heraclitus's view, but it is certainly close to Aristotle's exemplary account of science in *Metaphysics*, Book Gamma. The whole of pre-Socratic thought may, in hindsight, be taken to be a sort of preparatory labor for Book Gamma (which is Aristotle's own view, as it turns out)—together, of course, with the more than casual contribution of the numerous alternative solutions invented by other gifted Greeks (not merely pre-Socratic), notably Plato, whom Heraclitus somewhat anticipates.

Where Plato is concerned, we can only map the plausible options of interpretation, because we cannot be entirely sure of Plato's intent in the deep ironies of the *Dialogues*. On the sternest reading, the Parmenidean, we may say that Plato disjoins the orders of Being and Nonbeing, the changeless and the changing, and constructs rather pretty stories (but only stories) to suggest a way of linking the "one" with the "other" (or the "many"). Plato may not have meant "his" doctrine literally. We cannot say for sure. Our own world favors Aristotle in this regard because the notion of an invariant world of separable eternal Forms (whatever that may be interpreted to mean) is a formidably expensive conjecture we believe we can do without—in fact, we believe we had better do without.

You will have noticed how our topic sidles, without warning, from history to reality. To theorize about history *is* to theorize about reality, even if only (with Parmenides) to deny that change is real. And yet, of course, it would be hopeless to attempt, in this small review of the question of history, to insert the entire stunning question of just what *is* real—and why. It will be enough to fasten on the matter of what to mean by treating histories as real—if only to oppose those who presume that they are not in the least real, unless in the pallid sense that *stories* (narratives, histories therefore) are real . . . *stories*. The issue is clear enough: we must ask ourselves whether we should admit that there *are* real "things" that have or are histories, which certain narratives (history in the reportorial sense) are *about*.

III

Whatever we make of the usual remark that Herodotus is the father of history, there can be little question that Thucydides is a splendid historian, a historian of a remarkably modern sort.[2] There is every sense, in reading Thucydides, that he intends his narrative to represent, to correspond to, the actual history, the narratizable events (as we might now say—tendentiously), that he was engaged in relating. It is impressive, for instance, how many lengthy speeches and conversations Thucydides reports. There is the great speech he attributes to Pericles, the funeral oration for the first of those who fell in the war against the Peloponnesians,[3] and the lengthy exchange between the Athenians and the spokesmen of the island of Melos just before the Athenians began the military campaign against the island.[4]

Now, direct citation would, of course, have obviated narrative at the point at which it appears. But Thucydides sets every speech in the context of a larger narrative in which the cited material is clearly intended to be

congruent with a fuller account that is accurate regarding what is narrated: the cited material is meant to conform with (and perhaps confirm)
the accuracy of the latter. Thucydides invariably gives the impression that
the accuracy of what appears to be quoted is in accord with the speaker's
intention at the time. So, for instance, when he gives the lengthy exchange
between Nicias and Alcibiades regarding the advisability of the Sicilian
campaign,[5] Thucydides remarks at the close of a comment of Nicias's
(who opposed the expedition): "These were the words of Nicias. He
meant either to deter the Athenians by bringing home to them the vastness
of the undertaking, or to provide as far as he could for the safety of the
expedition if he were compelled to proceed. The result disappointed
him."[6]

In short, Thucydides construes direct discourse as a narrative device,
guided by the spirit and intention of the speaker of his picture, possibly
roughly accurate in some of its wording, but surely more seriously
accurate in the way that belongs to his own purpose—which, we may
fairly say, is narrative accuracy—and often instruction. The scruple of
his entire work would make no sense unless Thucydides could not have
been put off by the inevitably contingent inaccuracies of his reports of
speeches just where he believes he *is* accurately reporting what took
place. He must have supposed he was reconstructing the speeches themselves—accurately. There is no way to read his history without supposing the events he represents narratively are, accurately, narratively
formed.

In this regard, there must be a measure of convergence between
Thucydides' plan for his history of the Peloponnesian War and Aristotle's comparison, in the *Poetics*, between poetry and history. In fact,
Aristotle offers a brief account in the *Poetics* that is expressly about
the kind of device Thucydides uses. "From what we have said," he
remarks,

> it will be seen that the poet's function is to describe, not the thing that has
> happened, but a kind of thing that might happen, i.e., what is possible as being
> probable or necessary. The distinction between historian and poet is not in
> the one writing prose and the other verse—you might put the work of
> Herodotus into verse, and it would still be a species of history; it consists really
> in this, that the one describes the thing that has been, and the other a kind
> of thing that might be. Hence poetry is somewhat more philosophic and of
> graver import than history, since its statements are of the nature rather of
> universals, whereas those of history are singulars. By a universal statement I
> mean one as to what such or such a kind of man will probably or necessarily
> say or do—which is the aim of poetry, though it affixes proper names to the

characters; by a singular statement, one as to what, say Alcibiades did or had done to him.[7]

It would be hard to hit on a more apt defense of Thucydides' practice. For what Aristotle says of history he could have said—and in a way does say—of ethical judgment. It is also, by the way, not important for the Greeks that poetry might be about fictional characters, whereas history concerns itself with actual persons and events. The Greeks may never have supposed that Agamemnon and Oedipus were merely fictional. But Aristotle's intent is clear: even mere stories may capture what is changeless or essential in human nature (in a practical and normative sense). That explains the persistent theme (in Aristotle and his followers) that poetry functions to convey a high instruction.[8] In fact, by this distinction alone, Aristotle sets the stage for a troublesome puzzle that has engaged a number of recent theories of history. For, although he does not himself develop such a theory, Aristotle does not rule out histories that strengthen their grip on the realist standing of what they claim by embellishing their chronicles with fictional or near-fictional approximations to what is "probably" essential to the life and nature of particular historical agents. This is what Thucydides' practice begins to make plausible. But in a world very much less sanguine about essentialism than was Aristotle, the idea of a realist history that openly invites the extended use of fictionalized narrative seems distinctly paradoxical.

We're meandering a little, but we've gained some ground. For one thing, if the Greeks (Aristotle and Thucydides in particular) thought of history as a diminished science concerned with the singular ephemera of human life in terms of what is possible or plausible for men of this or that recognizable kind—a cut, therefore, below poetry—history (for them) would still be addressed to what was invariant in human nature (and good, with respect to action, at least "for the most part"), though always only among the most local contingencies and only in accord with the precision the domain was able to support. For a second, for the Greeks, history could not possibly be mere change—for they discounted change as being of no intrinsic interest in itself: change is interesting when it draws our attention to certain significant invariances. It must attract a bona fide science; and only changes of a certain order could support a narrative history. Finally, only changes of the right kind, changes in human affairs that could attract a Thucydides, could yield a narrative interesting enough to invite questions about its accuracy. So the Greek conception would make no sense if there were no narratizable reality that historical narrative could accurately represent.

Hegel, in fact, has this to say about the Greek historians in opening his "popular" lectures on the philosophy of history:

> As to the first mode [of history: "original history," the kind that provides the data for the other more advanced modes of history he mentions—"reflexive history" and "philosophical history"—which includes his own effort], the mention of a few names should give a definite picture of what I mean. *Herodotus, Thucydides*, and their like belong to this class—that is, to the class of historians who have themselves witnessed, expressed, and lived through the deeds, events, and situations they describe, who have themselves participated in these events and in the spirit which informed them. They have compiled a written record of these deeds and events, thereby transferring what were previously mere extraneous happenings into the realm of intellectual representation. What was originally mere existence thereby takes on an intellectual aspect and becomes a representation of the internal and external faculties of mind.[9]

Hegel's remark that the "original" historians "share" the spirit of the age whose history they report signifies that the narratized structure of the events they consider belongs already to those events.

The Greek conception obliges us, then, to distinguish between mere change and the real thread of human history. It does so on the strenuous thesis that human affairs show an invariant structure of their own, one that answers to the strong requirements of science. *We*, on the other hand, necessarily plying our trade late in the twentieth century, are more than doubtful about essential human nature, the recovery of the Aristotelian notion of a science, the supposed laws of history (the Marxist laws, for instance),[10] and even the separability of the laws of nature and historical contingency.[11] Consequently, *we* cannot redeem a full-blown theory of history as easily as the Greeks, one that would admit, uncontroversially, real history and its accurate representation; or, if we claim such a theory, then, admitting those doubts, we are bound to construe it in a very different way. That's not to say: (1) that history and change are indistinguishable, or (2) that history is no more than a narrative, a pleasant fiction or heuristic device, concocted to represent a selected continuum of change in narrative form (judged from this or that point of view). But if history is more than either option pretends it to be, we need to explain just how the new possibility can be made out—why it matters and how it can be legitimated.

We need not subscribe to the Greek view, of course. But even the Greeks held different views of history and change: certainly Herodotus and Thucydides could not have agreed less in their practice; and Plato seems to have held—at any rate, he puts the thought in Socrates' mouth—that political history, transformation through time of the known political

constitutions, takes a generally cyclical (that is, invariant) form.[12] Plato
was keen enough about the kind of science Aristotle and Thucydides
favored. They share the common genus of Greek history, though Plato,
of course, offers a much more radical option than the other two. At its
most extreme, where radical change is completely ungrounded, utterly
lacking in invariance, history becomes (would be judged by the Greeks
to be) entirely meaningless: history could then not sustain the minimal
narrative structures apt for the formation of a good life. No science,
Aristotle remarks, is concerned with the particular merely.[13] Tragedy,
then, constitutes a paradigm for intelligible history.

That is surely Plato's lesson as well. From our present vantage, however, it involves a drastic choice, the entrenchment of the one and only
range of possibilities the classical figures were disposed to explore—with
the single exception, always, of Protagoras, whose works are completely
lost. For, in recovering history in the modern world, *we* can either forge
a link between change and changelessness, or claim that *there is a stable
order in change itself that is not invariant*, or else confess the world to
be an utter chaos. The first option is the one Plato and Aristotle and Thucydides share (in different ways); the surprise is that that vision dominates
the modern world as well. The third belongs to Parmenides, but eliminates
history (together with familiar nature) altogether. The second has no clear
place in canonical Greek thinking, though something like it plainly
tempted the Sophists.[14] The fact is that the entire history of Western
thought has, with regard to narrative history, science, rationality, understanding in general, traversed twenty-five hundred years of laborious
theory moving in a direction away from the first and third options and
distinctly toward the *second*. The former have never been abandoned,
however, and the second has never been convincingly worked out.

There you have the central puzzle of the theory of history. All the
intellectual currents of late twentieth-century thought deny or contest or
admit to be contestable every form of invariance. They also affirm the
coherence of a science addressed to, and infected by, radical change. But
what are the possibilities of history according to the second option? And
can the first still be recovered consistently with contemporary views of
change?

IV

The Greeks considered history, then. But even Thucydides, who has a
much more informal view of principles and causes than Aristotle, claims
that a grasp of history—an understanding of how it is that "Athens is
the school of Hellas"[15]—falls under a generous conception of science,

and requires a grasp of what is invariant or probable relative to what is invariant. Otherwise neither the example of Athens nor of *Oedipus Rex* would be thought paideutic. That is the plain sense of the opening sentence of Aristotle's *Nicomachean Ethics*, the link between practical reason and science: "Every art and every inquiry, and similarly, every action and pursuit, is thought to aim at some good; and for this reason the good has rightly been declared to be that at which all things aim."[16]

But we need to understand the connection between change and history—that is, in our own world, where we have largely abandoned the ancient forms of essentialism and where the most insistent recent philosophical efforts have sought to retire every strong conception of invariance. If human nature had an essential structure (as Aristotle preeminently affirms), then history could claim a measure of scientific rigor by bringing the ephemera of life into accord with the narratizable structures native to the species. It could not be a science (in whatever measure we might press) unless the generic human career inherently possessed, whatever its vagaries, a narrative form that governed the valid explanation and direction of all individual lives.

Deny that thesis and three intriguing alternatives spring into view: (1) narrative history is no more than a concocted story answering to certain extrinsic interests and imposed for that reason on the recorded changes of particular human lives; (2) history is no more than the orderly chronicle of selected actual changes; and (3) narratizable structures are validly attributed to real lives and social events in the absence of invariance. Notice that the first and second options are compatible with admitting real invariances. They are also particularly favored in modern theories of history. The third option offers a radical departure from the ancient and modern canons. It is in fact favored in certain salient views in the late years of our century. But there is no fully articulated philosophical account of what a reasonable and coherent history of this sort would be like. Views of the first two sorts may be convergently associated with the work of Carl Hempel, Karl Popper, Thomas Kuhn, and Arthur Danto; the most radical versions of the third are associated with Friedrich Nietzsche and Michel Foucault, and a more moderate version may be reasonably associated with the work of Hans-Georg Gadamer.

There is reason to believe the ancient canon is no longer compelling. There is also reason to doubt that the modern option regarding invariance is sufficiently robust: for it characteristically denies the possibility of an objective history of cultural processes or reduces historical objectivity to no more than what would serve a science addressed to physical nature "apart" from man. (We shall pursue the matter in good time.) But there is also some doubt as to whether theories of history of the third sort *can* be coherently formulated. Our own age seems determined to find the answer. If it proved coherent now—when it is particularly attractive to theorists of all sorts—we should have reversed the entire history of conceptual thought running from Thales to the very threshold of the next century. And we should have altered thereby the trend of the history of the theory of history. Philosophically, that would be a piece of enviable good fortune.

The larger theme that looms behind the link between change and history and change and invariance is the notion of the flux. The pre-Socratics are obsessed with it and ask how it can be conceptually tamed. Parmenides denies that it is real at all. Plato makes it "resemble" as best it can the invariance of the Forms that never change and have no causal role. His story (in *Timaeus*, for instance) requires a *deus ex machina*, the Demiurge. The flux has no form of its own. This seems to be Heraclitus's view as well. Aristotle, catching up the causal concerns of the pre-Socratics, indissolubly embeds the invariant structures that make the flux intelligible, orderly, amenable to discourse, efficacious, and real, *in* the *materia* of the flux itself. Parmenides' flux (if we may call it that) "Is Not." Plato's lacks inherent structure altogether; so it would be "Not" in Parmenides' sense, were it not for the fact that it *can* (somehow) be stably formed but never imprinted with invariance. Aristotle's flux (again, if we may speak thus) is nothing but what, in scientific retrospect, we specify as the "distributed" portions of a hypothetical, formless *materia* (*hyle*) capable of sustaining the ordered changes of particular things that are themselves (the changes, that is) governed by the invariant structures of those same individual things. Hence, at one stroke, Aristotle retires (in part) both Plato's Forms and Plato's flux. We, now, at the end of our millennium, are tinkering with a more daring option that was already glimpsed in the ancient world—and outside the Western world, of course—namely, that the world is a flux, but a flux in which the discernible structures of things and the power to discern such structures are themselves inconstant, inseparable from one another, and apt (by reflexive testimony at least and at most) for sustaining a science loyal to the flux—where Plato's and Aristotle's science is not.

The thread of the argument that follows is straightforward enough, but it leads through a baffling labyrinth. The labyrinth *is* the flux. We can only acknowledge it as the house of the argument that follows. But the thread is a question: how (we may ask), if thinking *is* inherently historicized, can we recover the objective history of historied things? There's a puzzle to conjure with.

We cannot turn at once to offer a plausible account of histories in accord with the third option. A proper ground must be laid. The matter rests with two considerations: to succeed, we must, first, dismantle (if we can) the entrenched conviction that reality is invariant in its essential properties and structure—the conviction that we already possess adequate evidence to the effect both that reality is invariant and that denying that produces intolerable paradox; and we must, second, demonstrate (if we can) that the discursive resources a narrative history would need—serving reference, predication, individuation, reidentification, and the like—could be coherently applied even as we strengthen the denial of invariance. The required argument is less concerned with the actual structure of a history of the third sort than with its conceptual credentials; ensuring those credentials would—will—channel our labors in the direction of a great many questions practicing historians are likely to find irrelevant to their own close work.

This is indeed our task. It will take some ingenuity and tact to gain its end. The presumption of invariance has been so massively entrenched in the entire span of Western thought that the very idea of opposing it, as well as the patient preparation of a viable alternative, may strike many as bordering on the bizarre. But if we concede that the resources of argument are not entirely settled beyond standard deductive arguments, then the plausibility of the labor may benefit from a sustained reflection on the foundations of Western philosophy. The very meaning of argumentative validity is at stake. For if the perceived rigor of philosophical argument rests on our perception (and interpretation) of how the world is structured, the "logic" that serves invariance and the "logic" that serves the flux may prove quite different—wherever arguments are "dialectical," "ampliative," "pragmatic," "nonmonotonic," "legitimative," "inductive," "abductive," or the like. The structure of valid reasoning and the structure of the intelligible world could not then be altogether independent of one another; and, where arguments are conceded to be inherently informal, our sense of rigor could not then be altogether independent of the discursive practices of our society. In that sense, argument and rhetoric are consensually linked and may be artifacts of history. Here, at the beginning of our tale, it is enough to broach the possibility. For, if thinking is itself a historically constituted competence, then the ineluctable question of the bearing of the nature of history on the logic of science and philosophy will be acknowledged.

ONE

Some Modern Views of Change and Invariance

I

Increasingly, since the French Revolution, the Western world has pursued a curious line of thought. It has persuaded itself that, in human affairs, there is genuine historical novelty—novelty that cannot be described or explained or assessed in terms that remain essentially unchanged (committed to strict invariance). The rise of capitalism and the formation of the bourgeoisie appear to be novel, genuinely unique in this sense, however continuous with earlier social structures. They are entirely sui generis, possibly not subsumable under covering laws. Nevertheless, this new sense of history is characteristically not permitted to challenge the prevailing assumption that, through it all, purely physical events remain subject to the invariant, exceptionless laws of nature.

The modern world has been endlessly juggling these apparently irreconcilable doctrines. For instance, if the second held firm, it would be reasonable to doubt that the first was reliably in touch with all that was real. Otherwise, their compatibility suggests a profound dualism between the *natural* and *geistlich* "worlds" (*not* a dualism between the body and the mind). Even more radically, the straightforward reality reported in the first suggests that the seeming invariances of the second may be mere illusions, idealizations, fictions, conveniences of some sort subject to special longings internal to the world of the first.

The most extraordinary anticipation of this puzzle (hardly its solution) appears in Vico's *New Science*, possibly the first genuinely large conception of history that we think of as spanning the French Revolution and its aftermath and what, in advance of those events, dawningly prepared the Western world for them. Vico discovered an ingenious way of integrating the endless transient novelty of the human world and the invariances he firmly believed a suitable science rationally required. He domesticated historical novelty by bringing it under the control of a higher invariance. In this, Vico means to correct Descartes's very large mistake. Descartes disjoins *res cogitans* and *res extensa* (and then of course rejoins them); but he believes the natural light of reason proceeds in precisely the same way in both domains. Vico disagrees. He believes that human reason is not adequately guided or governed in the "geometric" way suited to nature—in its own sphere: history. The reason is that man is a kind of mortal god in human affairs. He understands human history because he is its true "creator":

> But in the night of thick darkness [says Vico] enveloping the earliest antiquity, so remote from ourselves, there shines the eternal and never failing light of a truth beyond all question: that the world of civil society has certainly been made by men, and that its principles are therefore to be found within the modifications of our own human mind. Whoever reflects on this cannot but marvel that the philosophers should have bent all their energies to the study of the world of nature, which, since God made it, He alone knows; and that they should have neglected the study of the world of nations or civil world, which, since men made it, men could hope to know. This aberration was a consequence of that infirmity of the mind . . . by which, immersed and buried in the body, it naturally inclines to take notice of bodily things, and finds the effort to attend to itself too laborious; just as the bodily eye sees and finds all objects outside itself but needs a mirror to see itself.[1]

Vico adds almost at once that the science he speaks of, history, like the science of the created world of which it is a part, must accord with "the orders established therein by providence [which are] universal and eternal."[2] Hence, though what belongs to history may well be "hidden from men, [that is,] the future, or . . . hidden in them, their consciousness," history is precisely what they should seek to know and what they alone can discern.[3]

Appealing to divine providence, then, Vico is able to reconcile the transient novelty and the invariance of human affairs. If we understood the providential "orders" established in history as in nature, he says, "our Science" (history) would penetrate "the affairs of the nations" and grasp the inevitability that collects them—that is, that "the course of [those] affairs . . . had to be, must now be and will have to be such as our Science demonstrates, even if infinite worlds were produced from time to time through eternity."[4] The necessity of history is not a form of external or reductive determinism—one merely in accord with the laws of physical nature (or geometrical reasoning); it depends instead on the providentially assigned nature of the human species, though *what* human nature is is only dimly perceived through history's inventions. Sifting through all that, Vico imagines that his Science "comes to describe at the same time an ideal eternal history traversed in time by the history of every nation in its rise, progress, maturity, decline and fall."

In this, history

> proceeds exactly as does geometry, which, while it constructs out of its elements or contemplates the world of quantity, itself creates it, but with a reality greater in proportion to that of the orders having to do with human affairs, in which there are neither points, lines, surfaces, nor figures. And this very fact [adds Vico] is an argument, O reader, that these proofs are of a kind divine, and should give thee a divine pleasure; since in God knowledge and creation are one and the same thing.[5]

Man is at once the creator and the discerning scientist of the singular events of human history. But his inquiries must also accord with the higher invariances of *his own nature*, as with those of every pertinent order of nature similarly ordained. Universal history is the recovery of the inclusive significance of the narrative history of the entire race, however opaquely instantiated in the local events of this or that society.

What Vico dazzlingly demonstrates is this: if we find it impossible to explain the events of the human world solely in terms of the invariances of physical nature, or if we distinguish disjunctively between the categories by which we understand physical nature and "geometric reason" on the one hand and those suited for understanding history on the other, then unless we link *the invariances of human history* to the power of God, to a power outside the created world altogether, *we shall find it impossible to justify the claim that there are such invariances in history at all*. Q.E.D.

In short, the idea of the universal history of the world is a privileged "theological" device for ensuring the extension of something of the classical conception of science to human history. *If* Vico had only acknowledged, in addition to acknowledging man's having "created" his own world, that *human reason is also a historical "product" of some sort*, a competence *not* immutably ordered, he would have anticipated all the daring themes that emerged shortly thereafter in the theory of history ranging from Hegel to Marx to Nietzsche to Heidegger to Foucault at least. This is not yet to approve the claims of these later theorists: Vico would doubtless have found their theories quite alien. But if we are to understand the rise of the contemporary view of history, we must realize that Vico was tempted in a way he could not rightly fathom. He takes a giant step in the direction of the moderns, but he falls back to the thought and speech of the ancients. He grasps the constructed historical nature of the human world but not the equally constructed nature of human reason. So he rightly claims a discovery Descartes had failed to make; and yet, for all that, his theory sounds more alien to us than Descartes's. The novelty of his history hangs in the balance.

Still, Vico *is* an original. His premise is the *sine qua non* of historical understanding: human events—the political and economic and artistic and technological and scientific and theological and linguistic and mythic and narrative elements *of the real world* (of human society)—*are "originally" (and thereafter) produced by men* and, *being their work,* their "creation," *those events are intelligible only in terms that reflect man's own nature and history.* Vico harbors no fears on that score: he believes the contingent changes of human history instantiate the invariant nature of man, which, as with the ancients, embodies a changeless moral and practical wisdom: "let him who would transgress the rules of social life binding on all nations beware [he says] lest he transgress all humanity."[6]

II

There is a gain here. For one thing, Vico establishes the commonsense rule that human events must be understood in human terms. Mankind "creates" its own history and seeks to comprehend it. Second, if, as alleged, the human world is a real "world," as real as any, then history can be objective: it can accurately represent the narratizable structures of human events. Third, there is no decisive evidence for supposing that the model of science suited to physical nature and geometry is equal to the task history sets before us. Fourth, although in understanding history we understand ourselves, history's structure remains opaque to bare sensory perception and must be recovered by a deeper understanding, one that is critical of first appearances. Finally, the customs of all peoples can be understood by a gifted mind, since "though this world has been created in time and particular, the orders established therein by providence are universal and eternal." It is for this reason that Vico concludes:

"In one of its principal aspects, this Science must therefore be a rational civil theology of divine providence, which [as he claims] seems hitherto to have been lacking."[7]

What we may now draw from all this is quite important: namely, sixth (to continue our tally), a science of the invariant structure of human history must (consistent with our third finding) admit a form of privileged access to what is essential and changeless in human nature as such. In the circumstances, since human reason is historically formed "in time and particular," the presumption of a science of history (of the sort Vico contemplates) must depend on a disclosure of God's own plan (or of some suitable substitute). What is intriguing is not that Vico admits the point: he's quite comfortable with that. He regards it as the triumph of his labors. What is more instructive is that every modern thinker who concedes the first four findings and who would characterize the science of history as capable of discerning what is invariant in the explanation and/or assessment of (variable) human affairs must be something of a "theologian" of Vico's stripe.

That comes as a surprise. Hardly any contemporary theorist of history would admit it. If human affairs are cognitively opaque to ordinary experience—in the way of a strict science—then either there is some (Cartesian-like) privilege by which a gifted intelligence may find the pertinent invariances, or else any suitably trained intelligence may count on being guided by providential disclosures. Alternatively, *we* are bound to admit that all distinctly human aptitudes, including cognitive and practical powers, *are themselves artifacts of a changing history.*

Our strategy, then, is clear: all those who admit that history is initially opaque and marked by endless novelty, but still suppose that it may be grasped by the changeless powers of human reason, favor some form of cognitive privilege: they remove human understanding (called into play in a scientific history) from the contingencies of history itself. That is certainly the Enlightenment vision, whether the competence of reason be divided in Vico's way or not. Vico theorizes that the unforeseen contingencies of "time and particular" are ultimately subject to the changeless "orders of human affairs," which also form the distinctive powers of historical cognition. Vico associates this with "theology"; but others, Wilhelm von Humboldt for instance, confirm that that particular extravagance may not be necessary.

There is a deeper point in all this. For, even where the invariant powers of human intelligence are not assigned an explicitly "theological" role, the would-be improvement comes to the same thing. Once you admit that historical novelty is causally efficacious and intelligible, but *not*, as such, explicable in terms of the invariances of physical nature (or the formal sciences), the assurance that human nature *is* invariantly structured must come from a higher source. Otherwise, history will always keep the conclusion at bay. Alternatively put, the presumption of cognitive privilege with regard to history is a secularization of Vico's "theological" theme.

We may put the point still more provocatively: if the argument holds, then thinkers as recent as Noam Chomsky and Jürgen Habermas (however different their views) *are* "theologians" of Vico's sort, though they would deny it. Whether along Enlightenment or Kantian lines (Habermas's option) or those of the Cartesian vision (Chomsky's), so long as the supposed invariances of the human world are recovered solely from the contingencies of history, one would need a privileged theory of some sort to ensure: (1) that there are indeed genuine invariances that historical contingencies embody, and (2) that those invariances may be objectively discerned. That's why the mere methodological dualism of the *Naturwissenschaften* and the *Geisteswissenschaften* that preserves the invariances proper to both inevitably threatens to invoke a God—explicitly in Vico, implicitly in Humboldt and Chomsky and Habermas.[8]

Chomsky is very careful, for instance, to distinguish the inquiries of linguistics from those of physics: effectively, the methods of the two disciplines are utterly unlike one another. But the invariances Chomsky claims to have discovered, in attempting to explain the features of a historically evolving and variable practice, he then assigns to an invariant *biology*—which is to say, he is only apparently "Vichian" in his fieldwork. He never abandons his "Cartesian" view of explanation. At one and the same time, he effectively denies that man creates language, though its contingent forms are plainly the work of social history; he assigns its invariances to a natural order that geometric reason can once again recover. In this sense, at the price of an uncertain melding of the sciences of culture and nature, Chomsky escapes "theology." Habermas is more consistent in this respect and therefore more obviously vulnerable. He is more loyal to the strong disjunction between theoretical inquiries into nature and a reflexive inquiry into the structure of practical reason. Hence, his optimism about the invariances of reason discerned, in "the long run," *through* the vagaries of history, *is*, inescapably, "theological." (We shall return to the issue in another setting.)

But perhaps it would be helpful to say that *if* history forms and re-forms human thinking—if thinking *is* historicized (as Hegel and Marx and Nietzsche suppose)—then, to be consistent, we should also interpret the apparent invariances of mathematics in accord with that constraint. Two suggestions are in order here: first, a mathematics meant to be "applied" to the data of the natural sciences is already an inseparable part of the empirical theories of those same sciences[9]—not an autonomous formal discipline that may satisfactorily be applied in an external way; and, second, the invariances of the formal sciences thus "applied" are themselves perceived to be such relative to the historical limits of a conceptual imagination competent enough to generate effective explanatory theories.[10] Both notions may be reconciled with a consistent historicism.

More profoundly still, the dualism of the sciences infects the whole of modern speculations about the flux of history. (Collingwood, we may anticipate, will prove an instructive specimen.) But the fact remains: if the would-be invariances of the physical world are inadequate for historical understanding, and if the constructed human world is marked by a novelty that cannot be explained in terms of geometric reason, then a merely human assurance that the contingencies of history bespeak an essential invariance nonetheless is either an illusion or relies (in Vico's opinion) on an independent revelation.

III

The lesson we have sketched may be drawn from Humboldt's inquiries as well. At the start of his masterwork, Humboldt introduces the idea of a "universal history," "the cultural history of the human race," in the course of developing his account of the general structure of the sentences of all natural languages. What he says reminds us of Vico, though he avoids anything like a "rational civil theology":

> The distribution of human beings into races and tribes and the variation in their languages and dialects [says Humboldt] are certainly closely related, but both of these result primarily from the productivity of human intellectual power in all its forms. It is in the creation of human intellectual power that they find their recognition and their explanation to the extent that research is able to penetrate the relationship between them. This revelation of human intellectual power about the earth during the course of millennia, varying in type and degree, constitutes the ultimate goal of all intellectual activity; it is, moreover, the ultimate idea which the history of the world must clearly strive to produce.[11]

In the process of summarizing his work, Humboldt makes an extraordinarily prescient observation, one that exposes the hidden "theology" he somewhat shares with the champions of more recent universalisms. "All creation," he says, "does not proceed in the simple direction of the original power, but its course changes, being affected by what was created earlier."[12] What he means is that in history, causes are sequentially connected *in* the very mode of their effectiveness and intelligibility. The causal efficacy observed in singular cases is a function *of their changing history*; our nomic generalizations fall short of anticipated invariances, therefore. Humboldt adds: "One can trace these obstacles [to a universal history and science] to that intellectual power whose nature cannot be completely elucidated and whose effects preclude prediction. This power emerges with its own product and that of its environment, yet shapes and modifies the product and that of its environment according to its own inherent peculiarity."[13] He's put his finger on the deepest problem of history: that is, the problem of *its* own historicity. Humboldt's thesis is very close to the terms of "structuration" in the theories of such contemporary sociologists as Anthony Giddens and Pierre Bourdieu: there is a "structuring" power in the living practices of a society that "structures" the effective aptitudes of every nascent generation, which, exercised in its turn, "restructures" the structuring powers of that same society.[14]

In Humboldt's hands, causality in human affairs is inherently historical. It is radically different, therefore, from the merely physical. So, although he acknowledges a universal "intellectual power" (in the species) implicated in the varied history of that power, he also admits "its origin is as inexplicable as its effect is calculable."[15] Presumably, its effect *is* calculable by the method of comparative linguistics he favors. Yet even there—ominously for his presumed science—Humboldt concedes its insuperable contingency. Summarizing a good part of his own work, he remarks in his candid way: "To analyze the factor of sentence structure we have established, with the exception of Chinese which is devoid of all grammatical forms, three possible language patterns: the inflectional, the agglutinizing, and the incorporating. All languages bear one or more of these patterns of forms in themselves."[16]

We need not follow Humboldt in his judgment on the Chinese language; and we cannot fail to see that his would-be universal patterns are bound to be less and less secure as his inquiries become more and more specific: "Languages cannot contain the selfsame factor in themselves because the nations speaking them differ and have an experience that is determined by different situations."[17] Universality and invariance, wherever they are wanted, are "inferential," never observed; they are inferential on the assumption of an idealized vision that already takes the invariant for granted. (As we shall see, this is the essential nerve of Collingwood's account. It is also in a way the nerve of Chomsky's.)

Again—now almost addressing Noam Chomsky's most dubious theme—Humboldt observes: "Insofar as languages are simply formal, only uniformity should be able to originate in them through this [universal] linguistic sense. For this linguistic sense requires in all tongues a correct and principled structure, which cannot be other than one and the same for all languages. In reality, however, matters are otherwise owing partially to the individuality of the intimate meaning in the phenomenon."[18] By this, Humboldt intends: (1) that these would-be universal uniformities are merely conjectured *from* the perceived differences in natural languages (centered on the relationship between apt speakers and their particular historical societies); and (2) that the putatively invariant formal structure of sentences is abstracted, if justified at all, *from* the seemingly variable structures of language in actual use (a structure that is *not* otherwise separately, modularly, hierarchically, or in any other ordered way, discernible in natural languages). In fact, Humboldt openly admits that (3) the study of language does not actually require a universalism of the sort just mentioned: "language in its intricacy is but an effect of the national linguistic sense."[19] There's a dawning boldness here, easy enough to overlook. To be sure, it remains committed to causal and historical invariance, but it begins to risk the *necessity* of such invariance. In effect, Humboldt is testing the weakness of Vico's theory—and, more intriguingly, its doubtful recovery in late twentieth-century thought. (In our own time, as already suggested, Chomsky has coopted the *inquiries* that seem initially Vichian, by way of a deeper economy committed to a Cartesian view of *reason*. Hence, history drops out of the Chomskyan analysis of language.)

In effect, Humboldt adopts the freest possible approach to Enlightenment "theology"; he believes in the essential (indeed, the "innate") invariance of human intelligence all right;[20] but, however that may be explained, the historical development of language (which, he says, "designates man as such") "is not [the development] of an instinct which could be simply explained physiologically."[21]

Here, one finds all the ingredients of Vico's account—except that Vico claims to discern *in* the diverse contingencies of human history all the universal elements of history itself, whereas Humboldt makes a mystery of the would-be invariances of his own science. He shows us a way of loosening (without abandoning) the grip of the Enlightenment conception of science; in doing that, he begins to shape the notion of history as a deviant science addressed to specifically human affairs. He is well on his way to abandoning "theology"—that is, the assumption of necessary invariances—although opposing the accepted mode of science was hardly Humboldt's purpose. In fact, in his well-known essay on history, Humboldt, seemingly beginning with something close to Aristotle's comparison between poetry and history, manages to extract a higher creative "individualism"—in language, mankind, nations, individual events—that cannot be captured by the "mechanical" laws of nature and that history is especially concerned to represent correctly. Humboldt's point is that the grasp of the "free" and inventive import of transient events marks the high distinction of the historian's calling. The historian constructs our sense of the significance of such events, by way of analogy with past histories. It is, Humboldt believes, reasonable to see in this both the "peculiar form" of historically creative phenomena and the "ideal" universality of mankind's unpredictable evolution.[22] The grip of this romantic notion on Humboldt's thought disallows his yielding in the direction of a nomologically closed, exceptionless linguistics. Language itself is inherently historicized.

IV

Now, the conceptual puzzle that Vico's and Humboldt's theories implicate, which spans the outlook of the last half of the eighteenth and the first half of the nineteenth centuries, has rankled in the imagination of our own century as well. This is not to say that Vico's or Humboldt's work explicitly sets our puzzle. Far from it. Still, on the reading given, a question can be seen to haunt their sort of theorizing—that *they* cannot satisfactorily answer and *we* feel compelled to answer. Vico "answers" by appealing to providential orders—an odd reminder of Descartes's equally curious "solution" to his own worry regarding the intrusions of the Evil Demon. Humboldt is frank to say he has no answer: moreover, he claims not to rely on exceptionless invariances. He works instead by analogy, extracting whatever common linguistic structures he can find; but these need never, he concedes, actually prove exceptionless. In this, he is *not* a forerunner of theorists like Noam Chomsky or Charles Sanders Peirce or Karl Popper—theorists who, in various ingenious ways, ultimately recover invariance from apparent contingency. On the contrary, Humboldt *retreats* from the strong Enlightenment interpretation of the classical conception of science. He retreats but he does not abandon the canon, and he does not strike out in an explicitly opposed way. His concern is not far from a late twentieth-century puzzle—one, say, that worries the potential need to invent a new model of science which could accommodate history and the historicizing of the physical sciences and which could coherently abandon the standard insistence on the world's invariances and the competence of science to discern them. Humboldt does not broach the possibility, but he sees the canon's presumption. Vico's shadow is longer than Humboldt's, but Humboldt's is more fashionable.

The difficulty may be put this way. If (1) history is a canonical science, then, presumably, it searches out whatever is changeless in its proper domain. But if (2) history is "autonomous," not bound by the model of explanation suited to the physical or biological or mathematical sciences, then what, granting the deep novelty of human life, can its sui generis method be? Most of the strong answers given in the twentieth century favor neither Vico's sanguine disjunction between history and physics nor Humboldt's incipient acceptance of something less than strict invariance in the cultural sphere. The latter theme (invariance in the whole of reality) is, of course, the option preferred by the advocates of the unity of science, whether by inductivist or falsificationist means. There is, moreover, one broadly Vichian strand of theorizing that still commands respect in our late age. In the English-language literature, it is undoubtedly R. G. Collingwood's distinction to have fixed its characteristic form. Collingwood's theory is often regarded as the English counterpart of Benedetto Croce's earlier recovery of the Vichian themes; also, in the Anglo-American philosophy of history, the famous quarrel between Carl Hempel and William Dray (which now seems dated) is also pegged to the viability of a Vichian-like option, though Vico himself is usually neglected in its recovery.[23]

Collingwood *is* a Vichian of sorts, although he replaces the appeal to "providential orders" with a model of rationality specifically suited to an autonomous science of history. He naturalizes Vico. He holds that a rigorous history is not possible except in accord with such a model. His only caveat supposes that idiosyncratic patterns of life and thought cannot by themselves support a genuine history—in the sense that a rigorous history must be grounded in the invariances of human reason. It needs to be said that Collingwood usually opposes "history" to "science," since the method of history is utterly unlike the method of the physical sciences.[24] But he does suppose that there *is* a rational method, a science, suited to history, sui generis, and entirely capable of capturing what is invariant in human thought. In that regard, he means to recover what, in Vico, is meant to constitute a scientific history.[25]

The point to bear in mind is that theorists as diverse as Vico, Humboldt, Collingwood, Hempel, Popper, and Habermas, though they are all committed to the invariances of human nature or human reason, are committed to them in very different ways. Vico and Collingwood, for instance, treat human reason as directly capable of discerning the invariant structures of human history. Humboldt assumes a universal structure but does not invoke it in his inductions regarding linguistic regularities. He also does not consider the meaning of the historical status of his own reflections. Hempel (as we shall see) does not really discuss the invariances of reason; but his assumption that the nomological invariances of physical nature are scientifically accessible entails the other. Hempel can afford to discount history because, for one thing, he inclines toward a strong version of reductive physicalism and, for another, he inclines toward a very straightforward form of scientific realism. The result is, history has no distinctive domain at all—neither methodologically nor metaphysically. (We shall review these issues more closely.)

Popper is remarkably sanguine about a progressive approximation to the real invariances of nature—presumably because of the constancy of reason—though he opposes essentialism (the presumption of an ultimate invariant "layer" of reality). Habermas plays a very curious double role because, at one and the same time, he believes historical inquiry can progressively approximate to the universal invariances of reason *and* because he believes that *reason, however much historicized, can still detect such progress.* We shall return to these strenuous options: they are certainly important. But, for the moment, it will suit us merely to link these earlier and more recent reflections as conceptual kin.[26]

The marvelous thing about Collingwood's theory (in *The Idea of History*)—a heroic account, by all odds—is that it is plainly cockeyed. It is certainly a little crazy in its insistence on the conditions it requires and the lengths to which it goes in offsetting every reasonable doubt about its plausibility. How, otherwise, one can imagine Collingwood protesting, could *we* understand, say, how *Humboldt* supposed *he* had correctly grasped the branching patterns of the natural languages he claimed to identify? The question is certainly the right one to pose—perhaps even the most strategic question for that context. But *our* failing to answer it in *our* way (if we fail) is hardly an endorsement of Collingwood's theory. Collingwood's theory (as we shall see) collapses of its own weight. For the moment, we need say only (by a sort of super-erogatory gossip) that the question just posed (or its generic version) remains unsatisfactorily answered down to our own time. It is certainly unsatisfactorily answered by Collingwood.

V

All right, so much for scaffolding.

In drawing on Collingwood's text, we must remember that the present composition of *The Idea of History* is largely the editorial labor of T. M. Knox made about ten years after Collingwood had (in 1936) partially drafted what he regarded as his principal work. His death intervened, and Knox has been entirely frank about the difficulty of deciding what to include and what not. In any case, the following short passages are more or less definitive of the theory we have, though there is abundant evidence that Collingwood favored other lines of speculation not alto-gether congruent with what we have here, and what we have here is baffling and ultimately unsatisfactory.

He says:

Of everything other than thought, there can be no history.

But there is another condition without which a thing cannot become the object of historical knowledge. The gulf between the historian and his object must be bridged, as I have said, from both ends. The object must be of such a kind that it can revive itself in the historian's mind; the historian's mind must be such as to offer a home for that revival.

Historical knowledge then has for its proper object thought: not things thought about, but the act of thinking itself. This principle has served us to distinguish history from natural science on the one hand, as the study of a given or objective world distinct from the act of thinking it, and on the other from psychology as the study of immediate experience, sensation, and feeling, which, though the activity of a mind, is not the activity of thinking.[27]

"The peculiarity of thought," says Collingwood, "is that it is not mere consciousness." What distinguishes "thought from mere consciousness is its power of recognizing the activity of the self as a single activity persisting through the diversity of its own acts."[28] The theme is plainly Vichian.

Collingwood had an excellent grasp of the central questions; but his answers were hardly proper answers. We shall pursue them down to their dreary dead ends. Their life lies entirely in their failure. The muddles are inescapable, but they teach us what to avoid. Collingwood is remakably persistent in turning up all the worries connected with the presumed competence of historical reason. *That* is his very large contribution. He never answers his own worries, because, for one thing, he simply assumes there is no alternative to the invariance of reason; for another, he never demonstrates that the doctrine is conceptually necessary; and, for a third, he never shows us just how it functions in historical understanding—beyond his mere say-so. So the failure of his thesis is genuinely massive, but it is not altogether total.

Collingwood claims that, just as an agent is able to "recognize" reflexively the "self's" identity through an act of thinking, so too the historian, bridging "the gulf of time," is able to recognize the identity of another active "self" of the past and can establish thereby the required connection between his own self and that other self sufficient for recovering an objective history. There's a great leap here. We lack the full picture (from Collingwood) of the supposed connection, but we may glean a sense of what it must supply.

Difficulties crowd in, of course—for instance, regarding the discerning of past selves, the grounds for knowing that one has rightly "recognized" a "self" from the past, the very idea of recovering an "act of thinking" somehow completed in the past. Collingwood's explanation is unabashedly idealist; so it invents (in that spirit) doctrines that would embarrass the belief under the most favorable circumstances. In any case, as knowledgeable commentators have remarked, Collingwood never treats these puzzles in a methodological way.

Consider, now, two constraints that Collingwood admits—one that he concedes, the other that he positively insists on:

> It is conceivable that different races of mankind, and for that matter different human beings, have had different ways of remembering or perceiving; and it is possible that these differences were sometimes due, not to physiological differences (such as the undeveloped color-sense which has been ascribed, on very dubious grounds, to the Greeks), but to different habits of thought. But if there are ways of perceiving which for such reasons have prevailed here and there in the past, and are not practiced by ourselves, we cannot reconstruct the history of them because we cannot re-enact the appropriate experiences at will; and that is because the habits of thought to which they are due . . . cannot be revived.[29]

The "thought" of other peoples and other times is said to have a history, though we may be unable to recover or reconstruct it; furthermore, it may not be true at all (it is not conceptually necessary) that particular "habits of thought" *be*, in whole or part, *of* any invariant sort;

and again, *we* should be unable to distinguish between genuine histories and fictive reconstructions unless we could legitimately claim to know that we share or do not share the "habits of thought" of those whose history we mean to reconstruct.

Collingwood does not show that we could never construct a valid history if we did not share, or did not know we shared, certain pertinent "habits of thought." Nor does he show that we do share, or know that we share, the "habits of thought" of any alien societies—or, for that matter, how we should ever tell the difference between a society or age that was alien and one that was not.

We may as well add a further worry here: Collingwood's idealism leads him to deny that there could ever be a history of, say, Michelangelo's *Pietà* apart from the history of Michelangelo's "thinking" involved in creating the *Pietà* (which, on the thesis, precedes chipping at the actual marble); or, for that matter, a history of World War II as distinct from the history of the "thinking" and "planning" of particular agents in the war. The argument, dubious enough in its own right, is buttressed by a related assumption drawn from Collingwood's notorious theory of art,[30] that, almost by its perverse refusal to admit any difference between the "actual" artwork (the marble *Pietà*) and the "thinking" (that is, Michelangelo's idealized thought) that produced it, invites us to pursue the advantage of just such distinctions. Notice that *Annaliste*-like histories would be precluded at a stroke by the unsecured presumption Collingwood's idealism entrenches.[31] *Annaliste* theories of history may be naive, but *Annaliste* histories are surely imposing and entitled to a better inning.

To return to the larger issue: what would it take to know whether or not we shared the same habits of mind with the ancient Egyptians or the prehistoric Lascaux peoples or the recent Nazis or contemporary Martians? Anyone familiar with the Japanese *noh* drama knows how impossible it is to say whether we definitely share the same habits of thought with the composers of the *noh*. And anyone familiar with West African masks knows that we simply assimilate and interpret their designs in accord with our own notions of their significance (even when we "recover" *their* conceptions).

The "objectivity" of interpreting an alien people is a matter entirely *internal to our own practices of objectivity*. We may adjust those practices where needed; but even the perception of discrepancy is internal to the ongoing practice. We never establish that we share the same habits of mind, *if* the test requires an altogether independent assessment of the supposed correspondence; apart from the interpretive effort itself, the issue is utterly vacuous. We cannot possibly discern such a correspondence. We cannot exit from our own language.

Or, if, more modestly, we ask (with Thomas Nagel) "what it would be like to be a bat," the answer returns: only humans know what that's like—bats certainly do not.[32] We know *that*, and *we* know why we say *that*, other people do not share our habits of thought. The question cannot arise in a way that would disallow this fresh possibility. There is no other possibility! If we interpret the thinking (that is, if we "re-enact the appropriate experiences") of others, then, trivially, we will have "shared" the same habits of mind; and whether (nontrivially) we have shared the same habits of mind can never be an independent question, a question independent of what *we* take to be adequate to establishing the validity of *our* histories and our interpretations of *them*.

A powerful finding lurks here. It's this: we have no independent way of contrasting "our" conceptual schemes and "theirs": they are "both" internal to "our" scheme—which is to say, *a scheme we cannot demarcate* but vacuously presume we inhabit. (This is Wittgenstein's point about the meaning of the image of the relationship between the eye and the world. But its admission subverts the entire structure of the *Tractatus*.)[33] Put less picturequely: the distinction never functions criterially except as an artifact of the encompassing schema we presuppose but cannot fathom.

To anticipate: this is the convergent theme of late twentieth-century thinking that, in its strongest form, refuses to distinguish between intra- and intersocietal (or linguistic) conceptual divergences. It appears, for instance, in remarkably different ways, in the pragmatism of W. V. Quine and the hermeneutics of Hans-Georg Gadamer and the genealogy of Michel Foucault.[34] But it circumvents completely the ineluctably self-defeating or question-begging maneuvers of Collingwood's idealism. We are still at Collingwood's level in the dispute, but we can already see what must be overcome. It *is* overcome in later inquiries, but we have still to arrange the full passage from the one to the other.

Now, Collingwood does admit

> there can be a history of warfare. In a general way, the intentions of a military commander are easy to understand. If he took an army into a certain country and engaged its forces, we can see that he meant to defeat it, and from the recorded account of his acts we can reconstruct in our own minds the plan of campaign which he tried to carry out. Once more, this depends on the assumption that his acts were done on purpose. If they were not, there can

be no history of them; if they were done on a purpose we cannot fathom, then we at least cannot reconstruct their history.[35]

But, surely, such "effects" and such "recorded accounts" enable us to reconstruct the history of events even where the agents' acts are *not* "done on purpose" in the strong sense Collingwood favors. For, *in* reconstructing that history, *we* "reconstruct" the agent's thought: there is no independent access to it, the "thought" is internal to the artifact that is the history. We do not assure ourselves that we have caught the agent's actual thinking (by some presumed recovery of the independent, invariant pattern of reason that "must" have formed it) and, in doing that, thereby justify the claim that we have recovered the history. Even the "failure" of an action, even the failure to have planned one's action, is interpreted as such on a model of rationality that refuses (or is unable) to discern any principled disjunction between what is suitable for an objective history and what is not.[36]

This may seem a poor quibble, until we remind ourselves of just how narrowly Collingwood means his own words to be taken. He expressly says that the historian "is only concerned with those events which are the outward expressions of thoughts, and is only concerned with them insofar as they express thoughts. At bottom, [he adds,] he is concerned with thoughts alone; with their outward expression in events he is concerned only by the way, in so far as these reveal to him the thoughts of which he is in search."[37] He baits us here for the sake of his idealism. But he confirms neither its necessity nor its viability.

VI

We have, let it be said, simplified Collingwood's argument a little. Look at it again. Collingwood might have meant: (1) that a genuinely objective history rests on the invariant structures of human thought ("acts" of thinking) discernible in the ephemera of actual life; believing that, he would have sought to isolate what was genuinely changeless *in* particular histories. Nevertheless, he might have believed: (2) that the historian's "scientific" reasoning imposes true invariances *on* the interpretation (or re-enactment) of past ephemera; believing that, he would have sought the ideal fit between the apparent thinking of past agents and what an objective history requires. These are very different notions: one is explicitly realist and the other, explicitly idealist; and though neither is cast in methodological terms, their differences would alter the meaning of an objective history. Collingwood does not rightly subscribe to either option. But, then, perhaps, the human world is a flux and human reason, a product of historical change. Collingwood makes no effort to explore this further possibility, namely, (3) that the acts of past agents may be validly interpreted despite the fact that human reason lacks an invariant nature. (He opposes this possibility.)

Collingwood (also) denies that there are invariant structures in the flux of history. That is, he denies it in the sense in which Greek realism and modern positivism would affirm it. He himself affirms it in a sense akin to Hegel's and Croce's taste:[38] first, because (having Hegel and Croce explicitly in mind) he affirms that "the real is the rational"; second, because he holds that "history is the coincidence of logical with temporal order." He goes on to explain: "the successive events of history form an order which, so far as it is genuinely historical (not all chronological sequences of events in human life are so), is a logical order as well as a temporal one. If it is temporal but not logical, the sequence is not historical but merely chronological—it is what Croce calls annals, or a mere series of events."[39] He equates "the principle of history" and "the thesis that reality may be found in the flux."[40] In short, he claims that the narrative structure of human history is a structure that, though it unfolds in time, manifests a real necessity in its evolution. So he construes the reality of history as a "drama, the unfolding of a plot in which each situation leads necessarily to the next."[41] Still, there is no sense in which Collingwood favors a world-historical teleology. He is no Hegelian in that sense. Also, *what* he means by the "necessity" of history, what is disclosed by "re-enactment," remains entirely obscure. Is there a better clue?

Try another strand of the argument. It offers a glimmer of a gain. Have patience. "Without some knowledge of himself [says Collingwood], [man's] knowledge of other things is imperfect. For to know something without knowing that one knows it is only a half-knowing, and to know that one knows is to know oneself . . . a condition without which no other knowledge can be critically justified and securely based." Such knowledge is "a knowledge of his knowing faculties, his thought or understanding or reason," not a "knowledge of man's bodily nature, his anatomy and physiology; nor even a knowledge of his mind, so far as that consists of feeling, sensation, and emotion."[42]

Collingwood is searching for something well beyond the classical Greek notion of science (the fixed Forms of intelligible things) as well as beyond the early modern, the seventeenth- and eighteenth-century, notion of science (the straightforward application of the invariant laws of nature): "in human affairs, as historical research has clearly demonstrated by the eighteenth century, there is [he says] no . . . fixed repertory of specific forms . . . the city-state itself [for instance] is as transitory a thing as Miletus or Sybaris. It is not an eternal ideal, it was merely the political ideal of the ancient Greeks."[43] Similarly, "just as history is not the same thing as change, it is not the same thing as 'timefulness,' whether that means evolution or an existence which takes time."[44]

But what of the positive theory? Try this:

> For history, the object to be discovered is not the mere event [event of nature, event of human action], but the thought expressed in it [hence, the thought that is the "inside" of suitable events—human acts]. To discover that thought is already to understand it. After the historian has ascertained the facts, there is no further process of inquiring into their causes. When he knows what happened, he already knows why it happened. . . . When an historian asks "Why did Brutus stab Caesar?" he means "What did Brutus think, which made him decide to stab Caesar?" The cause of the event, for him, means the thought in the mind of the person by whose agency the event came about: and this is not something other than the event. It is the inside of the event itself.[45]

This *is* Collingwood's notion. But what does it mean? We cannot flag now. We must go on. It must surely be captured by the following formula: "The history of thought, and therefore all history, is the re-enactment of past thought in the historian's own mind." But it also traces a great impenetrable circle back to the stubborn mystery of "re-enactment"; thus:

> The historian not only re-enacts past thought, he re-enacts it in the context of his own knowledge and therefore, in re-enacting it, criticizes it, forms his own judgement of its value, corrects whatever errors he can discern in it. This criticism of the thought whose history he traces is not someting secondary to tracing the history of it. It is an indispensible condition of the historical knowledge itself. Nothing could be a completer error concerning the history of thought than to suppose that the historian as such merely ascertains "what so-and-so thought," leaving it to some one else to decide "whether it was true." All thinking is critical thinking; the thought which re-enacts past thoughts, therefore, criticizes them in re-enacting them.[46]

Part of the notion's attraction lies in what it precludes. It denies in the most radical way all cognitive privilege to authority, to testimony, to documents. Thus, the historian, examining an emperor's edict in the context of the Theodosian Code, "must go through the process which the emperor went through in deciding on this particular course . . . and only insofar as he does this has he any historical knowledge, as distinct from a merely philological knowledge, of the meaning of the edict."[47] The result is that historical knowledge is profoundly "subjective": *it is knowledge of another's mind, and it is rightly achieved only in the historian's mind.*

Still, the impolite worry continues to nag: the mind of the "other" is historically formed, after all, by the same society that produces the opaque documents and testimony that Collingwood would penetrate; and the mind of the understanding historian is similarly formed by similar forces specifically different from those that formed the other's.[48] Collingwood does not hold that the reasoning of any past agent lies in some Platonic heaven waiting to be plucked by a talented historian. We have already established that much. The *historian* provides the "universal" pattern insofar as he "re-enacts" a past agent's thinking. The pattern *"is nowhere" until* it is re-enacted, *and* it may be re-enacted *in different ways* (given the open-ended flux of history). Collingwood is therefore no cartoon Hegelian.[49] He also hardly resembles Gadamer, with whom he has been so often compared. We may never know how to classify him. We hardly understand him at all. He is almost a counterinstance to his own doctrine. *We* cannot "re-enact" *his* thought! Certainly what he says cannot be easily reconciled with Gadamer's sense of the historical flux:

> Since the only way in which the historian can discern [the thoughts that are the "inside" of an event] is by re-thinking them for himself, there is [a] sense, and one very important to the historian, in which they are not in time at all. If the discovery of Pythagoras concerning the square on the hypotenuse is a thought which we to-day can think for ourselves, a thought that constitutes a permanent addition to mathmatical knowledge, the discovery of Augustus, that a monarchy could be grafted upon the Republican constitution of Rome by developing the implications of *proconsulare imperium* and *tribunica potestas*, is equally a thought which the student of Roman history can think for himself, a permanent addition to political ideas. If Mr. [Alfred] Whitehead is justified is calling the right-angled triangle an eternal object, the same phrase is applicable to the Roman constitution and the Augustian modification of it. This is an eternal object because it can be apprehended by historical thought at any time: time makes no difference to it in this respect, just as it makes no difference to the triangle. The peculiarity which makes it historical is not the fact of its happening in time, but the fact of its becoming known to us by our re-thinking the same thought which created the situation we are investigating, and thus coming to understand that situation.[50]

Apparently, we think the same thought that was thought—by ourselves or by another; and we can do so because every *such* thought is an "eternal object": "all knowledge of mind is historical";[51] "the so-called science of human nature or the human mind resolves itself into history."[52]

But this won't do at all. For one thing, any thinkable thought is, on the argument, an "eternal" object, even if we, for reasons of historical limitation, cannot think what others have thought. For example, can it rightly be supposed that the Neanderthaler could, in real-time terms, *have thought* the "thought" of quantum physics? Collingwood's curious doctrine does not help us there. For another, even if all rational agents "could" think any "thought" at any time ("time makes no difference"), *how* should we ever know that we had genuinely formed the right "thought" (of a given thought)? Would it ever make sense to say we were mistaken? And even if there were some sort of rational reconstruction to be had—suitable for "correcting" and "criticizing" another's thought—why should that ever disallow the possibility (1) that if there were one plausible reconstruction, there might be indefinitely many others incompatible with one another, or (2) that rationality was itself a historical product, so that the re-enactment of historical reasoning could not fail to be relativized to one's own (historical) horizon?[53]

There's no answer in Collingwood. Or, there's none that we can fathom. Collingwood deepens the sense of our question so as defeat "the very idea of a science of human nature" (that is, the idea of an autonomous science committed to changeless laws *in history*).[54] He also anticipates the entire theme of post-Heideggerian hermeneutics: "The historical process," he says, "is itself a process of thought, and it exists only insofar as the minds which are parts of it know themselves for parts of it. . . . History does not presuppose mind; it is the life of mind itself, which is not mind except so far as it both lives in historical process and knows itself as so living."[55] This draws him a little closer to Gadamer all right. But we have already seen that he cannot be read as that sort of hermeneut. Thus far, he remains an utter mystery.

VII

We must go a little further. We must satisfy the scruple of the hunt. The analogy so often drawn between Collingwood's and Gadamer's "hermeneutic" theories is misleading. (Of course, we have not yet prepared the ground for a proper comparison.) Collingwood's doctrine of re-enactment is not, as many have supposed, a methodological thesis.[56] Any potential disanalogy drawn along these lines may be rendered harmless. But that hardly touches the adverse fact that, contrary to Gadamer's thesis, Collingwood insists on the *necessity* of a particular past's matching a particular present: past and present appear (in Collingwood's theory) to be determinately individuated, crisply discerned, objectively linked, despite the flux of history; whereas Gadamer's doctrine of the "fusion of horizons" has no use at all for the determinate fixity of the historical present *or* the necessity of its being linked to a particular past. It is difficult to imagine a greater contrast between converging views of historical interpretation.

It's true that Collingwood repudiates every attempt to make the "science" of history conform with the "world of abstract universals":

> The things about which the historian reasons are not abstract but concrete, not universal but individual, not indifferent to space and time but having a where and a when of their own, though the where need not be here and the when cannot be now. History, therefore, cannot be made to square with theories according to which the object of knowledge is abstract and changeless, a logical entity towards which the mind may take up various attitudes.[57]

It's also true that Collingwood comes very close to "something" akin to Gadamer's *Horizontverschmelzung*:

> Because the historical past, unlike the natural past, is a living past, kept alive by the act of historical thinking itself, the historical change from one way of thinking to another is not the death of the first, but its survival integrated in a new context involving the development and criticism of its own ideas.[58]

But the polite analogy founders.

For one thing, in Collingwood's view, "every present has a past of its own, and any imaginative reconstruction of the past aims at reconstructing the past of this present, the present in which the act of imagination is going on, as here and now perceived."[59] It seems, therefore, that there *is* a recoverable past for every particular *present*. Admittedly, Collingwood holds that the historical present changes with continuing life, and so *its* re-enactable past must change as well. Still, *its* particular past, *every* such past, is, somehow, necessary to *that* (its) present. Its "Gadamerian" feature (the "past's" being "present" in the "present") is not meant to disturb that. What is changeless is the power of thought or reason to grasp what is the necessary re-enactable past for this or that specific historical present—where every such present is bound to the historical constancies of a particular society's life.[60] Gadamer (as we shall see) would never agree to that; and Collingwood never indicates how to "re-enact" such a past "scientifically."

For Collingwood, a historical past is a concrete, vital, changing, effective past. The historian captures its changing presence, its presence as change. Presumably, this is partly because of its effect in the processes of history that link it eventually to the formation of the historian's own thought. But also, *it can* be captured, though it is not fixed and though the historian's thought is not fixed, and though the two are historically different. Somehow, the latter is empowered (at least sometimes) to fathom the former.

It's quite true, also, that Collingwood construes "metaphysics" as the analysis or recovery of the "absolute presuppositions" of historically divergent peoples or of the changing phases in the life of a particular people. That is, Collingwood believed that "absolute presuppositions change"[61]—where we are to understand, by "absolute presupposition," that horizonal limit within the terms of which scientific questions are validly answered (may be assigned truth-values), but which is itself *not* a proposition that can rightly be said to take truth-values at all. Facts and truth, therefore, are relativized (it seems) to our absolute presuppositions; and (it also seems) *they* can be fathomed from different historical locations. For instance, we can see, by suitable analysis, that Newton, Kant, and Einstein worked with different absolute presuppositions regarding what a cause is.[62]

This suggests how Collingwood's view may be interpreted as anticipating themes in Gadamer and Foucault; but it hardly explains how metaphysics actually works, or why we are able to understand the presuppositions of other times (or of our own time), or how thinking and reason can change in any deep sense, or what ultimately accounts for historical truth. It is clear, however, that Collingwood is hospitable to the historical diversity and change of conceptual schemes.[63] In this respect, he departs from the Kantian themes he seems at times to favor; for Kant, of course, however tempted by empirical history, resists the idea that reason has an intrinsically historical structure.[64]

Collingwood's ultimate solution lies with what he calls "*a priori* imagination." The "imaginary" that historical reason can recover "is neither unreal nor real." *It is ideal.* What it seeks in history, as in fiction, is "a necessity internal" to the characters or the events supposed: "we cannot but imagine [he says] what cannot but be there."[65] It is the same with perceptual imagination, he claims—that is, imagining "the underside of this table, the inside of an unopened egg, the back of the moon"— except that "its special task is to imagine the past, to offer a picture [that] is meant to be true."[66] (The analogy is a poor one.) We may suppose that its mode of functioning has some affinity with Husserl's method, but we are never introduced to its actual process.

We have arrived at a stalemate, finally. But even that is a sort of resolution. It identifies what is insuperable for theories of history—and, therefore, where we must turn away from fruitless options. We can do no more than report Collingwood's claims. He offers no defense at all, and none can be imagined that does not entail the innate[67] hermetic power of human reason. There's the mystery. There is no counterargument to mount. Collingwood offers no argument to rebut. He's stretched the doctrine of invariant reason to its vanishing point. In doing that, he raises all the essential questions, but he utterly disables the power of reason to answer them.

He also ventures a weak analogy. He speaks of "the resemblance between the historian and the novelist" (having Aristotle in mind):[68]

> Each aims at making his picture a coherent whole, where every character and every situation is so bound up with the rest that this character in this situation cannot but act in this way, and we cannot imagine him as acting otherwise . . . nothing is admissible in either except what is necessary, and the judge of this necessity is in both cases the imagination.[69]

The mind has no other course, he says, but to function thus.[70] Just so. And yet, there *is* no way a historian could reliably reconstruct, *from* another's present, the unique or necessary past of *that* other's present: "historical thought is a river into which none can step twice—even a single historian, working at a single subject for a certain length of time, finds when he tries to reopen an old question that the question has changed." Is this a contradiction? In reconstructing history, we must consider "a second dimension of historical thought, the history of history."[71] But that now means that Collingwood's talk of "necessity" must be no more than a form of rhetoric—akin to the sense of right fit appropriate to drama.

There may be an argument here. Collingwood does not mean to trivialize history. *He* insists on the constancies of collective life. *He* opposes "caprice": "it is not enough," he says, "that science should be autonomous or creative, it must also be cogent or objective; it must impress itself as inevitable on anyone who is able and willing to consider the grounds upon which it is based, and to think for himself what the conclusions are to which they point."[72] He means that discerning what is "inevitable," what is "imaginatively *a priori*," belongs to one's own historical society. *Necessity is itself a historical artifact.* There can be no other reading. Not every caprice can masquerade as a necessity. But "necessity" is entailed in the sense of the structure of one's own historical world. It cannot be all that different from what, more deeply, Michel Foucault has labeled the "historical *a priori*."[73] But it never risks the thick public preconditions of Foucault's risk. It implicitly rejects them: the historian's task, says Collingwood, requires "the repetition by one mind of another's act of thought: not one like it (that would be the copy-theory of knowledge with a vengeance) but the act itself." "I am considering [Collingwood says] how history, as the knowledge of past thought (acts of thought) is possible; and I am only concerned to show that it is impossible except on the view that to know another's act of thought involves repeating it for oneself."[74] "The re-enactment of past thought is not [he adds] a pre-condition of historical knowledge, but an integral element in it";[75] "it is not only the object of thought that somehow stands outside time [ideally, or rationally]; the act of thought does so too: in this sense at least, namely, that one and the same act of thought may endure through a lapse of time and revive after a time when it has been in abeyance."[76]

There you have an inkling of the difference between Collingwood and Gadamer—as well as of the unfathomed mystery of the first. We dare not turn to Gadamer's theory without a fresh beginning. We have, however, the evidence, in Collingwood, of the full "theological" trust we discerned in Vico. We have more in fact: we have a sense of its utterly unacceptable extravagance. That, we must pretend, surely, vindicates our labor.

TWO

The Unity of Science Conception of History

I

Collingwood's idealism secures two advantages for the theory of history, however doubtful the argument on which they are made to rest: in the first place, it shows how natural it is to suppose that the historian's story corresponds to what, concerning the past, is already structured in story-like ways; in the second, it marks the plausibility of supposing that histories are rightly thought capable of being true about the world. The first, Collingwood believes, depends on the historical effectivity of actual "acts" of thinking; the second he interprets as leading us to see that, whatever the vagaries of history, there must be an essential rational aptitude in the species capable of recovering all infraspecies-wide forms of thought that happen to obtain in different histories. The re-enactment theory is an attenuated version of what, transcendentally, makes objective history "possible." There is little in Collingwood's papers to mark him as a full-blooded Kantian, but the "necessity" of which he invariably speaks is clearly meant in (some version of) the transcendental sense of the term.[1]

One is tempted to think Collingwood *is* a sort of Kantian about history, but it is not clear *what* "sort" he is. He tolerates some historical change in thought and reason, which Kant cannot allow.[2] But his skill in keeping the supposedly invariant structures of the natural and mathematico-logical world from bleeding into the radical provisionality of history subverts his own insistence on the necessary invariances of re-

enactive reason. For how could he have hoped to show that his attenuated "Kantian" notion was true? Only one option recommends itself:
he would have had to show that any departure from his re-enactive
model was necessarily incoherent, inconsistent, self-contradictory, self-
defeating, or insolubly paradoxical. He never supplies the argument.
No one ever has. Hence, to say he is some sort of Kantian is already
too sanguine. He has a penchant for the transcendental, but it is not
at all clear that it is, or could be, Kant's version. What he seems to
favor instead is some sort of a priori imagination that is not discernibly
bound by any structural invariances of human thought in the Kantian
way.

Now, the problem posed cuts very deep. What is at stake is nothing
less than the issue of whether there is, or must be, a structure of human
thinking that *is* "timeless," transhistorically constant, essential and necessary for rational thought, but *not* simply empirically keyed to any part
of the great body of the general commonalities of social life: kinship
relations, for instance, the perception of colors and shapes, the use of
tools, the possession of a language. These generalities, "indicative universals" (as we may call them), are philosophically neutral—entirely
benign—in the plain sense that it is *they* that *invite* (but hardly resolve)
the transcendental (second-order) question Collingwood poses.

The question insinuates itself everywhere. If, for instance, there were
pertinently invariant structures in the physical world, and if the world
of human history were rightly governed and guided by such invariances,
we should have to concede a very strong reason for believing that
rationality must also be invariant. There is no knockdown argument
here, but the notion is surely what Vico and Aristotle have in common.
(It softens the harshness of our previous charge against Vico.) But what
are its conceptual credentials? And what, we may as well ask, does it
establish regarding history?

Collingwood is emphatic on the matter: "The laws of nature have
always been the same," he says, "and what is against nature now was
against nature two thousand years ago; but the historical as distinct from
the natural conditions of man's life differ so much at different times that
no argument from analogy will hold."[3] Still, if, in the Kantian way (or,
better, in the contemporary post-Kantian way that still adheres to the
symbiosis of world and word but not to its putatively necessary constraints), the intelligible structure of the world is inseparable from the
"constituting" structure of actual human thought, then the would-be
invariances of nature cannot be more secure than those of history;

although, in practice, the one plainly supports prediction more reliably than the other.

Collingwood is prepared to say—really to insist—that "a positive science of mind will, no doubt, be able to establish uniformities and recurrences, but it can have no guarantee that the laws it establishes will hold good beyond the historical period from which its facts are drawn."[4] Yet, once we admit the historicizing of the natural sciences, as in Thomas Kuhn's influential view,[5] or (less explicitly) as in Bas van Fraassen's repudiation of nomic universals,[6] there is every reason to believe that what's good for the one is good for the other. Perhaps, then, there is "no guarantee" that, in the physical sciences—even in the formal sciences (logic and mathematics)—"the laws [they establish] will [always and everywhere] hold good." The human "mind" may continue to play its constituting role (if it may be assigned such a role at all), but it would be able to play that role only in a variable, profoundly contingent way—that is, from age to age—hopefully without conceptual disaster. Something akin to Collingwood's concessions about the provisional "laws" of history may then infect the entire order of nature. (It is not what Collingwood favors.) Is that conceivable? Is it likely to be true? These questions have been asked before, rather fiercely by Nietzsche for one. But they are more insistent now: they have the advantage of the drift of a full century of accumulating arguments and doubts.

II

The tendency to historicize physics and geometry and logic has always been resisted, of course. But historicism in science is now no longer a sign of conceptual illiteracy. It has its notable adherents. Still, even where the ubiquity of history is conceded—that is, at least the absence of assured fixity—it is often championed in paradoxical ways. After all, Collingwood himself insists on the invariant laws of (physical) nature. He cannot avoid the troubling question, therefore, of the full relationship between the natural and human worlds. For, if those worlds belong to one encompassing reality, then (one may suppose) either the invariances of physical nature must govern human affairs, or else the absence of strict invariance in the human world is bound to affect the logic of physical phenomena as well. The Kantian theme alone is intractably insistent. Collingwood would have it both ways and he cannot—at least not without an argument. In fact, a great many recent theorists known for their own views of history and inclined to favor something strongly resembling Collingwood's orientation—Gadamer, Habermas, Paul Ricoeur, Charles Taylor—similarly arrive at a duality regarding the *Naturwissenschaften* and the *Geisteswissenschaften*, and have done so with hardly more of a rationale than Collingwood's.

There are, however, those who insist on historicizing the inquiries of physics as well as of sociology and who, having done that, still mean to recover—in principle and through history—the ahistorical invariances of the laws of physical nature. The best-known exemplar among them is, of course, Thomas Kuhn. But there can be little doubt that other well-known theorists who would not agree with Kuhn about science or physical reality have, by other means, tackled the same task: Karl Popper, Imre Lakatos, Hilary Putnam, and (perhaps most imaginatively) that remarkable American genius, Charles Sanders Peirce.

The weakness of the first group may be termed *dualism*—for they never explain the duality of flux and invariance in the same world; that of the second may be termed *progressivism*—for they simply snatch the "true" invariances of the world, progressively, from within the flux itself, without so much as a by-your-leave. The two frailties are alternative versions of the same disorder: a bemused puzzlement about how to reconcile change and invariance under the condition of radicalizing human history. That question may be the single most important philosophical issue of our late century—very possibly of the century to come as well. It infects all our thought, but it is not even acknowledged as a conceptual puzzle in many of the goodly mansions of the scholarly world.

The scene before us has suddenly become quite complicated. The possibilities being hinted at are distinctly heterodox when viewed through the eyes of the unity of science movement. The unity vision has, of course, exerted a magisterial influence in our century down to the beginning of the 1970s. It is still immensely attractive to philosophers of science even as we approach the end of the century. Indeed, it may be said that the prestige of the unity movement—in physics and the formal sciences—has, until very recently, pretty well obliged all that "weaker" race of thinkers (the *geisteswissenschaftlicher* tribe, of course, who might otherwise be quite summarily judged to have been befuddled by history) to make the required obeisance to the settled "rules" of Science. Their usual solution has been to favor the "dualism" or "progressivism" we tagged a moment ago. But even that exertion may not always prove adequate. One certainly finds the theme formulaically intoned by theorists like Taylor and Ricoeur: it recalls Dilthey's vision respectfully of

course, but that alone can hardly protect them from the heartfelt contempt of the champions of the unity movement.[7] Gossip aside, the unity
champions have had their own share of difficulty in resolving the puzzle.

III

Consider Carl Hempel's justly famous paper on general laws in history.
First published in 1942, it quickly became a magnet for "informed"
philosophical discussions of the right relationship between the human
and natural sciences. It would still be true today, but for the fact that the
unity program has suffered its own reverses. The perceived need to
reconcile one's view of the human sciences with Hempel's model is
decidedly less compelling (even for "unity" loyalists) than it once was.

It is easy to be misled by the pretensions of the unity movement, but
we cannot afford to mount a wholesale challenge to its program here.
The better strategy lies with a certain indirection; the pertinent argument
rests more with what we may call its *modal* tenor than with its apparent
plausibility. Hempel himself provides the telltale clue:

> It is a rather widely held opinion [he says, opening the argument] that history,
> in contradistinction to the so-called physical sciences, is concerned with the
> description of particular events of the past rather than with the search for
> general laws which might govern those events. As a characterization of the
> type of problem in which some historians are mainly interested, this view
> probably cannot be denied; as a statement of the theoretical function of
> general laws in scientific historical research, it is certainly unacceptable. The
> following considerations are an attempt to substantiate this point by showing
> in some detail that general laws have quite analogous functions in history and
> in the natural sciences, that they form an indispensable instrument of his-
> torical research, and that they even constitute the common basis of various
> procedures which are often considered as characteristic of the social in con-
> tradistinction to the natural sciences.[8]

The operative word is "indispensable," that is, "necessary," "*sine qua
non*." Hempel has before his mind's eye the example of Maurice Mandelbaum, who apparently favors the "causal analysis" of singular historical events as opposed to the full "causal explanation" of such events
under scientific laws.[9] Mandelbaum is a curious counterexample, since
he never actually resists the thesis that causal connections fall under
universal laws; he "only" means to hold that such causal laws are not
also "covering" laws—in the context of history—in the plain sense that

they do not figure in *historical explanations*. He may well have been ill-advised to have pressed the desperate disjunction he does (which is not to say he is wrong about the difference between explanatory models of history and physics). But he holds a much weaker position than Collingwood (in one sense) and a stronger one (in another). That is, Mandelbaum is no "dualist" of the sort we identified a moment ago. Hence, Hempel's argument against Mandelbaum might well be irrelevant against the deeper duality—but for the modal intent with which he argues. He says for instance (against Mandelbaum): "every 'causal explanation' is an 'explanation by scientific laws'; for *in no other way* than by reference to empirical laws can the assertion of a causal connection between events be scientifically substantiated":[10] the expression "no other way" is meant in effect to disallow Collingwood's and Humboldt's kind of claim—as well as Mandelbaum's—because (on Hempel's argument) so-called *historical causes* cannot be rightly subsumed under the universal laws of physical nature. So the contest is joined.

There is some slippage here, however. Hempel is not careless, but he is too quick. First of all, there is all the difference in the world between a theory of causes and a theory of causal explanation. For, even if (invoking the modal term), we conceded that causes *necessarily* fall under causal laws, it would not follow that causal *explanation* (including historical explanation) necessarily invokes causal laws *as* covering laws. That would be a non sequitur, not merely because even if we were ignorant of the causal law a particular event fell under we could still explain the event satisfactorily, but also because we might reasonably deny that the right explanatory model in science (or history) *necessarily* makes reference to exceptionless covering laws. (It might well be impossible in the practice of the human sciences.) There is an obvious lacuna in the argument. Hempel concedes the first option when he introduces the notion of an "explanation sketch": "a more or less vague indication of the laws and initial conditions considered as relevant, [that] need 'filling out' in order to turn into a full-fledged explanation."[11] But he emphatically opposes the second, since, on the unity theory, covering laws just *are* necessary to every causal explanation, regardless of the nature of the events in question; also, such laws just *are* exceptionless universals. Still, Hempel never actually demonstrates that scientific explanations must or can always have this particular logical feature. *No one ever has.* For instance, no one has ever shown that causality entails nomologicality or a nomologicality rightly captured by strictly exceptionless universal regularities. In a sense, it is an entirely unearned advantage. In another sense, it may simply be a serious mistake.

IV

Collingwood's argument affirms that historical causes may support provisional empirical regularities but *not* "invariant laws," because the "historical past . . . is a living past" (though it harbors causes), because the causal regularities any would-be human science (of the "positivist" sort) might find could not be shown to be necessarily invariant in principle (or an approximation of some invariance), and because historical causes concern "the thought in the mind of the person by whose agency the event came about" (which "is not something other than the event [but] the inside of the event itself"). So Hempel may be flatly wrong—on conceptual grounds, not on the grounds of mere consistency with his own unity model—in holding that "in no other way than by reference to empirical laws can the assertion of causal connection between events be scientifically substantiated." (I am not, of course, endorsing Collingwood's argument here.)

There is a difficulty, to be sure, that dogs the use of the notion of "cause." Clearly, the unity conception does not fit Collingwood's sense of history, and Collingwood's notion of the "inside" of an event would require a conception of causality different from the unity conception. It is worth remarking that there *is* no single settled notion of causality suitable for the physical sciences, and there is none suited to both the physical and the human sciences or to the human sciences taken by themselves. Every account of what a cause is is, effectively, a theory of how to model causes in this or that sector of the real world: change the picture of the world and you risk changing the picture of the nature of a cause. There is no viable sense of causality that is not semantically affected by our theory of the processes of the real world.

The point is not adequately recognized by the likes of Hume and Kant; but it is obviously perceived in Hegelian and Marxist accounts of history as well as in recent views of the physical sciences.[12] There is no ramified sense of "cause" that forms an invariant part of the grammar of every natural language. Causality is an interpretive category. It may be "necessary" for a Humean world to exhibit Humean-like "causes," but whether the actual world favors the Humean notion is plainly an independent question. This sort of modest reminder is puzzlingly ignored in most of the strenuous debates about the "scientific" status of history and the human sciences. At best, an argument that deliberately relies on such neglect has a bit of mafioso charm.

In Hempel's hands—notoriously, also in the hands of his close adherent Donald Davidson (who is not a specialist in the theory of science)—the modal reading has come to mean that it is conceptually impossible to formulate an operative notion of "cause" (one that could sustain a practice we might reasonably label "scientific") that did not implicate, in principle, invariant causal laws (whether unknown or not).[13] *That* thesis cannot possibly be true—that is, the modal thesis—given the distinction between causality and nomologicality and given the mere coherence and admissibility of Collingwood's model (or Hegel's for that matter), regardless of whether we should ultimately favor it or not. Furthermore, the same admission shows the essential difference between characterizing causes and characterizing causal explanations; for, if Collingwoodian causes were admitted, then it would at once be impossible (in what *Collingwood* regards as scientific history) for historical explanation to invoke Hempel's covering law model despite being fully causal. In the same sense, Hempel's complaint against Mandelbaum may yet prove premature—although, there, the matter cannot be quite so interesting, since Mandelbaum (but not Collingwood) admits that historical causes do fall under canonical causal laws.

There is a second difficulty with Hempel's formulation that bears on the very idea of general laws. "By a general law," Hempel explains, "we shall here understand a statement of universal conditional form which is capable of being confirmed or disconfirmed by suitable empirical findings." (For Hempel, "general law" and "universal hypothesis" designate the same notion.) "In *every* case where an event of a specified *kind* C occurs at a certain place and time, an event of a specified kind E *will* occur at a place and time which is related in a specified manner to the place and time of the occurrence of the first event"—namely, such that "the object of description and explanation in *every* branch of empirical science is *always* the occurrence of an event of a certain *kind* . . . at a given place and time, or in a given empirical object . . . at a certain time" (connected, that is, by general laws).[14] (The italicized expressions identify Hempel's modal intent. Part of the point of Hempel's insistence on using the expression "kinds" is, of course, to emphasize the absence of all singular referents in genuine laws of nature. Yet, on an argument that can be easily supplied, such a stricture can be shown to be impossible to satisfy in any science. The issue is a strategic one.)

Notice that Hempel's formulation is explicitly deterministic (as in the use of the expression "will occur," in the indicative), though it is true enough that, later in the same article, Hempel admits probabilistic laws. If probabilized "laws" *are* laws, even where they cannot, in principle, be assigned an invariant or universalized limit of variation,[15] then it is false to hold that causal explanation conceptually requires the covering law model *or* that causality requires that there be true nomic universals. There has never been a satisfactory resolution of this matter. Furthermore, when Hempel speaks of "confirming" exceptionless laws, he plainly slights the logical consideration that there is no straightforward sense in which invariant and exceptionless universal regularities *can* be empirically confirmed, as well as the sense that the confirmation of "phenomenlogical" laws is not tantamount to the confirmation of strictly universal laws.[16]

Hempel's formula signifies that the expressions "*E*," "*C*," and so on, "stand for kinds or properties of events, not for what is sometimes called individual events."[17] By this, Hempel straightforwardly outflanks Mandelbaum. Fine. But he never shows: (1) that every cause necessarily falls under a universal causal law; (2) that all valid causal explanations are, necessarily, instances of the covering law model; or (3) that the kinds of events invoked in the context of history support pertinent general laws. Proposition (1) would oblige us to admit that causality entails nomologicality—which, on Collingwood's example and by independent conjecture, is clearly uncompelling; proposition (2) requires that universal causal laws can be "confirmed or disconfirmed by suitable empirical findings"—which is surely open to quarrel; and (3) raises a question normally ignored or answered in a most perfunctory way.

The complaint regarding proposition (3) is a straightforward one. *If* physicalist reduction or elimination of the terms (or phenomena) featured in human history—actions, intentions, purposes, thinking, institutions, traditions, meanings, and the like—fails, then *if* causes cannot be disallowed at the "human" level (at the "folk"-level, as it is now fashionably called),[18] Hempel must be mistaken in his blanket claim about the lawlike nature of causal explanation. The point is particularly telling in connection with Davidson's view, since Davidson makes an explicit show of admitting singular causes of the psychological or "folk" sort,[19] and utterly fails to establish the (token) physicalism (or "supervenience") he favors.

In the paper on history, Hempel does not really insist on physicalism. But elsewhere, for instance in his account of the logic of explanation, he shows his penchant for physicalism openly enough. There, he says:

> Certain specifiable biological phenomena cannot be explained, by means of contemporary physico-chemical theories, on the basis of data concerning the physical and chemical characteristics of the atomic and molecular constituents or organisms. Similarly, the thesis of an emergent state of mind might be taken to assert that present-day physical, chemical, and biological theories do not suffice to explain all psychological phenomena on the basis of data concerning the physical, chemical, and biological characteristics of the cells or of the molecules or atoms constituting the organism in question. But in this interpretation, the emergent character of biological and psychological phenomena becomes *trivial*; for the description of various biological phenomena requires terms which are not contained in the vocabulary of present-day physics and chemistry; hence we cannot expect that all specifically biological phenomena are explainable, i.e. deductively inferable, by means of present-day physico-chemical theories on the basis of initial conditions which themselves are described in exclusively physico-chemical terms.[20]

In short, Hempel regards every failure to resolve the description of "emergent" phenomena physicalistically as no more than "trivial," because it is due (he insists) to current cognitive limitations. He is entirely explicit about this: "emergence of a characteristic is not an ontological trait inherent in some phenomena; rather it is indicative of the scope of our knowledge at a given time; thus, it has no absolute, but a relative character; and what is emergent with respect to the theories available today may lose its emergent status tomorrow."[21] But how does Hempel know this? He certainly has not shown that it is necessarily true, and he certainly has not shown that it is even empirically likely. No one has, and no one yet can.[22] The importance of the physicalist maneuver, we may anticipate, lies in its intended economy. For, if physicalism were true, then (of course) universal, invariant, exceptionless causal laws could be reasonably invoked; one could always then claim some inductive approximation to such laws. With such an advantage, Hempel could afford to ignore all the familiar worries about context, intention, historical reference, and horizonal interest: those distinctions would never need to be more than heuristic devices. History would (in principle) be entirely eliminable from science! It's a nice thought, but is it reasonable?

V

We should not allow ourselves to drift too far into reductionist waters. The essential issues lie elsewhere.

Hempel had rightly taken exception to Mandelbaum's weak distinction between the singular and the general. No one can give a "*complete description* of an individual event," he says, neither in history nor in physics. But then, "there is no difference, in this respect, between history and the natural sciences: both can give an account of their subject-matter only in terms of general concepts, and history can 'grasp the unique individuality' of its objects of study no more and no less than can physics or chemistry."[23] Quite right. But two further considerations must be brought to bear: first, it is not always true that "kinds" identified in terms of "general concepts" enter, as such, into lawlike generalizations; second, it has never been shown that the "kinds" of events human history usually addresses *are*, in principle, the designata of general laws.

Apart from his physicalism, Hempel's treatment of causal explanations in history is puzzling—possibly even naive. The following makes this clear:

> Consider [says Hempel] the statement that the Dust Bowl farmers migrated to California "because" continual droughts and sandstorms made their existence increasingly precarious, and because California seemed to them to offer so much better living conditions. This explanation rests on some such universal hypothesis as that populations will tend to migrate to regions which offer better living conditions.[24]

This goes directly contrary to the sense of the considerations just adduced. No reason has been given for believing that categories like "human agents" ("farmers," "regions which offer better living conditions") *ever* function as the designata of universal laws; furthermore, no reason has been given for believing that such categories (or "kinds") *can* be suitably replaced or made more precise in the service of genuine lawlike statements.[25]

On the argument, Hempel should have concluded that history was not a science or that the unity model was incapable of absorbing history. For, consider that the *kinds* of events that enter into scientific *descriptions*, according to the unity model, are "natural-kind" kinds, that is, kinds known to be analyzable (or replaceable) congruently with the *explanatory kinds* that are the designata of covering-law explanations. The only "kinds" that (on Hempel's argument) could yield a "scientific" history are "natural-kind" (or "homonomic") kinds, that is, kinds that, ideally, could serve, in both descriptive and explanatory contexts, as the designata of valid laws. If we lacked grounds for believing that we could satisfy that constraint (by approximation, say), it would be utterly pointless to claim that "the methodological unity of empirical science" ranges over physics and history equally,[26] or that "general laws have quite analogous forms in history and the natural sciences," or that general laws "form an indispensable instrument of historical research" or "the common basis of various procedures which are often considered as characteristic of the social in contradiction to the natural sciences."[27]

Hempel's account cannot but collapse. He has nowhere shown that the "kinds" of events central to human history are (or could be) of the same *kind* of "kinds" he says are required in the physical sciences. We may as well say that the general presumptions of the unity of science model have absolutely nothing to do with demonstrating, piecemeal, the required reduction. They are no more than articles of faith.

It is perfectly clear that the phenomena of the human world tend to be catalogued in accord with the historically variable interests that different societies take in their own world. The categories of human history ("folk" concepts)—tools, medium-sized goods, marketable things—normally designate cross-category kinds (that is, kinds indifferent to the explanatory use of natural-kind and homonomic kinds), kinds that are selected informally in accord with salient interests. They "work," in an admirably stable and self-effacing way—descriptively, predictively, valuationally—without the least assurance of their conformity with the reductive needs of the unity model. We improvise in an ad hoc way about causal regularities involving them (folk medicinals, for instance, advice to cooks and gardeners and the lovelorn). We may always recommend their radical replacement or elimination, of course. The trouble is that the detailed plans for such a piece of clockwork (reduction or elimination in physical terms) tend to remain mysteriously vague.[28]

VI

If the unity model held firm, historical narrative would be no more than a fictional or heuristic interlude in the serious business of science. Hempel rightly says as much, scanning with a dose of contempt and skepticism the narrative strategies associated with the method of empathy, interpretive studies, the search for historical "meanings."[29] So there is, on the on the one hand, a large price to pay for the unity model's success, although we hardly want to rely on a blackmail argument. On the other hand, the "dualism" favored by Vico and Collingwood parades its own extravagant advantage: that of saving the objectivity of narrative history at the price of precluding altogether the unity model's entry into the sphere of history.

There's more to the lesson. The unity model treats the time of history as indistinguishable from physical time; causes are treated uniformly in physics and history, and for the same quarrelsome reason; and explanation is made to take the same procrustean form everwhere.

To resist the unity model, then, is to open history *and* physics—jointly and separately—to alternative conceptions of science. What we need to appreciate is that the principal objections to the unity model do not originate with the "dualist" conception of history. It's rather that the unity model misrepresents the actual work and accomplishments of *physics*—which is itself a historical practice, an actual way of exploring the world. The unity model is an idealization of some sort, a rogue conception that erases the marks of its own historical structure and makes itself fatally alluring to the modern imagination.

The serious alternative before us is this: *the work of science is conceptually inseparable from its historical praxis*—not merely in the sense that its accomplishments have a history of their own (which the unity program would be happy to admit), but in the deeper sense that *its methodological competence has an inescapably historical structure*. Classification, observation, induction, hypothesis formation, conceptual modeling, explanatory interpretation, approximation, idealization, testing, confirmation remain mysteries when separated from their historical context. *That* cannot be admitted in the unity theorist's gentle way.

So the game is hardly to reinstate the "dualist"—Vico or Collingwood; or to savage the "progressivist"—Hempel and his company. What we need is an entirely new conception of the sciences: not one that bifurcates the human and natural sciences, not one that imposes the encompassing vision of a single scientific Camelot for the play of both physics and history. There is no single methodology that fits each "single" science, or the "whole" of any one science, or the system of "all" the sciences together. That's not to say there is no method in the sciences: it only says there is no method separable from—transcendentally, timelessly, invariantly applied to, necessarily and normatively appropriate for—any and every contingent historical practice addressed to the question of the truth about the world. There can be no such method, once we admit: (1) that science and reality are inextricably symbiotized, that there is no principled distinction between the way the world is and the way it seems to us to be; and (2) that that symbiosis and the models of rational inquiry it happens to subtend are themselves the contingent "products" of the flux of historical life. The aptness or validity of any would-be method is a function of the validity of our conception of that part of the world to which it is to be applied; and *that* conception is ineluctably symbiotized. (This is not to say, however, that our symbiotized world cannot "resist" our would-be methods or claims. There's the touching feature of that tiresomely friendly—but important—quarrel between Imre Lakatos and Paul Feyerabend.)[30]

In bringing his own paper to a close, Hempel pertinently adds "two principles of the theory of science":

> First [he says], the separation of "pure description" and "hypothetical generalizations and theory-construction" in empirical science is unwarranted; in the building of scientific knowledge the two are inseparably linked. And, second [he goes on], it is similarly unwarranted and futile to attempt the demarcation of sharp boundary lines between the different fields of scientific research, and an autonomous development of each of the fields.[31]

He means this in the best spirit of the unity program; but, as we have been suggesting, the argument could easily have gone in an altogether different direction. We might, for instance, have refused to hold the unity ideal itself above the historical fray. Hempel never addresses the question; nor indeed do such younger theorists as Davidson and Hilary Putnam and Adolf Grünbaum and Wesley Salmon. The issue is more attractive to those philosophers of science who have quarreled with Karl Popper than to those who have sided with Hempel: Kuhn, of course, and Lakatos, and Feyerabend.

In a deeper sense, the issue is the same (though it is usually not so cast) as that raised in the quarrel between so-called "metaphysical realism" and so-called "internal realism"; except that—contrary to Hilary Putnam's too-easy optimism in formulating the distinction—*truth* can no longer function, on the "internalist's" view, *in a transhistorical, cognitively regulative way*. Putnam does not perceive (or does not acknowledge) the difficulty that a historicized science poses for his own version of "internal realism." The irony is that the very logic of internal realism narrows—enormously—the gap between the position he *should* now hold (for reasons of consistency) and the views of Kuhn and Feyerabend that he has always so happily castigated. (At one time, of course, Putnam was himself one of the principal champions of the unity program; here, he has become something of an ambivalent critic of Hempel's.)[32]

We must be careful. Mention of the realist controversy threatens to distract us into a detour that may well engulf the entire inquiry we intend.

We cannot entirely avoid it, because it confirms just how stubborn the notion of real invariances is in the declension of the unity model—from, say, Hempel to Putnam. For Putnam attenuates the invariances of reason (though that may not have been his intention) in a way that invites an unexpected comparison with Collingwood; it is also true, it must be said, that, as a "progressivist," Putnam does offer general assurances about the "Peircean" community of inquiry. More recently, he has given evidence of a distinct sympathy for Habermas's program, which one might have thought was completely out of touch with the problems of the methodology of science.[33]

Truth cannot function regulatively with respect to symbiotized inquiry. On the argument that concept is as "internalist" as the work of the sciences themselves, even if *we* posit (from our historicized perch within the symbiotized world) *that* the term "truth" signifies the favored standing of whatever can be discovered regarding the real world—the world as it (putatively) is "independent" of any human inquiry.

The short argument is this: truth is inoperative on the "realist's" or "metaphysical realist's" view of things (roughly: on the correspondence theory of truth), because, once we concede the symbiosis marked in the aforementioned (1), there is no access to a "noumenal" world at all; and because, once we concede the historicity of that symbiosis—the point made in (2)—truth-values cannot be restricted a priori in a bivalent way, and any logical laxity in the direction of many-valued values will provide for the possiblity of "incongruent" judgments (judgments that, on a bivalent model of truth but not now, would yield explicit contradictions or inconsistencies). But to admit that much is to admit relativism. In short, assuming symbiosis (1), "internal realism" cannot fail to win out over "metaphysical realism"; but assuming that rationality is an artifact of history (2), then internalism cannot but be historicized. If, furthermore, the symbiotized world is intransparent, then bivalence will be replaceable in principle, and relativism will be entirely eligible as an empirical option in this or that domain. So the advantage we have secured is a powerful one: it exposes at a stroke the twin frailties of Hempel's inductivism and Putnam's internalism. It does a good deal more, but we shall have to wait for the rest of the treasure to appear.[34]

Putnam presses his "internal realism" further (illicitly, on internal grounds *and* on the critique just sketched). For he says:

> If objects are, at least when you get small enough, or large enough, or theoretical enough, theory-dependent, then the whole idea of truth's being defined or explained in terms of a "correspondence" between items in a

language and items in a fixed theory-independent reality has to be given up. The picture I propose instead is not the picture of Kant's transcendental idealism, but it is certainly related to it. It is the picture that truth comes to no more than idealized rational acceptability.[35]

Putnam means that there *is* a sense, apparently not altogether "internalist" (not altogether "theory-dependent"), that, *despite the historied nature of inquiry*, ensures some sort of invariant rationality: it is said to yield what is *"warrantable* on the basis of experience and intelligence for creatures with 'a rational and sensible nature.'" In particular, Putnam explains: "in the tradition of James and Dewey, it is to say that devices [regarding seemingly competing truths] which are functionally equivalent in the context of inquiry for which they are designed are equivalent in every way that we have a 'handle on.'"[36] This, of course, is an excessively optimistic picture.

That such "devices" are "functionally equivalent" (*in the realist sense*) presumably is fixed by a rationality apt for discerning that *this* seeming incompatibility of truth-value assignments—but (perhaps) not *that*—may be allowed, given our present scientific undertaking. If so, then that same determination will inevitably be subject to historical change regarding what we take our rationality to be, and what, under such changes, we take to be functionally equivalent in truth-value. History will overtake every "functional" equivalence, or it will render those we continue to honor hostage to our horizoned rationality.

Putnam rejects the correspondence theory all right, but he still insists that "truth" is regulative *in a realist sense*:

> The most important consequence of metaphysical realism is that *truth* is supposed to be *radically non-epistemic.* . . . the theory that is "ideal" from the point of view of operational utility, inner beauty and elegance, "plausibility," simplicity, "conservatism," etc., *might be false.* "Verified" (in an operational sense) does not imply "true," on the metaphysical realist picture, even in the ideal limit.
>
> It is this feature that distinguishes metaphysical realism, as I am using the term, from the mere belief that there *is* an ideal theory (Peircean realism) or, more weakly, that an ideal theory is a regulative ideal presupposed by the notions "true" and "objective" as they have classically been understood.[37]

This cannot be right. For the regulative function of truth can obtain only distributively—otherwise, it is meaningless to speak of a regulative function at all. But the optimism of internal realism can never be more than holist or pragmatic—which is to say, specifically *not* progressivist or distributed. And yet, with all his caveats, Putnam is prepared to subscribe to a formula like the following:

> The pragmatist does not believe that correctness of the outcome of the procedures [of justice (in Putnam's discussion, cited here), though the procedures in question could as easily have been the procedures of science]— rational belief or just resolution of some conflict between demands—can be defined other than in terms of the outcome of the (*endlessly self-improvising*) procedure.[38]

This *is* progressivism, the recovery of a (historically unknown) telos of science. The short conclusion to this strenuous argument is this: Putnam cannot hold to the regulative function without being drawn back to the invariances of metaphysical realism that he rejects. (Is that a "theology" in Vico's sense?) He hesitates at the last step to concede condition (2), though he does not oppose (1). This is precisely what explains his recent endorsement of Habermas's notion of rationality.[39] It cannot be more than the lingering specter of real invariances captured progressively (by Peirceanizing Kant) through the indefinitely extended rational inquiry of the universal community of man. If it is more, we need the argument; and if it is not, it must fail. We ourselves are thereby led to grasp the full import of historicizing science. Putnam insists at one and the same time on the flux of science (the symbiosis and intransparency of its historically provisional blindness) and its capacity for a redemptive self-correction (the work of a regulative critique that brings its provisional findings progressively into line with the invariant structures of the real world). But the admission of the first precludes the necessity, even the plausibility, of the second. Putnam never addresses the issue.[40]

VII

We must take stock of things. Important questions keep surfacing that we cannot stop to answer. They need a genuinely fresh start in any case. But we have not lost our way. We are puzzling over the relationship between change and invariance in the context of theorizing about history, and we have now managed to identify certain pertinent polar tendencies in Hempel and Collingwood. We are weighing the prospects of a viable theory of history.

Both Collingwood and Hempel link history to science by featuring some sort of invariance. They pursue very different theories—which we have dubbed, unceremoniously, "dualism" and "progressivism." Hempel's option is the clearer of the two, since it flatly opposes the inclusion of history as a distinct science within the scope of the unity model. Collingwood features instead the invariant powers of reason. He acknowledges that the physical world has its changeless structures all right; but since he disjoins the human and the physical sciences, he makes very little of the theme he would otherwise seem to share with Hempel. Collingwood admits that "mind" or reason *is* "timeless"—"outside" historical time. (He means that it plays an "ideal" or transcendental role.) So it is not really subject to the laws of nature. Hempel would never concede such a possibility: for him, no sector of the real world escapes the invariances of causal law; the human world is ultimately no more than a part of the physical world. No doubt, it is a complicated part. But history signifies no more than a certain reflexive interest we humans take in ordering our own affairs in a narrative way. There's no science in it. History is at best an intuitive holding action employed in the context of human ignorance.

Much of this is inexplicit in what Hempel says. History is ultimately simply erased. But you do find an incipient appreciation of all this in Putnam, because Putnam calls into question all empirical invariances. It is not so much that (for Putnam) there are no invariances as that there are no invariantly correct formulations of such invariances. Putnam's entire philosophical effort is bent on finding the best possible way of saving the realist commitment to the invariances of the physical and formal sciences without appealing to the (now-) indefensible strategies of physicalism or apriorism or the unity program. That is the reason Putnam yields in the direction of Peirce and pragmatism. That's why the shift from "metaphysical realism" to "internal realism" is so important: it's meant to save the conjectured invariances of nature by progressive approximation—which (Putnam believes) can no longer be reclaimed on realist grounds alone. By this device, Putnam bridges the difference between the invariant power of reason and the invariant structures of reality—without losing either (he believes) and without risking either by "noumenal" sleights of hand. He "merely" champions scientific progress! He improves on Kant. We shall collect the evidence in a moment. But what makes Putnam's maneuver fresh is that it recovers part of the unity of science without insisting a priori on a lawlike world.

Once you abandon Hempel's vision, however, you must abandon Hempel's sort of progressivism as well. That's what Putnam means by Peirceanizing Kant: that's what he shares with Habermas, that's what explains the fatal weakness of his inability to ensure (against Michael Dummett's "antirealism") the independent regulative function of truth.[41] In a word, he ignores the role of real history. (Dummett, I should say at once, was Putnam's friendly antagonist through the early stages of the dispute regarding "metaphysical realism" and "internal realism" and the fate of the theory of truth relative to that quarrel. Dummett is himself opposed to "metaphysical realism," since he is an intuitionist in the mathematical sense. The irony is that both Putnam's pragmatism and Dummett's intuitionism fail to accommodate the role of history—Putnam's, in terms of truth's "regulative" role; Dummett's, in terms of the necessity of recovering bivalence or *tertium non datur*.)

We are still probing, in all of this, no more than two closely related versions of progressivism. One promotes a strong inductivism (Hempel's realism): it holds that there is a real world (a "metaphysically" real world), one that *is* invariantly structured, that rational inquiry has set itself to master. There's no idealism there. Once introduce a Kantian-like symbiosis, however, and historicize *that* (with Putnam)—the second option: you find that the goal of a nomologically exceptionless reality must turn idealist if it is to survive. It now requires that truth preserve a changeless *regulative* function—without "*noumenal*" assurances. That's just its fatal weakness. There is no internalism strong enough for that.

Putnam himself provides the proof. For one thing, he has recently retreated from the strong progressivism he once shared with Richard Boyd; and, for another, he now insists that there is no principled disjunction between "objectivity" and "subjectivity." What he does not yet admit is the ineluctable judgment that not only do these concessions undermine his progressivism, but they commit him to the relativist possibilities of history he had so fiercely conbatted in Kuhn and Feyerabend. The irony is now complete: Putnam must abandon the strong regulative reading of the role of truth he has always championed—both as a metaphysical realist (as a unity theorist) and as an internal realist (as a pragmatist). We need a little patience to see why this is so.

Some time ago, Putnam had joined forces with Richard Boyd in advocating an empirical realism of the internalist sort, one in accord with the following two principles:

1.   Terms in a mature science typically *refer*.

2.   The laws of a theory belonging to a mature science are typically approximately *true*.[42]

Bear in mind: this *is* the "regulative" principle Putnam speaks of. He adds: "My knowledge of the *truth* of (1) and (2) enables me to restrict the class of candidate-theories [in the sciences] and thereby increases my chance of success."[43] Nothing could be simpler (or sweeter or more Peircean), except of course that Putnam has now collected the deepest doubts about reference (in tandem with Davidson) and has abandoned the effort to explain just how it is he knows (emprically) that (2) is true.

Putnam now treats reference (against Boyd's view) as constrained by the following ("internalist") difficulty: "objects are theory-dependent in the sense that theories with incompatible ontologies can both be right."[44] He takes the trouble to point out that this warning must be read in the pragmatist's way, not in the metaphysical realist's way. But if that is so, then of course the grounds for claiming to know *that* (1) and (2) *are* true must elude us. Putnam then retreats to the supposed invariances of "idealized rational acceptability"—that is, to whatever is compelling to "creatures with 'a rational and a sensible nature.'"[45] (He notices an incipient agreement, here, with Habermas, though he finds it in an area of inquiry Habermas usually does not explore.)

Putnam then affirms that, "epistemologically at least, the attempt to draw this distinction, [the attempt] to make this cut [between what is 'simply true' and what has only 'assertability conditions,' or between what is already conceded to be true or false and what is only an 'extension of previous use,' or between what is a 'projection' and what is an independent and unitary property of things in themselves], has been a total failure. The time has come to try the methodological hypothesis that no such cut can be made."[46]

He goes on to say: "My own view is that the entire enterprise [of converting a 'continuum' into a 'dichotomy,' of making a 'Dedekind cut'] isn't worth the candle. The game is played out. We can make a rough sort of rank ordering (although even here there are disagreements), but the idea of a 'point at which' subjectivity ceases and Objectivity-with-a-capital-O begins has proved chimerical." This is now "the essence of the 'internal realism'" Putnam is prepared to defend.[47] But if we allow the improvement, we must give up the sort of "functional equivalence" Putnam first pressed regarding the "truth" of "theories with incompatible ontologies." For, we should already have abandoned (with Putnam) any principled distinction between subjectivity and objectivity. Hence, Putnam's entire undertaking is fatally compromised. This is hardly to say that science or rationality (or metaphysics, for that matter) is compromised; it is only to say that, conceding (1) and (2), science and rationality must be interpreted in accord with a sense of history that eschews all putatively timeless invariances, whether real or conceptual.

In a word, if we historicize "internal realism," we cannot fail to endorse relativism. Putnam resists of course: that is the point of his insisting on the "regulative" role of truth. But if we abandon that thesis (as we must), then we cannot preclude a relativistic view of science as well as of history. We cannot pursue the matter in depth.[48] But only a warning and a suggestion are needed. As regards the warning: we need only avoid those relativisms that entail self-referential paradoxes—in particular, those that define "true" relationally, as relative to thee and me or relative to this language and that. As for the suggestion: we need only retire or restrict a bivalent logic, admit many-valued truthlike values, and acknowledge that, on that replacement, some judgments which, on a bivalent logic, would be incompatible, would now be what may be termed "incongruent." On the argument, "incongruent" judgments may be jointly validated. Admitting that much, we may then claim that historicism *is* a form of relativism: one in which *science*—all inquiry, in fact, regarding truth—is (epistemically, *not* alethically) historicized within the terms of symbiosis and intransparency. The argument here is that Putnam effectively concedes the point, though he denies it. All that is needed is to shift the argument from alethic considerations to epistemic ones (from the definition of truth to the question of supporting evidence).

VIII

The foregoing helps to explain the difference between dualism and progressivism and to map the forms of the latter favored in the unity of science program. Collingwood saves history, we saw, by disjoining history and physics. In doing so, he neglects to consider (or to consider the import of admitting) both that human reason and inquiry are historically formed in a way that varies from age to age and that physics is inseparable from the historical formation of inquiry. So he falls back to a disarmingly thin invariance in order to penetrate the truth of history. He requires no sense of progress, and he allows for none. The human world, he believes, is indeed a world of change. Furthermore, only the transcendental power of reason can grasp the intentional acts of past historical agents. But *how* that can be, Collingwood never quite explains.

In the unity account, the real world exists independently of human inquiry and, there, it is invariantly structured. Hence, progress marks the genuine achievement over the course of time of an improved grasp of just such structures. History, therefore, is no part of science. It may be a chronicle of our efforts to gain the goal of science; otherwise, it provides no more than a temporal summary of some sort, of some extrinsic interests in the actual world. But Hempel has no need of history. It does no more than narratize our idiosyncratic involvement with whatever is real. (This slim formula actually identifies the nerve of an attractive contemporary theory of history, Arthur Dantos. But we cannot address it now and will touch on it only briefly much later in this account.)

The themes of twentieth-century philosophy, we may conclude, are hardly prepared to honor Hempel's "noumenal" optimism. (Here, we are applying Putnam's term in its deliberately derogatory sense.) The world is said to be cognitively intransparent, symbiotized, subject to the contingencies of history. Fine. But if so, then progress and nomological invariances and the invariances of reason become entirely unsatisfactory notions. Hence, by the force of his own philosophical odyssey, Putnam signifies not only the passing of invariance but the nostalgia for it that infects the robust pragmatisms of the twentieth century: Peirce's, his own (at an earlier moment), and now, most instructively, Habermas's. (In Putnam's case, it is the stubborn "regulative" function of truth that betrays him; in Habermas's, it is the function of practical reason.)

In bringing this little summary of the remnants of the unity conception to a close, we must remind ourselves that there are other ways of theorizing (besides Putnam's) regarding the recovery of invariance in human history. There is, for instance, a much more developed conception of history in the work of Hans-Georg Gadamer, which attempts to recover (something very much like) invariance in human history, after having abandoned strict invariance in all of the human sphere. Gadamer's theory is hardly a progressivism, however. It's only in the declension from Hempel to Putnam that the progressivist tag seems right. Within the menagerie of theories leaning in Gadamer's direction—post-Heideggerean, hermeneutic, late phenomenological, possibly even early Frankfurt Critical, certainly Nietzschean—what we find in place is not a measure of progress in grasping the invariant structures of an independent reality but only a sense of the mysterious constancy with which a tradition of invariant human norms and values can always be recovered from the swirling flux of history. There, metonymically, Habermas and Gadamer are pitted against one another in a larger contest. For both of them, there *is* no "independent" human world that inquirers simply happen upon in a fit of scientific zeal. Inquiry is historicized, and what it investigates is similarly historied.

We have now left Vico and Collingwood far behind, just as we have left Hempel. But it is certainly not clear how invariance or invariantlike constancies could possibly be recovered within the space of an inconstant history. In any case, we may suggest, for the sake of closure, that whereas Habermas champions a form of *progressivism* distinct from Hempel's (somewhat less distinct from Putnam's), Gadamer's thesis is no progressivism at all. We shall call it instead a form of *traditionalism*—meaning by that that, in spite of his historicism, Gadamer recovers the abiding verities of the human condition.

We musk ask ourselves how he manages to do that.

THREE

The Declension of Progressivism

I

It is a fact that nearly all the latest versions of progressivism have been inspired by the work of Charles Sanders Peirce: some directly, like Putnam's, Habermas's, and Karl Popper's; others, surely through their mediation, like Kuhn's, Lakatos's, and Larry Laudan's. It is an even more important fact that Peirce's vision—his progressivism, not his general philosophy—is a conceptual disaster. No matter. It is its optimism that has carried its colors triumphantly through the entire Western world. That failed optimism, often overlooked in its generous acceptance and influence, has obscured an important part of the puzzle of history.

One might suppose that Peirce's doctrine was no more than a gloss on the old tale of loosing a band of monkeys to pound on typewriters an infinite amount of time, supposing that they would eventually produce the corpus of Shakespeare's plays. That would be a mistake. It was much more than that, and it was certainly not stupid. But it was and remains wrongheaded, impossible to redeem; and its failure affects the fortunes of the theory of history in a most profound way. For, in failing, it leads us to conclude that if there are no discernibly invariant structures in our symbiotized world at any contingent moment in a blindly historicized inquiry, then there cannot be any compelling (or plausible) reason for supposing that such structures are, in principle, discernible at the end of an infinite process of inquiry, no matter how thoroughly self-corrective and rational it may be on the way. For, on the argument, self-correction is itself historically blind, and reason is no more than a (high) artifact of historical forces. Without an effective telos inhering in the continuous process of temporal change, Peirce's vision could not but fail. No mere society of human inquirers (no infinite "community" of cosmic inquirers—to favor Peirce's image) could rightly claim to have grasped, at any particular time, what would accord with *that* telic order that, on the thesis, dawns only at the infinite limit of history's completion—when, that is, the rational order of the whole may be judged to have been served piecemeal through the gathering movement of its temporal parts. This, of course, is just what Putnam's theory of the regulative function of truth could never overcome. It is also what Hegel's theory could never overcome if ever Hegel had meant—which is doubtful—to posit an actual telos at the end of history. (Hegel's theory of course is hardly an open book.) Peirce, we may conjecture, was somewhat victimized by the salient notions of evolutionary progress in his day and the irresistible charm of Emersonian transcendentalism.

This means that progressivism (fallibilism, in Peirce's idiom) is impossible to defend in any but an arbitrary way.[1] On the "pragmaticist's" theory, *some* set of the self-corrective intervals of inquiry would have to count as a determinate (humanly determinable) gain over other (errant) intervals in the same process, if Peircean fallibilism were to be *humanly* vindicated as we moved, in ignorance, toward the limit of infinitely extended rational self-correction. Fallibilism could succeed only on the knowledge of the pragmatic equivalence (if the term be allowed) of the temporal ordering of the aggregated blind perspectives of every society's self-correction and whatever an omniscient reason at the end of time would require of the whole process.

The significance of this gnomic judgment is considerable, but it needs scope. It shows, for instance, that the first and greatest philosophical effort to defend progressivism—Hegel's immense project (if that was indeed its primary purpose)—could not but have failed. It cannot help Peirce's more recent argument, though it makes it nobler, to know that neither Hegel nor Peirce had held that there was a determinate telos governing the whole of history, discernibly effective *in* the distributed parts of the temporal process. The logic of Hegel's and Peirce's argument precludes the possibility. If they had presumed such a telos, their projects would have been palpable shams: there would then have been a changeless structure built into the very flux of history. In resisting that, they refused, however, the only grounds on which progressivism could thrive.

It was indeed Heidegger's arbitrary judgment that *that was* the point of Hegel's philosophical cheating.[2] Heidegger fails to make good his claim or even to make it fully plausible: Hegel could not possibly have deceived himself so simply. But it serves us, now, to mention Heidegger's conception of history—to confront every historicism and progressivism with the unyielding logic of the flux. The result is startling. For, if it makes sense to speak of the inclusive history of the world, then it also makes sense to speak of interpreting the finite bits of time in accord with the proper parts of that encompassing history; and if that's conceded, then there cannot be a telic structure discernible at the end of history *if the unfolding parts do not at least share already*—as they contingently evolve through the blind interventions of human societies—*a proper and humanly discernible place* (a progressive place but not a finally telic one) *in that ultimate structure*. That is what Heidegger should have pressed but did not. That is the site of Hegel's mystery.

The importance of Hegel's account lies there. (Kierkegaard's complaint is essentially idle.)[3] For what Hegel demonstrates is *the insuperable contingency of the rational ordering of the whole of any human inquiry*: the power of reason to recover the normative order of the real intervals of history must itself be a creature of the uninformed parts of such a history. But *that* is impossible without conceptual cheating. The glee with which we refute Hegel again and again obscures the deeper lesson of the sheer historicity of thinking. Hardly any theorist dares embrace the full implications of Hegel's "failure" (or Peirce's). Literal-minded progressivisms—those invented by Jürgen Habermas and Karl Popper, for instance—are no more than betrayals of Hegel's conceptual daring. But let that pass: *Hegel* failed, if he ever meant thus to succeed.

Gillian Rose, for one, has put the point effectively enough: "Hegel's philosophy has no social import if the absolute cannot be thought."[4] Rose construes the lesson in terms of Hegel's anticipation of the failed presumption of the universalism (or universalized rationalism) of the neo-Kantians—Max Weber, Emile Durkheim, the phenomenologists, the Marxists, the Frankfurt Critical School, and, of course, Habermas read as a progressivist.[5] Still more important is the discovery that *we* cannot step out of Hegel's philosophical shadow.

Hegel's seemingly alien argument entails, without the least effort, the complete refutation of progressivism. If we turn back to Hempel's and Putnam's views, we cannot fail to see that Putnam's thesis is a pale instance (possibly the coyest) of a Peircean-like recovery of the unity of science program. If so, it must be internally inconsistent or arbitrary.

However, Hempel's inductivism is not in the least inconsistent; it is, nonetheless, incompatible with the flux and untenable under the conditions of symbiosis and intransparency. We of course are nearly all Kantians now, leaner by design than the Kant of the first *Critique*: that is, *we* mean to avoid (as that "first" Kant cannot) the progressivism (or "methodologism") of the neo-Kantian interpreters of Kant. Hegel shows the way. We abandon, with Hegel and against Kant, the very idea of a uniquely correct conceptual order within which the real structure and significance of the world can be *humanly* discerned. In that sense, Rose has exaggerated the lesson she draws from Hegel's ("failed") effort; for it may just be that Hegel means to instruct us about the infinite openness of every human effort to capture Absolute Spirit. That is, perhaps Hegel means to draw attention to the impossibility of historicized thought's grasping absolute history, though the human mind (Hegel's, for one) *can* conceive of the sweep of absolute history. (There is that equivocation in what Rose says, though her intention is clear enough. She does not give Hegel sufficient credit, however. Surely Hegel understood what Rose would explain.)

We begin, as Hegel observes, with our contingent perspectives and experience, and, in every attempt to encompasss an "absolute" history, we are bound to concede that there always looms a larger totality that we cannot fathom. Hegel's theme may be construed as signifying the *historical relativity* of all human cognitive claims—but not (alethic) *relativism*, that is, as signifying the contingency and diversity of truth-claims relative to our history, but not a "relational" definition of truth. In this, the *Phenomenology* serves to define the insuperable relativity of human claims: it does *not* define "absolute" truth as an achievement that is humanly accessible. Epistemologically, Hegel is a historicist—which is to say, a theorist who views ascriptions of knowledge as relativized to the resources of our cognitive horizon. Clearly, Hegel does not define (absolute) truth in any relativistic way; but his account is certainly compatible with a relativistic theory *of* truth (though not one that produces self-referential paradox). In a curious way, Hegel's insistence on Absolute Spirit and on defining "truth" from the "perspective" of Absolute Spirit confirms his own sympathy with a historicist account of *knowledge*.[6]

Hempel's version of progress presupposes, as Putnam's does not, that there *are* invariant structures in the real world that science asymptotically grasps in its punctual work at particular stages of inquiry. Hempel "places" the structure of physical reality entirely outside history—outside the Kantian symbiosis altogether. Hempelian progress, therefore, is internally consistent, though bought at the heavy price of denying that history is an ingredient of reality; Putnam's progressivism, however, is internally inconsistent, wherever Putnam's increasing vagueness on the matter of methodology (and truth) functions as a sign of his Peircean-like acceptance of the real indeterminacies of the world.[7] His progressivism depends upon it.

Hempel and Putnam have already made their appearance here as the champions of the two main forms of progressivism in science. Hempel is no historicist, but Putnam is. Hempel accepts the legible invariance of an independent physical nature (inductivism), whereas Putnam is sanguine about its recovery within the space of an asymptotic blindness. The space between them is made to yield (by Hans Reichenbach) still another form of progressivism. For Reichenbach falls back to the spare resources of a neo-Kantian inductivism—without benefit of Hempel's ontology.[8] But we need to proceed more slowly in this matter.

II

The best-known exposé of Peirce's fallacy belongs to W. V. Quine. Peirce had characterized logic as "the doctrine of truth, its nature and the manner in which it is to be discovered." Logic, for Peirce, becomes the theory of inquiry—the theory, preeminently, of "abduction."[9] Under this umbrella notion, Peirce supplies the famous pragmatist formula:

> The real . . . is that (more exactly: the object of the opinion) which, sooner or later, information and reasoning would finally result in, and which is therefore independent of the vagaries of me and you. Thus, the very origin of the connection of reality shows that this conception essentially involves the notion of a *Community*, without definite limits, and capable of definite increase in knowledge.[10]

This is a most carefully crafted progressivism. First of all, Peirce relies on the image of an entire self-correcting "community, without definite limits" to offset (to be "independent of") the particular inputs of "you and me." That already harbors a non sequitur, a desperate maneuver that Peirce cannot do without. Second, Peirce maintains that the infinite community of inquirers, working on and on without assigned limit, is quite capable of a "definite increase in knowledge," which, once again, is a completely gratuitous posit. "The final Interpretant [of what is real, Peirce adds,] does not consist in the way in which any mind does act but

in the way in which every mind would act." Here, "the whole com-
munion of minds" may well include the intelligence of the creatures of
other planets.[11] Here, the play with actual and ideal minds and aggregated and collective consensus cannot be very reassuring.

Peirce intends no irony. I am tempted to say that there is an irony in
Hegel, even in his extravagant philosophy of history, where the project
of "the philosophy of world history" is taken most literally. For the seed
is admitted in Hegel's reflection on two kinds of history:

> The sole end of history is to comprehend clearly what is and what has been,
> the events and deeds of the past. It gains in veracity the more strictly it confines
> itself to what is given, and—although this is not so immediately evident, but
> in fact requires many kinds of investigations in which thought also plays a
> part—the more exclusively it seeks to discover what actually happened. This
> aim seems to contradict the function of philosophy; and it is this contradic-
> tion, and the accusation that philosophy imports its own idea into history and
> manipulates it accordingly, that I wish to discuss.[12]

Hegel surely fails to prove, either as an empirical hypothesis or as a
necessary philosophical truth, that "reason governs the World, and
that world history is therefore a rational process."[13] The theme, of
course, is that of the "cunning of reason." Apart from my own temp-
tation, I must say that J. N. Findlay offers the most succinct reminder
of Hegel's excellent grasp of the "formal" inadequacy of the "logic" of
teleology:

> Hegel now points [in the *Science of Logic*] to a radical defect in teleological
> mediation: it entails the same endless intercalation of Middle Terms that we
> saw in the case of the Syllogism of Existence. The End passes into execution
> only by way of the Means, but this implies that the Means must itself be
> "worked up to" by further Means, and so on *ad infinitum*: a Purpose, it might
> seem, cannot get under way at all, since every step in its fulfilment requires
> another step to be first made. (This is not intended to be a practical Teleol-
> ogy.) . . . Whatever we achieve, being only contingently related to the End,
> can embody it only in a one-sided, inadequate and temporary manner: it is
> itself merely a Means which will require further Means to be added to it, if
> the End is to be persistently pursued. . . . Strictly speaking, we have no finite
> Ends, but only "the End." This End, says Hegel, never finds a true Means,
> since it will always require a prior execution in order that this Means may
> bring it into being.[14]

On this reading, progressivism can be no more than a peculiarly optimistic variant of Hegel's teleologism. Hegel, of course, is hardly indifferent to the conceptual puzzle of ephemeral constructions forming

determinate parts of a telic invariance completed and discerned only at the limit of history (or worse, discerned, however incompletely, in the flux of time itself).

There's no way in which Peirce could have validly recovered his "logical" optimism. But it is plain enough that he shaped his formula with an eye to eliminating every objectionable privilege *"in the short run."* It's not the "short run" or the "long run" that betrays Peirce, however: it's the supposed conceptual connection between the two. At best, Peirce could have hoped that his optimism regarding the long run was formally coherent: it might have been, had he not muddled it with the extraneous idea that, *in the short run, the long-run hope entails the inquiring community's capacity for "definite increase in knowledge." That* could never have worked. It's the same difficulty that worries Popper. It's the fallacy Quine identifies (in Peirce) in his elegant way:

> Peirce was tempted to define truth outright in terms of scientific method as the ideal theory which is approached as a limit when the (supposed) canons of scientific method are used increasingly on continuing experience. But there is a lot wrong with Peirce's notion, besides its assumption of a final organon of scientific method and its appeal to an infinite process. There is a faulty use of numerical analogy in speaking of a limit of theories, since the notion of limit depends on that of "nearer than" which is defined for numbers and not for theories. And even if we by-pass such troubles . . . still there is trouble in the imputation of uniqueness ("the ideal result").[15]

"Scientific method is the way to truth," Quine adds, "but it affords even in principle no unique definition of truth. Any so-called pragmatic definition of truth is doomed to failure equally."[16] On the argument, every provisional gain in a developing inquiry remains forever risked in principle. There are no gains that, once made, are safely fixed come what may. Peirce could not have shown that the fallibilistic correction of whatever procedure appeared to lead in the short run to a significant gain would also hold in any longer run, or would politely fit in the ultimate long run into a single continuous series of incremental improvements convergently projected from any point in that same series. *The very method of correction* (in the short term) *may require correction or invite a radical turn* (in a later *short run*). There is no "linear" improvement to be had. (Fallibilism can make no sense of it.)

In analyzing Peirce's notion of an "infinite progress," Quine inadvertently tumbles onto the deeper weakness of Peirce's "Hegelian" theme: for it must be the case, on Peirce's view, that *some* particular discoveries at *some* stages of human inquiry (but which ones and why?)

must form the *henceforth* reliable phases of the evolving process whose *telos* can be discerned only at the end of inquiry.

This is the same point Putnam had championed in the version of scientific realism he once shared with Richard Boyd.[17] The doctrine of the (transhistorical) regulative function of truth is simply a commitment to the ultimate telos of (the history of) inquiry. But Putnam effectively disallows his own right to appeal—*criterially*—to such a telos. So Putnam equivocates (as does Peirce) about the relation between reason and the flux of history. Quine takes note of the fallacy but without the slightest interest in the theory of history: he simply reduces Peirce's pronouncement to a formal non sequitur.

Still, it is the same Quine who, in his own voice, had urged an indivisible holism (in science) deeper than any Pierre Duhem had ever dreamt of—one impenetrable to cognitive privilege of any sort. Quine even disallows a principled disjunction between analytic and synthetic truths.[18] In that attenuated sense, he may be read as having compressed our historicized theme into a synchronic slice of scientific practice (for the sake of his formal treatment of the matter). This is hardly Quine's intention, of course: it's no more than a sly way of explaining the congruity between Quine's criticism of Peirce and our own recovery of Hegel's mastery of the historicist theme. But it would not be amiss to mention that the fatal weakness of Hegel's telic theme regarding the cunning of reason is the mate of the fatal weakness of the analytic theme of the cunning of extentionalist logic. There you have the compendious *reductio* of nearly the whole of Western thought. It's pleasant to record the charge, but we cannot stay to chat about it.

The weakness of Peirce's theory is precisely its commitment to determinate progress. History, then, is the record of that progress: hence, history has a telos, even if at any moment we cannot fathom its particular increments. Peirce's "thirdness," which counts toward the symbiosis of world and word, does not (as it does in Putnam) entail intransparency (or, radical intransparency) as well.[19] Progress is palpable for Peirce; it is unclear how it could be for Putnam (once he parts company with Hempel and then with Boyd).[20] Hegel construes history teleologically and progressively, but he does not hold that there *is* a telos in actual history or a discernible order of real progress in actual history. The telic and progressive are the normal structures of history all right, but they are what they are when retrospectively *mapped* by human historians *onto* the chronicle of appearances. That is the only conceptual option by which Hegel could escape Peirce's unfortunate mistake. However, there is an explicit teleologism and progressivism in Marx, insofar as Marx contends that the real engine of history lies (progressively) in the dialectical contests of the class struggle. But, even in Marx, there is a deeper strand of thinking that, as in Hegel, is neither telic nor progressivist in any naive realist sense.[21] (We shall return to the issue.)

III

Karl Popper's falsificationism is even more transparent than Peirce's doctrine. There is evidence of Popper's interest in Peirce, but his references to Peirce tend to be confined to Peirce's indeterminism.[22] The fact is that the falsificationist method makes no sense without something like Peirce's mythic speculation that the human mind is the cognitive organ of the whole of nature—which, of course, is needed to make Peirce's "abduction" plausible. (Peirce's doctrine is an ingenious version of the process of *Geist's* self-discovery.)[23] Imre Lakatos hints at some dependence on Peirce, on Popper's part, in developing his "method of free, creative conjectures and empirical tests";[24] he characterizes Popper's conception of scientific progress, particularly in *The Logic of Discovery*, as "increased awareness of ignorance rather than growth of knowledge. It is *'learning'* without ever *knowing*."[25] Lakatos's reading is a kindly letter with a devastating message.

Still, the question nags: how can we know that science is progressive if we are blindly bound to an infinite space of hypotheses, even if some limited conjectures appear (to us) to be falsified by our present resources? Popper answers by linking falsification to his curious doctrine of verisimilitude:

> Intuitively speaking [Popper explains], a theory T_1 has less verisimilitude than a theory T_2 if and only if (a) their truth contents and falsity contents (or their measures) are comparable, and either (b) the truth content, but not the falsity content of T_1 is smaller then T_2, or else (c) the truth content of T_1 is not greater than that of T_2, but its falsity content is greater. In brief, we see that T_2 is nearer to the truth, or more similar to the truth, than T_1, if and only if more true statements follow from it, but not more false statements or at least equally many true statements but fewer false statements.[26]

Apart from the utter unworkability of this proposal (the measures compared are obviously no more than transient artifacts of our historical horizon and verbal conventions), the point of the intended linkage rests with Popper's so-called "modified essentialism," which is itself an attack *on* essentialism proper (that is, the strong realist reading of the laws of nature): "I do not think." Popper says that "we can never describe, by our universal laws, an *ultimate* essence of the world. I do not doubt that we may seek to probe deeper and deeper into the structure of our world or, as we might say, into properties of the world that are more and more essential, or of greater and greater depth."[27] On the one hand, essences are taken to be noumenal; on the other, *we* somehow manage to approach these properties asymptotically through the work of science. It is as if Popper had economized on Peirce's extravagance; for Popper construes the laws of nature "as (*conjectural*) descriptions of the structural properties of nature—of our world itself" but as neither "inherent in the singular things [of the world nor as] Platonic ideas outside the world."[28] Popper advocates an inductivism *manqué of* his own falsificationist method. In fact, Popper has himself admitted, more recently, the unsatisfactory standing of verisimilitude, without (however) abandoning the notion itself.[29] The result is the sheer drift of his own progressivism.

IV

Now, Popper has a theory of history as well, but it is equally baffling. In his historical note to the third edition of *The Poverty of Historicism*, Popper straightforwardly declares: "The fundamental thesis of this book is that the belief in historical destiny is sheer superstition, and that there can be no prediction of the course of human history by scientific or any other rational methods."[30] But in the preface to the first edition, he had already concluded: "The argument does not, of course, refute the possibility of every kind of social prediction; on the contrary, it is perfectly compatible with the possibility of testing social theories—for example, economic theories—by way of predicting that certain developments will take place under certain conditions. It only refutes the possibility of predicting historical developments to the extent to which they may be influenced by the growth of our knowledge."[31] Of course, wherever the formulaic view of verisimilitude fails, Popper can offer no measure of the "growth" of knowledge (or the "reduction" of ignorance): he would not then be able to show that "science" had any advantage over "history," he would not even be justified in dismissing the belief in "destiny." Remember: Popper has never shown that increases in verisimilitude accord with the "growth" of knowledge (via falsification).

One cannot be sure of Popper's meaning. If we take him to mean that some predictions may be "rational" though not "scientific," that to be scientific entails complying with falsificationism, then the note and the

preface are clearly incompatible. If, on the other hand, we favor Lakatos's reading (offered a moment ago), then we can never speak reliably
of "the [positive] growth of our knowledge." The complaint against
history would then be utterly fatuous: not even the prediction of physical
events could then be shown to be "influenced by the growth of our
knowledge."

In a recent review of his own long-held views, Popper claims that "the
rationality of science and of its results—and thus of the 'belief' in
them—is essentially bound up with its progress, with the ever-renewed
discussion of the relative merits of new theories; it is bound up with the
progressive overthrow of theories, rather than with the *progressive corroboration* (or increasing probability) resulting from the accumulation
of supporting observations, as inductivists believe."[32] But here, "progressive overthrow" surely means no more than "successive overthrow";
otherwise, it is as arbitrary as the inductive measure of progress itself.
In that case, science cannot be shown to be "rational" at all. (Needless
to say, both falsificationism and inductivism require a reliable measure
of progress.) "No society," Popper insists, "can predict, scientifically, its
own future states of knowledge."[33] Of course he's right.

These quibbles are hardly negligible. They show how carelessly Popper dismisses the possibility of a "theoretical [or scientific] history."[34] It
was Popper, after all, who disallowed the realist's reading of the laws of
nature and conceded (however equivocally) that historical prediction
was possible. It's the same Popper who objects to every pretense at
fathoming "the growth of our knowledge" and who yet affirms that
"The course of human history *is* strongly influenced by the growth of
human knowledge."[35] We are lingering over a few lines of print, it's true;
but if they help to recover the possiblity of a "scientific" history, they will
have been worth our patience.

It may be that, when officially affirmed by Popper, "growth of knowledge" never means more than what is meant by "progress," by increased
"verisimilitude," "elimination of error . . . by nonviolent rational criticism."[36] If so, then the elimination of a world-historical telos or destiny
or special laws of history may actually advance the prospects of a
scientific history—not, to be sure, in accord with Popper's view of science
and history, and certainly not in accord with Hempel's. But there's
reason to believe that those two gentlemen are wildly wrong about what
the sciences can deliver. Hempel, you remember, had concluded that
history is little more than a heuristic exercise: genuine science is hero-
ically committed to eking out the invariant laws of nature. Popper was

always an opponent of that inductivist view; but his own doctrine of verisimilitude (that is, "modified essentialism") simply reinstates, along falsificationist lines, another realism for our nomological "conjectures" to be *about*. Neither maneuver seems entirely propitious, and neither quite vindicates its contempt for objective history.

V

Consider the following pronouncement of Popper's:

> Sociology, to the historicist, is theoretical history. Its scientific forecasts must be based on laws, and since they are historical forecasts, forecasts of social change, they must be based on historical laws.
>
> But at the same time the historicist holds that the method of generalization is inapplicable to social science, and that we must not assume uniformities of social life to be invariably valid through space and time, since they usually apply only to a certain cultural or historical period. Thus social laws—if there are any real social laws—must have a somewhat different structure from the ordinary generalizations based on uniformities. Real social laws would have to be "generally" valid. But this can only mean that they apply to the whole of human history, covering all of its periods rather than merely some of them. But there can be no social uniformities which hold good beyond single periods. Thus the only universally valid laws of society must be the laws which *link up the successive periods*. They must be *laws of historical development* which determine the transition from one period to another. This is what historicists mean by saying that the only real laws of sociology are historical laws.[37]

We know Popper holds that what makes a conjectured hypothesis scientific is that it is genuinely falsifiable. Popper does not envisage that universal lawlike hypotheses in physics will be *true*; also, he never shows (he cannot show) that generalizations restricted to historical "periods" cannot be treated as falsifiable. It's true enough that Popper opposes essentialism in all our nomological conjectures. That's the point of his war against "methodological essentialism" (which, he claims, "was founded by Aristotle, who taught that scientific research must penetrate to the essence of things in order to explain them").[38] But even verisimilitude is really committed—committed even methodologically (against Popper's express denial)—to some such doctrine.

Furthermore, Popper never shows that a commitment to universal invariances is really needed to sustain (in at least a formal sense) the realist pretensions regarding physics or history; nor does he show that historicists could never formulate (if they cared) their own conjectures

in a vacuous universal form, all the while they simply tested their conjectures for the "periods" for which they were really intended. In fact,
physics cannot do better in principle or in practice.[39] Certainly, biology
cannot.[40]

Third, on Popper's say-so, historicists "accept" the "unity" conception, since they suppose that "success in sociology would . . . consist,
basically, in the corroboration of predictions. It follows [Popper says]
that certain methods—predictions with the help of laws, and the testing
of laws by observation—must be common to physics and sociology."[41]
But if all this is true, then there is no principled disjunction between
physics and sociology or history, though there are differences in effective
prediction of course. Remember: on Popper's theory, the "degree of
corroboration of a theory (which is something like a measure of the
severity of the tests it has passed) cannot be interpreted simply as a
measure of its verisimilitude. At best, it is only an *indicator* . . . of verisimilitude, as it appears at the time *t*. For, the degree to which a theory
has been severely tested I have introduced [he says] the term 'corroboration.'"[42] So, a temporally indexed "corroboration" of a theory does
not logically require the exceptionless invariance of its would-be laws,
and it does not directly bear at all on confirming such laws (or confirming
their verisimilitude). It certainly does not settle the question whether
invariant laws *are* necessary to science, and it exposes how gratuitous the
doctrine of verisimilitude is.

In any case, all this constitutes Popper's closest approximation to
Peirce: it's the poor fruit of a strenuous labor. It confirms at a stroke that
the *method* of corroboration at *t* may well need to be altered at *t′* in ways
that cannot *ever* be rationally determined at *t*. So Popper is effectively
reclaimed by Aristotle (whom he despises). There's a lot of flummery
here.

VI

We are tracking the career of a strange concept—from Hempel's high
discipline to certain increasingly arbitrary claims about invariant laws
and real progress. Its declension depends on historicizing the accomplishments of science and on challenging the grounds for involving
invariant laws. We are, in effect, defining a middle ground between the
extravagances of Vico and Collingwood on the one hand and those of
Hempel and Popper on the other. The first would save history by disjoining its invariances from the invariances of physical nature; the second

would diminish or dismiss history altogether by exposing its inability to bring its explanatory work into accord with the covering-law model. Progress in physical science becomes irrelevant to the first, and the second simply precludes history as a serious discipline.

The disjunction has proved intolerable since the appearance of Thomas Kuhn's *The Structures of Scientific Revolutions*, for Kuhn infects the analytic philosophy of science with the deep worry that human reason and inquiry must be as much subject to the flux of history as any particular picture of the world our science might confirm. In this, Kuhn himself was surprised, even dismayed, by the gathering appeal of the subversive possibilities of his theory. More locally, his intuitions about history—which are hardly systematically developed—became more and more entangled with all sorts of Hegelian, Marxist, Nietzschean, Weberian, Durkheimian, Foucauldian currents, possibly through a connection with the prescient inquiries of such figures as Ludwig Fleck and Gaston Bachelard.

Kuhn confesses that he too, once upon a time, subscribed to the covering-law model of history. (He does not actually name Hempel.)[43] He observes that historians cannot be denied access to the covering laws of their own field of interest—if there are any such laws. He claims only that the usual specimen "laws" are trivial and that the historian's *explanatory* task lies elsewhere:

> When [social scientists, imitating the physical scientist] draw examples from historical writings, [he says,] the laws they educe are at once obvious and dubious: for example, "Hungry men tend to riot." Probably, if the words "tend to" are heavily underscored, the law is valid. But does it follow that an account of starvation in eighteenth-century France is less essential to a narrative dealing with the first decade of the century, when there were no riots, than to one dealing with the last, when riots did occur?
>
> Surely, the plausibility of a historical narrative does not depend upon the power of a few scattered and doubtful laws like this one. If it did, then history would explain virtually nothing at all. . . . I am not claiming, [he goes on,] that the historian has access to no laws and generalizations, nor that he should make no use of them when they are at hand. But I do claim that, however much laws may add substance to an historical narrative, they are not essential to its explanatory force.[44]

There is a distinct gain to be collected here, although Kuhn himself has "no alternative philosophy of history or of historical explanation to offer."[45] For one thing, Kuhn affirms that the historian's task is not the same as the social scientist's: it is, he says, a narrative task. Second, he favors a realist sense of narrative. Third, he insists that the historian is subject to constraints of rigor and may be said to explain the events he collects. Finally, he offers a sketch of the useful sorts of explanatory work in history that cannot be provided by the physical or human sciences, that play a consequential part in the ongoing work of the sciences themselves and the philosophy of science. That is something of a small windfall.

We are taking advantage of Kuhn's resistance—as an insider—to the automatic application of the covering-law model (and any of its analogues) to history. Kuhn admits he has no ramified theory of history. (Some would say he has no theory of science.) He believes there are laws of nature, but he has no argument to show that there must be invariant laws. He is candid enough to favor the possibility of objective (narrative) history,[46] but he does not work out the relationship between science and history. He adds very little more. He mentions inviolable "rules" that "limit but do not determine the outcome of . . . the historian's task": the historian must not falsify the facts to be explained; he works (somewhat as a child does, putting the pieces of a puzzle together) "to fit [those pieces] to form a familiar, if previously unseen, product." Kuhn says the historian is neither a prophet nor a seer. "If history is explanatory," he says, "that is not because its narratives are covered by general laws. Rather it is because the reader who says, 'Now I know what happened,' is simultaneously saying, 'Now it makes sense; now I understand; what was for me previously a mere list of facts has fallen into a recognizable pattern.' I urge [Kuhn adds] that the experience he reports be taken seriously."[47] He offers little else.

Kuhn calls the historian's work "global." It incorporates discrete events into an inclusive pattern that: (1) *resembles* the narratizable patterns of ordinary life, and (2) strikes us as *explaining, by making familiar*, the scattered historical facts that otherwise form "a mere list." Thus far, there is no real difference between Kuhn's and Collingwood's accounts, except that Collingwood is quite clear about his theory of human reason, and Kuhn is not. What we have is rather inchoate as a theory, but the pieces are important.

There is a troubling element in Kuhn's account—the jigsaw puzzle analogy. Apparently Kuhn believes: (1) that historical "facts" are relatively independent of *the historian's theorizing intervention in piecing them together in his narrative*; and (2) that *the historical facts are facts in no more complicated a sense than are the facts of the physical sciences*. In the Preface to *The Essential Tension*, he also risks an admission to the effect that he has only begun to realize he is practicing "the hermeneutic method."[48] But he hardly seems to have grasped that this itself calls into question the jigsaw model in regard to items (1) and (2). (Of course, his view of the *physical* "facts"—remember Priestley and Lavoisier!—requires a much more radical conception of the role of history than the jigsaw model would ever allow. "Facts" are theoretical constructions. Surely Kuhn sees that.)

So from these small potatoes, a thicker brew begins to form. Even where Kuhn admits that causal laws "enter science as net additions to [empirical] knowledge and are never thereafter entirely displaced," he admits that "it is no longer clear just what it would be for a law to be purely empirical." He also says (but does not stay to explain): "Nevertheless, as an admitted idealization, this standard account of empirical laws fits the historian's experience quite well."[49] We may, therefore, suppose that "idealization" collects physical events within the scope of a covering law analogously to the way in which the historian's narrative collects historical events. But that already invites a sense of the hermeneutic method richer than any Kuhn supplies.

VII

Kuhn's deep prejudice lies in this: he is committed a priori to some ultimate invariant structure of nature; but his own historicized picture of the actual work of science makes it increasingly difficult to ensure any realist (or "idealist") reading of such invariance.

The obverse side of his conviction appears in his discussion of Karl Popper. First, he acknowledges that neither he nor Popper is an inductivist; then he criticizes Popper for speaking so easily of "testing" "revolutionary" theories by his falsificationist method (or speaking of anyone's simply "learning from our mistakes" in replacing "Ptolemaic astronomy, the phlogiston theory . . . or Newtonian dynamics"):[50]

> Quite possibly Sir Karl's sense of "mistake" can be salvaged, but a successful salvage operation must deprive it of certain still current implications. Like the term "testing," "mistake" has been borrowed from normal science, where its use is reasonably clear, and applied to revolutionary episodes, where its application is at best problematic. That transfer creates, or at least reinforces, the prevalent impression that whole theories can be judged by the same sort of criteria employed when judging the individual research applications of a theory. The discovery of applicable criteria then becomes a primary desideratum for many people. That Sir Karl should be among them is strange, for

the search runs counter to the most original and fruitful thrust in his philosophy of science. . . . I fear that he is pursuing a will-o'-the-wisp born from
the same conjunction of normal and extraordinary science which made tests
seem so fundamental a feature of the sciences.[51]

"Testing" and "mistake" prove to be no more than vague bets made
within the transient process of historical science—however "salvage-
able" may be the fruits of a fallibilism continuously committed to the
"*normal*" science of some past interval. In this sense Kuhn implicitly
undercuts both Peirce's and Popper's claims. But in doing that, he inadvertently undercuts his own optimism. The difficulty is this: Kuhn
cannot draw a principled line between normal and revolutionary science.
Progress is impossible to measure. (The reasons are no more than a gloss
on Hegel's text.)

Popper too is caught, but for different reasons:

Since I have used the word "progress" several times [he says], I had better
make quite sure . . . that I am not mistaken for a believer in a historical law
of progress. . . . The history of science, like the history of all human ideas,
is a history of irresponsible dreams, of obstinacy, and of error. But science is
one of the very few human activities—perhaps the only one—in which errors
are systematically criticized and fairly often, in time, corrected. This is why
we can say that, in science, we often learn from our mistakes, and why we
can speak clearly and sensibly about making progress there.[52]

The difference between Kuhn and Popper is this. Kuhn believes in
progress because he believes in an invariant order of reality that we
somehow fathom; but he never imagines he could construct a methodology valid for different histories; and he never ventures an assured claim
about any large invariances. He does, it's true, adopt certain generic
marks of what it would be reasonable to construe as scientific reason.[53]
Popper, however, advances a timeless methodology, though the actual
process of science depends on the sheer contingency of our candidate
hypotheses. He insists, therefore, that *any* successful string of falsifica-
tions accumulates in such a way that we may claim to approach, progressively, the noumenally inaccessible invariances of the real world.
Kuhn's progressivism is a mere hope that never functions criterially;
Popper's is criterally determinate—and therefore untenable.

For Kuhn, the physical laws are inseparable from their encompassing
histories, though they may be "salvaged" moving from one theory to
another.[54] Popper has no sense at all of the historicized nature of the

hypotheses he means to test by falsification. Hence, like Peirce, his argument depends on a sort of diminished teleologism that he never perceives.

Kuhn has a more powerful insight into history:

> When [the historian] looks at a given period in the past [Kuhn says] he can find gaps in knowledge later to be filled by empirical laws. The ancients knew that air was compressible but were ignorant of the regularity that quantitatively relates its volume and pressure; if asked, they would presumably have conceded the lack. But the historian seldom or never finds similar gaps to be filled by later theory. In its day, Aristotelian physics covered the accessible and imaginable world as completely as Newtonian physics later would. To introduce the latter, the former had to be literally displaced. After that occurred, furthermore, efforts to recapture Aristotelian theory presented difficulties of a very different nature from those required to recapture an empirical law. Theories, as the historian knows them, cannot be decomposed into constituent elements for purposes of direct comparison either with nature or with each other. That is not to say that they cannot be analytically decomposed at all, but rather that the lawlike parts produced by analysis cannot, unlike empirical laws, function individually in such comparisons.[55]

There may be difficulties with Kuhn's conception of science; but if there are, the pertinent corrections would strengthen his picture of history's function. For what he means here is that scientific "theories are in certain essential respects holistic" (relatively undecomposable),[56] "global" (meant to unify a society's entire experience), *and* already narratized in structure (apt for indicating the train of rational thought by which the scientists of a given age made just the conceptual linkages they did among observable data, would-be laws, and explanatory theories). As he says, "[t]he overwhelming majority of historical work is concerned with process, with development in time. . . . About these processes we know very little, and we shall not learn more until we learn properly to reconstruct selected theories of the past. As of today, the people taught to do that job are historians, not philosophers."[57]

Theories, then, have two salient interests: one is concerned to link explanatory laws to "empirical" laws (themselves connected, though not inductively, to the scattered data of some scientific work); the other is concerned to preserve, by way of a synchronic summary, the historical movement of the rational, self-critical process by which the first comes to be favored (in its time). The historical pattern of past science is plainly hidden, partially erased, difficult to fathom. So history has always had its distinctive role to fill. Where it succeeds, it explains, as Kuhn says, by making the pattern of reasoning "familiar." Hence, Kuhn's excursion into the theory of history inclines him to dismiss the invariant (real) structures of nature (as in Hempel) *and* the invariant (real) structures of human reason (as in Collingwood and Reichenbach). But he relents, at least far enough to recover his party credentials.

What Kuhn shows by indirection is the coherence and plausibility of joining *a realist reading of narrative history, on the concession that the world may be a flux, with the conviction that human reason cannot claim an invariance greater than the other's.* There you have a summary of the entire thrust of Western philosophy—focused, in terms of methodology, at the end of the millennium.

VIII

Finally, we need to offer a better sense of the tension in Kuhn's conception of the history of science, since there is every reason to believe related difficulties will surface in other accounts. The clue is a nice one: it appears almost at once in the Introduction to *The Structure of Scientific Revolutions*. One could, Kuhn says there, construe the "history of science [as] the discipline that chronicles both [the] successive increments [to an ideally adequate science] and the obstacles that have inhibited their accumulation."[58] To go that far would be to agree with Hempel and Popper. But then, as he also observes, *that* very effort is hopelessly stalemated by the fact that, if "[o]ut-of-date theories are not in principle unscientific because they have been discarded"—that is, if, say, Aristotelian dynamics "can be produced by the same sorts of methods and held for the same sorts of reasons that now lead to scientific knowledge"— then "science has included bodies of belief quite incompatible with the ones we hold today."[59]

Here, Kuhn anticipates the account of history he gives in *The Essential Tension*: it leads, he says, to a "historiographic revolution in the study of science," in which, as in the work of Alexander Koyré (whom he features), historians "insist upon studying [not the relation of Galileo's views to those of modern science], but [the opinions of Galileo's group, i.e., his teachers, contemporaries, and immediate successors in the sciences, and] the opinions of that group and other similar ones from the viewpoint—usually very different from that of modern science—that gives those opinions the maximum internal coherence and the closest possible fit to nature."[60] So a strong narrative conception was already in place in Kuhn's first account. On the summary we have been pursuing, it must have signified that Popper completely falsified the historicized nature of the very concepts on which the progress he reports depended. He cannot have been aware of it; and yet its recovery requires in principle the same "historiographic" attention due Aristotle and Galileo.

Nevertheless, at the end of the original monograph, Kuhn raises and answers the same question of progress. He tries to save the notion and, simultaneously, to oppose Popper's doctrine of verisimilitude. Progress in science must meet at least "two all-important conditions," he says: "First, the new candidate must seem to resolve some outstanding and generally recognized problem that *can be met in no other way*. Second, the new paradigm must promise to preserve *a relatively large part of* the concrete problem-solving ability that has accrued to science through its predecessors."[61] Here, Kuhn certainly eclipses Popper's doctrine; for, even for progress, we need only "preserve a relatively large part" of science's past achievements. The deliberate vagueness of the phrasing scuttles any hope of precision in measuring verisimilitude:

> A sort of progress will inevitably characterize the scientific enterprise so long as such an enterprise survives. [This is apparently because, within the scope of an enterprise for solving the problems or puzzles that its paradigms define, such solutions must inevitably be progressive; and because "(scientific) revolutions close with a *total victory* for one of two opposing camps."] In the sciences there need not be progress of another sort. We may, to be more precise, have to relinquish the notion, explicit or implicit, that changes of paradigm carry scientists and those who learn from them closer and closer to the truth.[62]

Some difficulties remain. For one thing, Kuhn still insists on a very strong sense of the victory of one paradigm over another; but though that shores up a realist reading of progress all right, it cannot dispel the impression of the transience of the "total victory" it claims to discern. In this regard, Kuhn is a lesser ally of Peirce's and is caught up in the same "Hegelian" web. For another, Kuhn signals that we may have to avoid speaking of "truth"—in the sense of "verisimilitude"—when assessing the outcome of contests between divergent, incompatible, sometimes incommensurable paradigms. But he does not seem to realize that, in principle, he cannot disjoin the two notions: progress in the "short run" implicates and is implicated by verisimilitude in the "long run." He is doomed to be Popper's apprentice here. In fact, there is no evidence that the contest of paradigms ever yields a truly "total victory"; or that, among the advanced sciences, "recognized problems . . . can be met in no other way" than by applying this or that exclusive paradigm.

Furthermore, in the important Postscript to the second edition of *The Structure of Scientific Revolutions*, Kuhn considerably weakens his declared sense of the logical play of "incommensurable viewpoints":

> There is no neutral algorithm [he says] for theory-choice, no systematic decision procedure which, properly applied, must lead each individual in [a given scientific] group to the same decision. In this sense it is the community of specialists rather than its individual members that makes the effective decision. . . . Two men who perceive the same situation differently but nevertheless employ the same vocabulary in its discussion must be using words differently [within the same community, perhaps from two different communities]. They speak, that is, from what I have called incommensurable viewpoints. How can they even hope to talk together much less to be persuasive.[63]

This surely means that the fate of the notions of "progress" and "verisimilitude" go hand in hand: Kuhn's instinct for abandoning the second should have instructed him to abandon the first as well. (It is, we may say, Hegel's revenge.) Kuhn himself concedes the point obliquely: "the superiority of one theory to another is something that cannot be proved in the debate . . . each party must try, by persuasion, to convert the other."[64]

The center of gravity shifts now, away from the question of progress to that of communication and linguistic understanding—that is, shifts to the incommensurability question. Our puzzlement concerns the fact that

> because the words about which difficulties cluster have been learned in part from direct application to exemplars [roughly: from "the concrete problem-solving solutions that students encounter from the start of their scientific education"], the participants in a communication breakdown cannot say, "I use the word 'element' (or 'mixture,' or 'planet,' or 'unconstrained motion') in ways determined by the following criteria." They cannot, that is, resort to a neutral language which both use in the same way and which is adequate to the statement of both their theories or even both those theories' empirical consequences. Part of the difference is prior to the application of the languages in which it is nevertheless reflected.[65]

Let us be open enough to admit that objective judgments of progress are no longer possible here. Kuhn falls back to an unacceptable objectivism—in fact, he sounds remarkably Quinean. He claims for instance that those who experience "communication breakdowns must . . . have some recourse," and he offers the following reassurance: "The stimuli that impinge upon them are the same. So is their neural apparatus, however differently programmed."[66] But the recovery can be no more than an illusion, for the "neural apparatus" thought to be cognitively pertinent must be subject to the same quarrels, the same incommensurabilities, the same divergence of educative "exemplars" Kuhn has just been telling us about. The incommensurabilist issue is much deeper than he can admit—or fathom.

We need another moment to collect our gains. We have been tracking all the progressivists to their lair. They cannot make their doctrine plausible: certainly, they cannot make it compelling. Behind all the verbiage, what we glimpse is the not-so-secret insistence on the invariances of nature. Kuhn remains "a convinced believer in scientific progress," but he also confesses in effect that he must worship progress from afar. At any rate, there's no necessity in it (in the Hegelian sense): there's "no theory-independent way to reconstruct phrases like 'really there'; the notion of a match between the ontology of a theory and its 'real' counterpart in nature now seems to me [Kuhn admits] illusive in principle."[67] Invariance, then, is no more than a provisional posit within a fluxive inquiry; and science collects our best conjectures without ever exiting from history. Progress, therefore, is not a principled distinction. The theory of history must take note of that.

FOUR

Progressivism and Traditionalism

I

We must reverse course now. We have been tracing the consequences of weakening an unqualified insistence on the invariant structures of reality. We have suggested that the strong unity of science bears a remarkably close resemblance to the dominant conviction of classical Greek thought despite the separation of centuries. It is a little unnerving to glimpse in that linkage the deep inflexibility that has yielded only grudgingly to the pressures of the changing experience of the Western world. It suggests how untrustworthy our intuitions of the eternal verities may be, for they are clearly most at risk in coming to terms with the theme of history.

The journey of philosophy now seems to have gathered a new force, passing through the following phases at least: first, prioritizing the analysis of knowledge over the (ontic) assurance that reality is changeless or that change is intelligible only within the context of what is changeless (roughly: the modern ascendency of Descartes over Aristotle and Thomas Aquinas); second, symbiotizing the analysis of knowledge and the world (roughly: Kant's Copernican revolution); third, historicizing that symbiosis (roughly: Hegel's interpretation of world history); and fourth, extirpating, within the context of contingent history, every trace of cognitive privilege or transparency, or any assured invariances associated with either (roughly: the contemporary struggle that appears already in Marx and Nietzsche and therefore in figures like Heidegger and

Merleau-Ponty and Foucault and the late poststructuralists and post-modernists).

We must reverse course, then. We must consider whether and how invariance is recoverable from change. Progressivists begin with the invariant order of nature or human reason and attenuate in a game way their hold on such order by inscribing the process of their own inquiry and understanding within the flux of history. They sometimes reach a point of puzzlement at which they are no longer certain that what they mean to preserve *is* still a form of progress. Kuhn, for instance, is so unguardedly open to the radical possibilities of history—for instance, conceptual and methodological discontinuities following shifts in par-adigms, incommensurabilities among competing conceptual schemes, historicized preformations of our conceptions of what is real—that he can no longer locate the evolving practices of science within the older canon *he* means to *adjust* historically.

The literature that includes Kuhn's *Structure of Scientific Revolutions* as its most subversive specimen (already an extravagant notion in its own right) may therefore be read instructively in the "reverse direction." The question then becomes: how, within the vagaries of empirical inquiry (where no presumption of invariance is yet permitted) *can* we recover the invariances of nature and rational inquiry? Merely to pose the question conveys a sense of the danger of relying too heavily on our self-corrective powers—*a fortiori*, a sense of the dawning need to subordinate pro-gressivism to a stronger ("ontic") doctrine—one, say, that links it to the deeper assurances of something like Aristotle's *Metaphysics*. (Plainly, the suspicions of positivism regarding metaphysics must now seem a fool's gold.) A philosopher of science like Wesley Salmon for instance, loyal to the larger vision of the unity program (particularly, Hans Reichenbach's variant), finds himself forced to turn away from history, epistemology, methodology in order to save what the progressivist claims in just those regards. Within the unity tradition, Salmon functions as the diagonal opponent of Thomas Kuhn, once we search the world in accord with a reading that moves *from* empirical change *to* the discovery of invariant structure. Except, of course, for the "minor" fact that (if he could) Salmon would completely erase the effect of Kuhn's having already introduced the relevance of radical history.

There's the clue we need: moving from invariance to change, we dare not stray too far if we mean to recover progress *in* the unity sense (Kuhn's dilemma); and moving from change to invariance, there must already be (discernibly) an independent order of invariances if ever we are to claim to have found them *in* the transient self-corrective process of the sciences (Salmon's dilemma). The problem is the same in both directions. Yet there are important differences: the first produces an illicit optimism we have called *progressivism*; the second produces an (equally illicit) optimism we shall here call *traditionalism*. They are the Spain and Portugal of the newly discovered continent of history: they divide and assign themselves a moiety of history in accord with the old fixities of the laws of nature—but for quite different reasons.

Traditionalism is noticeably protean, more so than progressivism. Wherever we bracket the nomological invariances of nature and turn instead to the would-be invariances of human thought (the invariances of reason and action), entirely new possibilities and new dangers appear. Our own age favors the practical over the theoretical—speculating on the dependence of supposed invariance on perceived change. Contemporary discussions of reason are likelier to concede that reason is a "product" of history than a constant capacity apt for discerning the structures of an independent reality. Put another way: progressivism is the special darling of the sciences—except for occasional odd figures like the art historian E. H. Gombrich; but then Gombrich construes painting quite literally as a science of realist representations of nature.[1] Gombrich is an ally of those who posit the realist invariances of nature. Otherwise, of course, Gombrich's own question about progress in painting, progress in composing visual images, would be entirely pointless.

The progressivist treatment of practical reason is rarer. Its current champion is Jürgen Habermas, plainly a Peircean (a Peirceanized Kantian) who admits (who really insists on) the strong role of history in the *recovery* of the invariances of reason. There is an unavoidable complexity in our story, therefore. For Habermas's account (also, Karl-Otto Apel's, which it opposes on fundamentals) is deliberately disjoined from any realist account of nature: it adopts, in effect, the Kantian disjunction between the spheres of theoretical and practical reason.

The traditionalist treatment is currently more usual than the progressivist: it favors a stronger role for history in the recovery of invariances. One sees this, for instance, in Hans-Georg Gadamer's inquiries. In fact, Habermas and Gadamer have debated the adequacy of the other's attempt to reclaim the normative invariances of practical life from the same supposed contingencies: the one, from the side of Frankfurt Critical and Enlightenment speculation; the other, from late hermeneutics; both, in deep sympathy with the Diltheyan division of the sciences; and each, profoundly opposed to the other's attempt.

We opened these remarks with a modest enough objective: to provide a measure of closure by rethinking the connection between change and invariance, by reversing direction against the bias of the classical world (and the unity of science). Closure still seems possible here, but it has plainly become more elusive. We have also gerrymandered things a little, though not for the sake of trickery. We have been quietly testing a conceptual template for collecting the scattered analyses that are bound to follow. In the briefest terms, if we now divide the question of the link between change and invariance (1) along the lines of the two opposed directions of thought, with an emphasis (2) on theoretical or practical reason, and in accord (3) with the unity or the Diltheyan model of science, then Kuhn and Salmon will be seen to oppose one another, respectively, from progressivist and traditionalist sources regarding the physical sciences (though Salmon is hardly a traditionalist), in a way remarkably parallel to that in which, regarding the human sciences and practical life, Gadamer and Habermas oppose one another as, respectively, full-fledged traditionalist and progressivist. These alternatives should afford us a measure of closure and may direct us effectively to the implications of radicalizing the role of history.

But the issue is a complicated one. We shall need some patience. One sees, for example, that as human reason is construed more and more radically as a "product" or artifact of contingent history, the accelerating processes of the "fourth" stage of modern philosophy (the rejection of cognitive privilege) must make it increasingly difficult to get back to the would-be invariances of nature. One should expect, therefore, a conceptual backlash, a certain uncooperativeness on the part of some in acknowledging a world that harbors no such reliabilities.

II

We can track the theme effectively from the sanguine expectations of Hans Reichenbach, relying essentially on the logic of probability as interpreted for empirical science, to the more insistent "ontic" commitment that his principal champion Wesley Salmon has recommended in order to buttress the other. What is at stake, roughly, is a shift in confidence away from the inherent progressivism of a method of inquiry (Reichenbach) to the realization that no mere *method* could possibly function, under the condition of history and symbiosis, in a reliably progressivist way without the prior assurance of an invariant order *that* such a use could claim to fathom (Salmon).

That is, to catch up what we have already suggested: Salmon construes Reichenbach's adherence to an isolated method as risking the deep contingencies of a changing historical practice. In this sense, as a disciple of Reichenbach's, he begins (unwillingly) from what we have called a traditionalist position (one foisted on him by the circumstances of his entry into the field). As a result, he takes steps to supersede the limitations of traditionalism by shepherding us back to an explicit realism of invariant structures. In that way, he illustrates, diagonally, the need for a strong opposition to Kuhn's explicit progressivism, which is akin to the unnecessarily thin resources of Reichenbach's strategy. That is, on Salmon's view, Reichenbach's progressivism appears more like a (risky) traditionalism, precisely because it relies so heavily on the inherent powers of reason. Since reason is subject to the formative forces of history, Reichenbach's sanguine emphasis on "logic" alone may well be too thin for its purpose: Salmon insists, therefore, on an explicit commitment to the invariances of the physical world.

The shift is intended to be a loyal one: history and change are seen to risk unnecessary conceptual disorder, unless inquiry is rightly directed to the recovery of what, antecedently, is reliably conjectured to be unaffected by the vagaries in question.

Thus, in a much-admired discussion, Reichenbach begins an account of nomological statements with a reflection on what to construe as the sense of " 'reasonable' implication." The term "reasonable" is "a challenge to the logician [he says] for finding rules delineating a usage [informal or specialized] that follows unconscious rules." The problem, therefore, goes beyond deductive concerns in seeking the invariances of rational order; in particular, pertinent implications are not "restricted to implications expressing [merely] a *logical entailment*," they "include what may be called a *physical entailment*" (for instance, as in affirming that "if a metal is heated, it expands"). Reichenbach characteristically concludes: "Since the latter kind of implication expresses what is called a law of nature, whereas the former may be said to express a law of logic, I have proposed to include both kinds under the name of *nomological* implications."[2] Nevertheless, Reichenbach seems to have assigned to the inherent powers of reason invariances that should perhaps have been more explicitly assigned to the order of nature that reason seeks to grasp.

The requisite invariances are apparently to be drawn from the reflexive work of reason itself, probing its own competence in an autonomous way. This is quite a bold conjecture, riskier by far than one might wish. (That is Salmon's worry, of course.) It may also prove inadequate for recovering the real invariances *of nature*. (There's the traditionalist theme.) For there can be no assurance that the self-correction of our would-be rational conjectures is inherently progressive or that the exercise of intrinsic powers can be counted on to accord with the discovery of the invariant laws of nature. One sees at once how disruptive it would be to suggest that reason is itself a changeable artifact of historical forces: Reichenbach's entire plan would strike us instantly as naive, as no more than an extreme form of Kantian simplicity. But that *is* the daring lesson hesitantly advanced by Kuhn. Reichenbach's would-be economy is simply the most extreme scruple of inductivism.

Reichenbach favors the inductive verification of nomological statements by means of probabilized evidence. For him, "probability is always interpreted as the limit of a relative frequency within a sequence [of a class of events involving a 'reference class' (say: twenty-one-year-old persons) and an 'attributive class' (say: dying within the current year)]." The problem of such invariances concerns the empirical accessibility of a proper limit of a given frequency within a well-formed sequence of relative frequencies. Reichenbach's program requires both that the pertinent sequence *be* of the right sort for a real limit to obtain and that that limit *be* accessible to probabilistic strategies. The two questions are said to be disjoint: one concerns the independent order of physical nature; the other, the inherent powers of reason.

Reichenbach is frank to admit that induction by enumeration cannot help here: "The value p of the limit [of a given frequency, he says] cannot be ascertained by counting the whole sequence [of the events in question], because the sequence is either infinitely long, or too long to be actually counted; in fact, [he adds,] if a probability is to be used for predictions, we have to know the limit long before the sequence is finished." He says that "the value of the limit is found by counting an initial section of the sequence and extending the observed relative frequency to future observations in terms of an indicative inference. We speak here of a direct method [he explains], or a *direct probability*."[3] But his sense of the real difficulties is already too sanguine: he already assumes that, even apart from the technical difficulties that are bound to arise, the match between the inherent powers of reason and the invariances of nature is somehow assured. There *can* be no good grounds for such a conjecture. Also, the historicizing of reason is obviously against it.

This is close to what Salmon divines—always in a way loyal to the spirit of Reichenbach's program. Salmon disjoins the necessity of logical entailment from that of physical entailment; doing that, he throws into the most profound doubt the adequacy of Hempel's explanatory model as well—in fact, the adequacy of all models of science that rely primarily on *"epistemological"* considerations alone. In this, Salmon explicitly follows one of Laplace's clues (although he himself is committed to an "indeterminate world"):

> Nomological necessity [he says], derives from the laws of nature in much the same way as logical necessity rests upon the laws of logic. *In the absence of knowledge of the explanatory facts, the explanandum-event* (the appearance of Halley's comet, say) was something that *might not have occurred for all we know; given the explanatory facts it had to occur.* The explanation exhibits the nomological necessity of the fact-to-be-explained, given the explanatory facts. Viewing the matter in this way, one need not maintain that an explanation is an argument showing that the explanadum-event had to occur, given the initial conditions. . . . In the epistemic conception, the relation of *logical* necessity obtains between the entire explanans and the explanandum by virtue of the laws of deductive logic. In the modal [what Salmon later calls the "ontic"] conception, the relation of *physical* necessity holds between particular antecedent conditions and the explanandum-event by virtue of the general laws, which we are taking to be part of the explanans.[4]

However coherent Salmon's "ontic" commitment may be, there is no obvious logical necessity in accord with which we must admit that physical necessity (nomological invariance) actually obtains in the real world. Salmon sees the need, therefore, to buttress Reichenbach's conjecture if it is to pass muster; but he offers no compelling reason for his own recovery. His own principle has in effect now been opposed in the strongest imaginable way—for instance, by Bas van Fraassen;[5] and it is surely no more compelling on its face than the (failed) ancestral conjecture of Aristotle's *Metaphysics*, Book Gamma.[6] All this may be surmised from the penny history we have already adduced. The point is simply that, to "save" science or to make it "reasonable," it is *not demonstrably necessary* to subscribe to nature's necessarily possessing invariant structures. It is not only not necessary, it may be positively arbitrary, in the light of science's history.

That is a lesson obviously unpleasant for many.

III

In a larger vision of science, Reichenbach's (and Salmon's) arguments would not be taken to be terribly different from Hempel's (or even Popper's): for they ensure progress as the proper consequence of a science rationally pursued within an order of nature hospitable to self-corrective conjectures and committed to the discovery of invariant laws. We may even say that Reichenbach's program is designed to offer the thinnest concession possible (in the direction of real invariances) in order to rest its case entirely on what it takes to be the rational methodology of science. There's the thrust of its Kantian-like economy. (To speak of Reichenbach's "Kantian" theme is not, however, to ignore his well-known opposition to Kant's conception of time and space and the synthetic a priori.)[7] It submerges the invariance of nature, via a Kantian symbiosis, *in* the invariances of reason. That is what worries Salmon, of course. But it also signifies that the change of direction within the unity program (from metaphysics to logic, let us say) is something of a sham: for invariance is assumed to be accessible in the match between the two. The only difference is that in the one direction, progress seems quite remarkable, almost chanced upon by sheer intellect, and in the other, its prospects are structurally ensured by the a priori match of the power of reason and the underlying fixity of nature.

Salmon, who is not disposed to rely (like Reichenbach) on Kant at all, and who is distinctly opposed to Hume, is quite prepared to fall back to something more like Aristotle's robust distinction in *Posterior Analytics* (71b14–25, 33). So Salmon offers the following ("ontic") conception: "*To explain an event is to describe it as occupying its (nomologically necessary) place in the discernible patterns of the world.*"[8] Both Reichenbach and Salmon have already conceded (fatally, as far as invariance is concerned) that the work of induction depends on making the right partition within a given sequence of contingent events, linking thereby its observed relative frequency and the nomological projection rightly made from it—which, within some ideally self-corrective limit, we are to suppose *would* explain the regularity in question. That is, Salmon sees quite clearly that even if the Kantian model were (formally) capable of accommodating nomological invariances in nature, its symbiosis (under the condition of history or usual practices) could never ensure that the putative invariances of a "correctly" employed *reason* could effectively ensure our discerning invariances that we could then reasonably take to be the determinate invariances *of nature*. That linkage must be already presupposed.

Salmon sees the matter in terms of a strong disjunction between the invariances of reason and the invariances of nature. So he makes no concession to history. Reichenbach is committed to a very strong Kantian-like symbiosis, so the vagaries of history never enter his theorizing in any way that could seriously upset his progressivism. It's only when theoretical and practical reason are rather loosely linked, when the (supposed) invariances of nature are initially set aside, bracketed, made empirically problematic, that, restricting ourselves *methodologically* to the invariances of reason, a specifically historical and artifactual conception of reason (as in Kuhn) threatens progressivism irreparably.

It is just the distinction of Jürgen Habermas's philosophical program to have set itself to recover a strong progressivism from such (or similar) unpromising beginnings. In that sense, Habermas proceeds in the opposite direction from Salmon's. If he had elected to consider the problem of the physical sciences (the problem of "theoretical" reason), he would have been obliged to confront the same question Reichenbach sets himself (the problem of scientific realism—however "metaphysically" attenuated). But since he assumes a Kantian-like symbiosis, since he begins from Hegelian, Marxist, and Frankfurt Critical concessions to history, *and* since (unlike Reichenbach) he confines himself to ethical, political, and similar "practical" matters, Habermas needs to recover "only" the invariances *of reason*. In that sense, Habermas distinguishes (a bit like Reichenbach) between a "logical [or deductive] entailment" and an ampler sort of practical entailment (which, of course, Reichenbach never considers, but which is the only relevant counterpart to his notion of "physical entailment"). Because of his Kantian orientation, Habermas treats the problem of practical reason as entirely distinct from anything like the "physical entailment" issue. That is, he separates the search for the invariances of practical reason from any presumption of scientific realism. (We are taking Habermas at his word here.)

There is a good reason for juxtaposing these very different philosophical programs. They are convenient specimens of the contemporary Kantian-like attempt to come to grips with the troubling contingencies of history—in the one, in order to save the invariant structures of nature; in the other, to save the invariant directives of practical reason.

Salmon's honest uneasiness about the supposed adequacy of Reichenbach's reliance on the "rules" of inductive reason, his retreat to a frankly Aristotelian assurance about the ("ontic") order of nature beyond *any* mere "epistemological" or methodological confidence (Hempel's, for instance, and now, sadly, Reichenbach's as well), exposes the illicit theme in the would-be Kantian recovery of that deeper invariance. We have already glimpsed the same maneuver in Peirce and Popper and Putnam. The charm of these latest unity-program specimens (Reichenbach's and Salmon's, playing mentor and disciple) is just that they betray a certain loss of confidence that suggests how to extend the defeat of scientific progressivism to the field of practical life. It is no accident that Salmon is so adamantly bent on exposing the "mistake" in Hume's conception of causality.[9] For, at some intuitive level of reflection, he is conceding (it was already a concern of Rudolf Carnap's)[10] that, apart from the fortunes of deductive logic, it is hard to formulate the "rules" of (inductive or general) reasoning: (1) in a way that would be entirely free of psychological or historical contingencies, or (2) in a way that preserved physical necessity. (Hume has no satisfactory answer for the empirical sciences; Kant wonders whether Hume had anticipated the synthetic a priori; and Salmon will accept none of that, in the work of Reichenbach.)

The failure of all programs committed to the discernible nomological invariances of nature may be very strongly defined now: (1) such programs cannot be legitimated on the strength solely of an inductive logic claiming "physical entailments" (in Reichenbach's sense) or a priori principles of scientific methodology (in Popper's or Carnap's sense); (2) merely "epistemological" programs (Hempel's, say, or Carnap's, or Popper's) must be buttressed by a deeper and independent ("ontic") commitment to the invariances of nature (in Salmon's sense) if they are to work at all; and (3) no such commitments (classically, Aristotle's and Kant's) can be shown to be necessary or ineluctable. Hence, no union of Kantian and Aristotelian arguments (regarding the invariances of either nature or reason) can now ensure the progressivism of theoretical reason vis-à-vis the sciences. We may anticipate that progressivism with regard to practical reason will fail as well. The economy is an accountant's dream; but the calculations remain to be completed. A review of Habermas's undertaking should enable us, therefore, to write *finis* to progressivism.

IV

We are confirming that the entire tail-end of our century is obsessed with the threatened loss of invariance. History (via Kant and Hegel) has begun to penetrate our conception of the entire intelligible world and the structure of inquiry set to understand that world. That penetration was bound to deepen with time, not only empirically but conceptually, not only in terms of accuracy about the past, change, the context and meaning of events, but also in terms of the ineluctable horizontal perspective and limitation from which all claims of objectivity and truth are generated. *History penetrates the legitimation of facts as well as the would-*

be facts themselves—which is a most disconcerting truth, you must admit. Many of the strongest thinkers of our era, eager to accommodate a radical sense of history if they can, manage to blink philosophically at the right moment in their own work. They draw back in order to claim to be able to discern the hidden invariances on which the truth of their own accounts of contingency and change somehow rely. All this suits our penny history, of course.

Perhaps the most touching specimen of this widespread loss of nerve may be found in the late work of Edmund Husserl. For Husserl mobilized his formidable analytic powers—for the last time—to bring his entire phenomenology to bear on the meaning of what he called "the crisis of European sciences," as much (he realized) a crisis of mankind and world politics within the context of the rise of Nazism as ever it was a crisis due (as Husserl would say) to the "positivistic" conception of the sciences. "We make our beginning," he says at the start of the *Crisis* volume, "with a change which set in at the turn of the past century in the general evaluation of the sciences. It concerns not the scientific character of the sciences but rather what they, or what science in general, had meant and could mean for human existence."[11] In an almost ceremonial way, Husserl had theorized that the conceptual invariances his phenomenological method could unearth *were* ultimately grounded in the contingencies of the life of the human species, including its history. (In that sense, there is a touch of traditionalism in Husserl.) But it was Husserl's inability to provide a convincing analysis (through every particular phase of that conceptual practice) of its "existential" beginning and continuation that explains Heidegger's early dissatisfaction with his mentor's work, as well as Merleau-Ponty's more gradual, more tactfully acknowledged, but also more genuinely distressed dissatisfaction as his own inventive inquiries began to take form.

This is not to say that Husserl first turned to the theme of the *Lebenswelt* only toward the end of his career. There is good reason to believe he was occupied with the question of the lifeworld—or *Umwelt* or *natürliche Umwelt*—throughout all of his work. It is to say, rather, that, whereas the lifeworld "is prior to the world of science in the (particularly Husserlian) order of '*Seinsgeltung*,'" and whereas the lifeworld (or *Umwelt*) is "a world I share with a community of other persons whom I recognize as other persons and who recognize me as such, and with whom I can communicate, agree and disagree,"[12] Husserl never managed to construe the work of *phenomenology* itself as embedded in, inseparable from, and horizonally affected by the tacit structures *of* the lifeworld. He never showed how that side of the story plays its part. That's the complaint of the later phenomenologists and of others otherwise sympathetic to Husserl's heroic effort to correct the extravagance of the Kantian theme. (There is a bit of a parallel here between the very different ventures Reichenbach and Husserl favored.)

In any case, it seems to have been Husserl's intention, in part at least, to respond to the implicit challenge of Max Weber's historically centered sociology—to reconcile phenomenology, finally, with the processes of actual history, not with the mere concepts of time and history (which had, of course, already been adapted within Husserl's ahistorical method of analysis).[13] That attempt utterly failed: the *Crisis* volume is the irrefutable proof. The deeper conceptual possibilities of history eluded Husserl's systematic work. They were implicitly poised in Husserl's challenge to the "objectivism" of Descartes and Kant.[14] But Husserl relented too quickly; he confined history to serving as little more than the transient setting for the phenomenological undetaking—the very *process* of which effectively denies (in Husserl's hands) the deep constitutive relevance of history itself. And yet, rightly understood, the essential problem of phenomenology *is* the problem of the historical nature of what we should mean by conceptual necessity. In this sense, Husserl betrays the nerve of his own extraordinary work. He falls back to the canon he himself had put at permanent risk.

For his part, at the beginning of his career, Merleau-Ponty had found a simple formula that demonstrates at a stroke the coherent possibility of recovering a historicized phenomenology, even as he remained loyal to the spirit of Husserl's immense invention:

> Man [he says, in the *Phenomenology of Perception*] is a historical idea and not a natural species. In other words, there is in human existence no unconditional possession, and no fortuitous attribute. Human existence will force us to revise our usual notion of necessity and contingency, because it is the transformation of contingency into necessity by the act of carrying forward.[15]

That may not unreasonably be construed as Merleau-Ponty's anticipation of Foucault's ("archaeological") finding regarding the "historical *a priori*." For it shows how the Hegelian theme may be construed in phenomenological terms; and, contrariwise, it shows how the Husserlian theme may be construed in historicist terms.

We cannot pursue the matter further. (We have already risked too much scatter.) But we need to hold one thought in place: two radically different conceptions of history are contending here, two opposed visions are beginning to take explicit form. The strain between Husserl and Merleau-Ponty is, we may surmise, really no different—as far as the nature of history is concerned—from that between Salmon and Kuhn (via Reichenbach) and that between Habermas and Gadamer (which we have yet to broach). The topic, you see, cannot be confined, it touches every larger philosophical option. It collects the common anguish of all those who, recalling the Aristotle of *Metaphysics* Book Gamma, worry (as late progressivists or traditionalists) about the loss of the world's invariant structure.

Progressivists and traditionalists, we were supposing earlier, are theorists who mean to reclaim invariance from within historical change. They have proved more vulnerable than either Aristotle or Kant (or, belatedly, Husserl) because they concede the *real* intrusion of history *into the very structure of human reason and/or the symbiotized world*. They regard thought as an artifact of history. We are betting, therefore, that science and morality (or, theory and practice) cannot be coherently recovered under that condition (historicized symbiosis) without developing a conception of history entirely different from the one that serves the partisans of invariance so well. In the canonical account, *history* implicates invariance. Extraordinary! Remember: a progressivist is one who: (1) acknowledges the invariances of nature but (2) denies that those invariances can be directly discerned. Instead, the progressivist (3) admits that reason or inquiry, reflecting on its own powers, cannot directly discern any invariances there either, and yet (4) concludes that it can, by the exercise of those same powers, progressively approximate to the invariances of nature or the invariances of reason.

Still, not all the theorists mentioned are progressivists. Reichenbach is of course a progressivist. He is, after all, a straightforward inductivist. Popper is a progressivist, because he construes the serial defeat of false hypotheses as enhancing "verisimilitude." Habermas begins as a progressivist and he remains one to the extent that he remains a Peircean. Under the "darker" influence of Karl-Otto Apel's interpretation of Kant, however, Habermas is inconsistently tempted to abandon his progressivism at times in favor of something rather like apriorism. (He resists, it's true, but we have still to judge the force of his maneuver.) Apel is no progressivist at all: he begins with a frank apriorism. Neither is Salmon: he commits himself to the invariances of nature. So the picture is rather clouded.

Now, Husserl is no progressivist either, though it is indeed possible (in the spirit of his ahistorical vision) to interpret the continuing self-corrective play of phenomenological inquiry as yielding "progressive" approximations moving toward some ideally convergent array of the invariant categories of thought that fit the thinking of our own particular species. Such a maneuver would be the phenomenological counterpart of falsificationism.[16] It is, therefore, opposed to Merleau-Ponty's historicized conception, and it suggests again the dawning distinction between the two conceptions of history that we have been hinting at.

Husserl has a great need to neutralize the challenge of history. On Husserl's example, history threatens the validity of phenomenology whenever it constitutively determines the process of actual phenomenological work. For Heidegger and Merleau-Ponty, however, history is (in different ways) phenomenology's life's blood. That is why Husserl merely "introduces" history. It is never permitted to play a constitutive role (as it does, for instance, in Merleau-Ponty)[17] in the *historicized* recovery (step by step) of the salient categories of our conceptual life. History is always and absolutely overcome—phenomenologically. Husserl's "turn" (or "re-turn") appears quite early in the *Crisis* volume:

> Our first historical reflection [Husserl declares] has not only made clear to us the actual situation of the present and its distress as a sober fact; it has also reminded us that we as philosophers are heirs of the past in respect to the goals which the word "philosophy" indicates, in terms of concepts, problems, and methods. What is clearly necessary (what else could be of help here?) is that we *reflect back*, in a thorough *historical* and *critical* fashion, in order to provide, *before all decisions*, for a radical self-understanding: we must inquire back into what was originally and always sought in philosophy, what was continually sought by all the philosophers and philosophies that have communicated with one another historically; but this must include a *critical* consideration of what, in respect to the goals and methods of philosophy, is ultimate, original, and genuine and which, once seen, apodictically conquers the will.[18]

We may claim to find, here, the bare beginnings of our contemporary contest regarding history.

In any case, the passage joins three telltale clues: first, that history sets a conceptual problem but is not in any way the source of its solution; second, that historical reflection reveals a certain constant, unchanging concern for self-understanding that must be permitted to guide us in a critical review of our own history; and third, that that very exercise calls into play a rational aptitude capable of reaching genuinely universal, genuinely *apodictic* findings. In this, so far at least, there is no difference at all between a Cartesian, a Kantian, and a Husserlian use of native reason. Ultimately, for Husserl, reason is a synchronizing competence— timeless in that sense, however tethered to the contingencies of the natural species—which functions unvaryingly, *by* variably testing whatever norms and concepts may arise in the course of the species' history. (Of course, there is no other species to consider, and infraspecies divergences are no more than occasional obstacles to be overcome. So history has no role affecting legitmation.)

Relax Husserl's relentless insistence however, yield in the direction of the historied nature of human life, adopt an agnostic view of invariance: you will have inhaled the breath of traditionalism. Remember: the traditionalist denies real invariances in this or that domain or is completely agnostic regarding them, but "discovers" the analogue of such invariances in the very contingencies of history and practical life. The progressivist approximates the real invariances of the world. The traditionist cannot make sense of approaching to what he does not concede obtains, and yet he is surprised to find that history yields effective saliences that are as good as invariances!

Husserl was never so concessive, for he was adamant about the inherent powers of reflexive reason:

> Together with the new task [the one just cited] and its universal apodictic ground, the *practical* possibility of a new philosophy will prove itself: through its execution. But it will also become apparent that all the philosophy of the past, though unbeknown to itself, was inwardly oriented toward this new sense of philosophy.[19]

We may, in this, pretend to find some vestigial attraction to the Hegelian theme of historical progress—which, of course, would have disallowed any appeal to apodictic sources. Husserl's method precludes any appeal to history, even as it traces its way through history. Phenomenological "progress" is a conceptual change inherently directed to a deeper constancy: possibly, then, a kind of platonism, via Kant, cast as the analysis of the cognizing structure of the human "subject."

There you have the vulnerable heel of the argument. For, *if the human "subject" is a "product" of historical forces, then all the presumptions of ideal or asymptotic invariance collapse at once.* For the moment, keep the possibility before you. It suggests how to recast the contest we have been hinting at: a truly radical theory of history could not possibly avoid historicizing human nature and human reason directly. Husserl is himself that odd proto-traditionalist who, having once admitted that reason cannot escape the contingencies of the human condition, nevertheless formulates every conceptual necessity so as never to need to trace its legitimation to its own *inconstant* historical source. The true traditionalist means to recover the (historical) analogue of invariance more sparely—*within* the flux of history alone and *without* appeal to cognitive privilege; he means to recover some ahistorical invariance or near-invariance or quasi-invariance or effective invariance or approximate invariance or historical analogues of invariance *through the resources of history alone.* Can he succeed?

There is a timelier quarrel than the one that collects Merleau-Ponty's relationship to Husserl. We are approaching it—it was mentioned before. Our question spreads through all the currents of the day: the unity of science, phenomenology, pragmatism, and (soon) a pragmatized Kantianism, and a hermeneutics. With the resolution of the quarrel that still remains, then, we may be able to bring this line of analysis to a close: that is, the option concerning the generic relationship between invariance and change under a strong conception of history. We may here anticipate (as has been remarked before) Foucault's notion of the "historical *a priori*" as a first attempt (on Foucault's part) to fix (at least implicitly) a viable sense in which Kantian and Husserlian invariances may be reclaimed (in diminished form) within a historicized phenomenology (Merleau-Ponty's theme).[20] In any case, Foucault himself moves on from the limited data of an "archaeological" inquiry to a "genealogical" undertaking.[21] There, the would-be "necessities" of thought are made to acknowledge the radical (and radically changing) contingencies on which they rest.

V

Quite frankly, the purpose of introducing Husserl was to set the stage for a more fruitful maneuver: to offer a plausible example of the attempt to recover invariant structures from within the flux of history, but not by progressivist measures.

Husserl never plays the game at all: he exits from history at the first sign of the pressures of contingency. Habermas, we were suggesting, is a more instructive specimen. He begins as the most important philosophical optimist of our time; still, not unlike Salmon with regard to Reichenbach, he retreats, or is strongly tempted to retreat, to some alternative to progressivism. Salmon finds comfort in an Aristotelian-like realism, as we have seen; Habermas finds it in a Kantian-like critique, though he is uneasy about apriorism. Habermas begins as a progressivist but ends as something of a traditionalist—or worse. It is for just this reason that we treat the Kantian and Husserlian options as bearing dialectically on the assessment of all those thinkers (there is an army of them) who, though more profoundly committed to the historicized nature of human life (and reason) than frank progressivists (particularly regarding the physical sciences), nevertheless manage, magically, to snatch the victory of invariance from the defeat of change: they manage to recover, you see, what appear to be the invariant norms, the invariant values, the invariant rational constraints of practical life from the very flux of history. How do they do it?

The principal exemplar of this traditionalist strategy is surely Gadamer. Gadamer is no progressivist. For Gadamer, the norms and values of human life are never actually lost: if they were, they could never be rightly recovered by *approximation. That* would make no sense. And yet, they *are* recovered. They're not recovered by exercising some timeless competence: they're recovered, it seems, by reflecting on the historical tradition.

On Gadamer's view, human subjects—hence, human reason and human commitment—*are first formed by tradition*—formed contingently and variably, constituted historically, and yet also (somehow) reclaimed in a universally unchanging way. There's the paradox.

Habermas and Gadamer are two explicitly opposed, conceptually very canny philosophers who are profoundly committed to the flux but who are also bent on recovering certain normative invariances apt for the direction of practical life. Those invariances are said to be drawn: (1) *from* the deep contingencies of history itself, and (2) *without* exercising any cognitive privilege of Kant's or Husserl's (or Aristotle's or Hegel's) kind. The programs of both fail utterly; but, in failing, each manages to expose the fatal maneuver of the other. Gadamer proceeds by invoking the universality of the hermeneutic condition in the space of practical life and the human sciences: there are then no invariances that can be initially presupposed. Habermas explicitly disjoins the rigor of practical reason from whatever theoretical reason may be said to discern regarding the real structures of nature: there are similarly, then, no invariances that can be rightly assumed. Both embed human life in history.

Nothing could be neater. Theirs is the classic contest between progressivists and traditionalists and, within each camp, between the contending visions of what the flux of history might yield. They draw in in one small quarrel all the grand themes we need to tame, though their conjoint lesson was never really hidden, never really in doubt. Traditionalism proves leaner than progressivism, but it fares no better. Both fail and, in failing, jointly relieve us of all the failed presumptions of recoverable invariance. The question will haunt us once again: what is history? How could the best work of theoretical and practical reason— science and morality, say—possibly be legitimated if wedded to the flux?

It's not too much to say that *that is* the philosophical puzzle of the next century.

Habermas begins, then, as a strong progressivist; and Gadamer, as a strong traditionalist. Each fails, defeating the other out of the resources of his own failure. Their joint defeat and the admission of the historied nature of human life mark the perception of a great lacuna in the entire inclusive tradition of Western philosophy. Everything so far considered has been premised on the possibility of reconciling change and invariance. We have traced the matter back through a declension of invariance itself; and now, reversing the argument, we must ask whether the requisite forms of invariance can be recovered from sheer contingency and change.

Our finding is plain enough, both prospectively and retrospectively, and the argument by which we mean to join progressivism and tradi- tionalism is also plain. Methodology (it is said) bends to a sense of the real world to which it applies (Salmon); conversational exchange aspires to install by consensual stages whatever universal constraints it contends are necessary to its own work (Habermas); and the vagaries of diverse human histories are happily discovered to have always and everywhere preserved an unchanging adherence to the humane values of the entire race (Gadamer).

All three maneuvers prove completely arbitrary, utterly incapable of the strong legitimation they require. Their collapse, however, instruc- tively directs us to more radical possibilities—which, as we shall see, are already incipient in Gadamer and Habermas.

What could we possibly mean, for instance, by speaking of the his- torical formation (and preformation) of actual persons and selves? Is it possible that persons have histories rather than natures? Could they, lacking fixity, *be* histories compressed as agents? What if rationality were an artifact of history? And what if the theorizing capacities of science and morality, of art and religion and economic life, were no more than the slowly changing transient forms of the viable praxis of our species, now congealed sufficiently to judge themselves constant for a time?

These are strenuous questions, to be sure; but they begin to challenge the entrenched convenience of the idiom of invariance. To honor them is to begin to fashion a fresh conception of history, one that enters into the metaphysics of human existence and the thick but fragile world of human culture. The grand contending theories are beginning to take form: on the one hand, we imagine a human world as constant as the physical world to which it is tethered, to which, that is, we assign, reflexively, whatever particular local histories we may require heuristically (Habermas's conjecture); on the other hand, we imagine a human world that is nothing but a congeries of shifting histories, from which, again reflexively, we extract whatever salient constancies of theoretical and practical life we believe we can legitimate (Gadamer's conjecture). What is saved in the first is precluded in the second; and what is gathered in the second is lost in the first. They cannot be reconciled, but their joint fate is the prize of the contest we are now facing. Dare we say it is a new contest?

VI

Mercifully, these swirling issues prove entirely manageable. Habermas and Gadamer have seen to that. So let us look to them.

We could have begun this inquiry with their particular debate, and then traced a path back to all the analogies of the recent past we have already supplied. But we should have lost the sense of the gathering history that has made their question so compelling. We chose instead to show how naturally the contest arises. That contest is in fact much more important than the particular convictions Habermas and Gadamer harbor. For, once we concede (1) that there is no necessity to suppose that either reason or the world is invariantly structured, (2) that reason and the world are inextricably symbiotized, (3) that our understanding of that symbiosis is an artifact of contingent history, we see at once that their resolution of the puzzle linking change and invariance cannot possibly succeed. They prove thereby to be no more than a pair of late messengers—"modernists," in the current slang—who (by their failing) unwittingly announce the need for an entirely new conception of history that will eclipse their own. The irony is that they had actually meant to contribute to its formation.

The contest is a classic one. Gadamer insists that all distinctions, all rational inquiry and claims, obtain within the bounds of history; they must be subject *to* its flux and cannot exit *from* it. Habermas maintains instead that history is itself the product of deeper forces in the natural and human world that cannot be reduced to such contingency: those forces cannot be the sport *of* history. Each construes the pair formed by their respective views as exhaustive and exclusive options. If either is right, we are faced with a grave dilemma: for each insists that opposing *his* option entails the incoherence of the other's; the two are plainly irreconcilable. What is to be done?

Consider the matter a little more carefully. Habermas had opened the quarrel with a review of Gadamer's *Truth and Method*.[22] He begins with more than a word of approval for Gadamer's innovation: "Wittgenstein [he says] subjected linguistic analysis first to a transcendental and then to a sociolinguistic self-reflection. [Habermas is thinking of the *Tractatus* as superseded by the *Investigations*.][23] Gadamer's hermeneutics marks a [further] third stage of reflection, which conceives the interpreter and his object as moments of the same context." By this device, Gadamer is said to defeat at one stroke the false objectivism of Wittgenstein, Hegel, and Husserl: "The hermeneutic self-reflection of linguistic analysis [Habermas continues] overcomes the transcendental view that Wittgenstein had maintained even in the face of the diversity of grammars or language games. [And] Hegel's experience of reflection shrinks to the consciousness that we are delivered over to a process, itself irrational, in which the conditions of rationality change with time and place, epoch and culture."[24] Gadamer's innovation apparently scuttles phenomenology together with historicism: "Gadamer's excellent critique of the objectivistic self-understanding of the *Geisteswissenschaften* applies to historicism and to the false consciousness of its phenomenological and linguistic successors as well. The pluralism of lifeworlds and language games is only a distant echo of the worldviews and cultures Dilthey projected onto a hypothetical place of simultaneity."[25]

Habermas's remarks collect these generous gains at the same time they claim to detect a self-defeating muddle in Gadamer's own account:

> Hermeneutic self-reflection . . . gets lost in this irrationalism [the irrationalism marked in Hegel as a result of objectivizing historicism] only when it posits hermeneutic experience as an absolute and fails to acknowledge the transcending force of reflection that is also at work in it. Certainly, reflection can no longer reach beyond itself to an absolute consciousness that it then claims to be. The path to absolute idealism [phenomenology as well as historicism] is barred to a transcendental consciousness that is hermeneutically mediated and has fallen back into the contingent context of traditions. But must it for that reason [that is, hermeneutics] remain on the path of relative idealism?[26]

So Habermas concedes that reason, intelligence, reflexive understanding, inquiry itself belong to the historical practice of some society. They cannot escape; and, if they cannot, then, as Gadamer shows, they cannot legitimately raise themselves up beyond the horizoning limitations of those same practices either. And yet, says Habermas, rather mysteriously, there is a "transcending force . . . also at work" in history. What is *that*?

If Gadamer had actually thought that historical tradition functioned—criterially, so to say—to settle pertinent cognitive claims beyond the flux of history, then Habermas's charge would indeed be devastating. For, then, Gadamer would have inconsistently affirmed an "absolute" foundation for knowledge that he himself had demonstrated was impossible. He would have stepped outside the flux of history. Remember that *Habermas* endorses the lesson of his own charge: *he* accepts the "medium" of history in all human affairs. (It's "hermeneutics" he opposes.) So the tribute to Gadamer stands. But why should Gadamer have ever supposed that the hermeneutic process could recover what it had exposed as irretrievable? The answer is plain enough: Habermas must be mistaken in his complaint (against "idealism")—which is hardly to say that *Gadamer* wins hands down. (There's more to be considered.) Furthermore, the extravagance of Habermas's charge raises serious doubts about his own way of escaping the apparent paradox.

There is a "transcending force" in hermeneutic work, says Habermas, which Gadamer never noticed. Having missed that and having realized that there must be some recoverable ground of objectivity, Gadamer irresponsibly throws himself into supporting some hermeneutic absolute. That's Habermas's story all right; but there's no evidence for it, and it's quite incredible.

The truth is altogether different: Gadamer simply dismisses the foundational question. It is not, as Habermas supposes, that he resurrects an absolute standard of knowledge from the flux of history: it is rather that he is unwilling or unable to address the question of objective hermeneutics at all. That's curious enough; for a good part of Gadamer's argument (in *Truth and Method*) is, as Habermas rightly observes, intended to undermine the absolutist and objectivist currents of the European philosophies of the day (including the romantic hermeneutics originating with Schleiermacher, whom Gadamer explicitly opposes):[27] Gadamer defeats those currents by demonstrating that *if* we historicize human life and reason, we cannot *ever again* claim for ourselves a vantage from which to retrieve any form of knowledge that escapes the flux of history. (Remember that *we* must admit that we are bound by the same constraint.) But Gadamer is hardly interested in reclaiming objectivity here. He needs it, it's true; but he's concerned only with the existential significance of man's being in that historicized condition ("ontically," that is), in whatever way affects the natural pursuit of knowledge.

Gadamer nowhere denies objective knowledge (even of the hermeneutic sort), but he does not pause long enough to explain what an objective hermeneutics would be like. He is certainly no skeptic. The important thing (for him) is that knowledge could never arise as the objectivists suppose. If that be granted (he thinks), it no longer matters whether we insist on "recovering" objectivity or not. (Gadamer cheats in this; but that is a matter that is not yet at stake.) The effect of his "epistemology," then, is no more than a mere byproduct of his theory of existential history. In fact, he comes perilously close to having no epistemology at all.

There is, it is also true, a deeper difficulty in Gadamer's account that needs to be exposed. But if the tale we are telling is close to the truth, then Habermas has utterly misread his rival. That may suggest a possible escape from the multiple dilemma we have set ourselves; and that escape is more important than the local quarrel between our two champions. There's no doubt that Gadamer's hermeneutics has its radical side. Perhaps we may enlist a bit of evidence in its favor.

Gadamer affirms that "Language is the fundamental mode of operation of our being-in-the-world and the all-embracing form of the constitution of the world."[28] Here, the theme is clearly metaphysics, not epistemology or methodology. But then, against Schleiermacher's objectivism, he goes on to say:

> We say . . . that understanding and misunderstanding take place between I and thou. But the formulation "I and thou" already betrays an enormous alienation. There is nothing like an "I and thou" at all—there is neither the I nor the thou as isolated, substantial realities. I may say "thou" and I may refer to myself over against a thou, but a common understanding [*Verständigung*] always precedes these situations. . . . Our task [he adds] is to transcend the prejudices that underlie the aesthetic consciousness, the historical consciousness, and the hermeneutical consciousness that has been restricted to a technique for avoiding misunderstandings and to overcome the alienations present in them all.[29]

To grasp the full force of this instruction, a further word is needed: that word is "*prejudice*." "Prejudice" is the key to Gadamer's entire theory of history. "It is not so much [he says] our judgments as it is our prejudices that constitute our being. . . . Prejudices are biases of our openness to the world. They are simply conditions whereby we expe-

rience something—whereby what we encounter says something to us."[30]
In Gadamer's idiom, "prejudice" signifies: (1) the social construction of
any "I" or "thou" within the practices of a historical society; (2) the
preformed horizon of its cognitive and affective powers vis-à-vis the
encountered world; (3) the symbiosis of the encountered world within
the course of history; (4) the inherently historical nature of meaningful
experience itself, fusing conjectured past and encountered present wherever the world is judged to be meaningful; and (5) the inescapability of
this condition, changing, however it must, through changing history.
Presumably, these are themes that Habermas also accepts. But Habermas
adds at once: *there is* a "transcending force . . . at work" in all that.
Gadamer says only that we must "transcend" our prejudices. So there
is a contest here. For Habermas believes we can *escape* our hermeneutic
limitations by that "transcending" (progressivism); whereas Gadamer
means only that we can "transcend" *our* prejudices *though not by
escaping prejudice*: we "transcend" this or that prejudice (Gadamer
claims) by recovering, within our prejudices, some insight that captures
"a comprehensive life-phenomenon that constitutes that 'we' that we all
are"[31] (traditionalism). This is obviously not a methodological (or objectivist) achievement of any sort. What is it?

The answer (to which we shall come in a moment) would, among
other things, explain Habermas's extraordinary misreading of his rival.
It would also be the key to the bankruptcy of both theories—which, in
effect, would signify the bankruptcy of progressivism and traditionalism
altogether. That alone would be a fair enough prize. Beyond that, it
would show the way to a new conceptual possibility regarding history:
in bringing closure to the question of reconciling invariance and change,
we should find that we had launched a new and deeper inquiry into the
viability of theorizing about science and morality—and philosophy for
that matter—completely within the terms of the flux of history, without
appealing at all to any vestigial dogma regarding invariance. It's hard to
grasp how much would be changed, conceptually, by that. But, for the
moment, we are struggling to gain the rim of that new space. The last
few inches are almost within our grasp.

VII

In attacking Gadamer, Habermas combines two objectives: first, he
means to displace all idealist conceptions of the human condition—
Hegelian, Husserlian, Diltheyan, Wittgensteinian, and now, Gadame-

rian—by a materialist account (or an account sufficiently tempered by "materialist" considerations—Marxist or Frankfurt Critical for instance) that could provide a ground for an objective human science; and second, he means to identify, within the (benign) constraints of history, a specific rational discipline apt for recovering, *as necessary*, certain *normative invariances* regarding the legitimate direction of practical life.

For his part, Gadamer means to defeat every version of "objectivism" or cognitive privilege that fails to *historicize reason intrinsically* and to interpret the human condition comfortably. Gadamer construes *Habermas's* account of rationality as violating his first concern, though he himself has no interest in methodology or epistemology; and Habermas construes *Gadamer's* metaphysical reading of the hermeneutics of human life as reinstating a cognitive absolutism that Gadamer's own philosophical program could not possibly countenance, though it is true enough that he (Gadamer) is concerned to demonstrate the validity of certain universal norms of practical reason without violating the constraints of history.

We need to establish two findings here: first, that Habermas is mistaken about Gadamer's objective (and achievement) though it is also true that Gadamer fails to persuade us as to what the universal norms of humanity are (*not*, however, by way of the mistake Habermas attributes to him); and, second, that Habermas fails utterly to legitimate the rational process by which his own would-be universal norms prove valid and binding in practical life. The first would bring closure to the fate of traditionalism; the second, to the fate of progressivism. Together, they would yield a compelling picture of the conceptual lacuna in our own age's theorizing—that the insistence on invariance has regularly papered over. To come to the end of the story would be to urge an entirely new beginning. So let us bring it to a close as neatly as we can.

Habermas insists that "the empirical sciences do not represent an arbitrary language game. Their language interprets reality from the viewpoint of possible technological exploitation, a viewpoint that is, anthropologically speaking, deeply anchored." By contrast, he claims that "an interpretive sociology that hypostatizes language as the subject of life forms and of tradition binds itself to the idealist presupposition that linguistically articulated consciousness determines the material being of life-practices."[32] This is reasonable enough. It is certainly true that Gadamer ventures almost nothing regarding the effective forces of historical change: Habermas is right to challenge him in this, though that is not the point of Gadamer's argument. Also, Habermas himself is nearly as vague as Gadamer about the ("material") dynamics of social existence.

Furthermore, the admission of the effectivity of language need not be treated as a form of idealism. It may be construed instead as a concession to the realism of the cultural world. What metaphysics would be required to sustain the point remains an open question. But surely Habermas would hardly deny the causal force of languaged behavior. That's all that Gadamer requires. Gadamer's objective is to show the universality of the hermeneutic constraint: if he could make that single point stick, he would have effectively subverted Habermas's attempt to recover objectivism—beyond objectivity. Habermas fails to see this, and, for that reason, he fails to answer Gadamer's objection to his recovering what looks suspiciously like a Kantian apriorism all over again. It's in this sense that each defeats the other, that each demonstrates (in doing that) that their joint failure is more important than their local clamor and success.

Look at the matter more closely. Habermas is entirely right to affirm: *"The objective context in terms of which alone social actions can be understood is constituted conjointly by language, labor and domination. The process of tradition is relativized both by systems of labor and by systems of authority."* He adds at once (the fatal misreading): "It appears as an absolute power only to an autonomous hermeneutics. Sociology may therefore not be reduced to interpretive sociology."[33] There is, however no reason for Gadamer to reject the first part of this: it's only that he has no interest in it (although *we* do—and must); *he* cannot accept the second: but it is misguided anyway. Gadamer nowhere champions an "autonomous hermeneutics."

For his part, Gadamer is right to affirm that "history is all of a piece . . . in the sense that there is nothing one might call a pure description in contrast with something else to be called an interpretation. . . . History as an imitation or duplication of the past is an impossible ideal [for not] occasionally only, but always, the meaning of a text goes beyond its author."[34] Habermas ought to have accepted this in the spirit in which it was advanced. The irony is that he misreads it, construing it as an assertion of a cognitive absolutism (which it plainly is not), and that he recovers his own absolutism (somehow) as an antidote to Gadamer's alleged excess. Both thinkers entrap themselves by their common Kantian and Hegelian heritage. Gadamer believes he is justified in supposing that "in history and tradition" there *are* universal norms and values suited to the entire species (perhaps better: suited to the entire population) of human persons (which, in Kant and Feuerbach and Marx, is identified as *die Gattung*); and Habermas believes he can recover, pragmatically, what (in Kant) would otherwise have required a transcendental a priori, that is, the necessary principles of practical life. Each, therefore, illicitly claims a normative invariance under the constraint of historical change: Gadamer, in the traditionalist's way; Habermas, in the progressivist's.

We are nearly at the end; we have a little further to go. Stay a moment more for Gadamer's attack on Habermas. It has its distinctive charm. "Habermas's use of hermeneutics," Gadamer says,

> stands on the premise that it shall serve the methodology of the social sciences. [But] hermeneutics teaches us to see through the dogmatism of asserting an opposition and separation between the ongoing natural "tradition" and the reflective appropriation of it. For behind this assertion stands a dogmatic objectivism that distorts the very concept of hermeneutical reflection itself. In this objectivism the understanding is seen . . . not in relationship to the hermeneutical situation and the constant operativeness of history in his own consciousness, but in such a way as to imply that his own understanding does not enter into the event. . . . Habermas sees the critique of ideology as the means of unmasking the "deceptions of language." But this critique, of course, is in itself a linguistic act of reflection [and so invites a hermeneutic understanding].[35]

The simple point is that Gadamer catches Habermas in a palpable contradiction: Habermas cannot refuse Gadamer's claim, *on his own acceptance* of Gadamer's attack on objectivism: he cannot show that *he* is not an objectivist himself; any supposed recovery of the invariant norms of reason will either be a priori (which Habermas means to avoid) or, by some sort of doubtful consensual process, will achieve an increasing approximation to the required "transcendental"—or universally valid—norms of discourse. The details of Habermas's argument (borrowed essentially from K.-O. Apel) are genuinely interesting.[36] But it is enough to remark here that if Habermas's intended argument depends (as it clearly does) on disjoining the required "emancipatory" function of critical reason from the hermeneutic complexities of an inquirer's history, then that argument cannot fail to be illicit, no matter what its details. In fact, Habermas nowhere demonstrates how the intended argument comes to grips, step by step, with the historical diversity of human cultures and the diachronic processes within any of them.

For his part, Gadamer fails to reconcile his admission regarding the historically constructed nature of any "I and thou" with the particular universal values he claims to find in the whole of human history. It is for this reason that he mentions the distinctive "combination of the normative and the historical elements in the 'classical' [that is, the 'classical' of classical Greece]."[37] He is quite eloquent on the matter, and he brooks no doubt as far as the diversity of Asian, African, Amerindian, and other native cultures is concerned. The account is entirely Eurocentric and lacks any legitimative rationale at all:

> [T]he classical [he says] is a truly historical category, precisely in that it is more than a concept of a period or an historical stylistic one and that yet it does not seek to be a suprahistorical concept of value. . . . What we call "classical" is something retrieved from the vicissitudes of changing time and its changing taste . . . something enduring, of significance that cannot be lost and is independent of all the circumstances of time, in which we call something "classical"—a kind of timeless present that is contemporaneous with every other age . . . the concept of the classical is capable of being extended to any "development" to which an immanent telos gives unity.[38]

Gadamer's claim is utterly undefended—as of course it must be, on the conditions of the argument. That is the heart of traditionalism. But the "authority of tradition" that Habermas fastens on, in the odd criticism he mounts against Gadamer, is never, in Gadamer himself, offered in cognitively privileged terms: it is never more than the historical and existential matrix within which we live and make the judgments and commitments we do. It bears only on the metaphysics of the human condition, never on the methodology of interpretation, except (once again) in the negative sense of opposing objectivism—the Enlightenment conception of reason, for example.[39] *We* cannot be satisfied with Gadamer's defection here; but Gadamer himself is unconcerned. He offers no responsible theory of interpretation or of the norms of practical life, but he presupposes that there is some ground of objectivity in the disputes he acknowledges. It will not serve to say that Gadamer falls back to familiar (and adequate) philological practices (in the sense favored by romantic hermeneutics). He *cannot* do that, having vigorously supported a radical conception of history that subverts the other. There is the difficulty in his recovery of the classical.[40]

We are entitled at least, therefore, to the strong presumption that progressivism and traditionalism fail in regard to the powers of theoretical and practical reason. What could anyone offer, we may ask, in the way of a more adequate theory of history—or, for that matter, of science or morality or philosophy?

VIII

The important point about Gadamer's appeal to the "classical" is that, in *Truth and Method*, the "classical" is entirely arbitrary, isolated, lacking in any developed rationale at all. It is simply announced. One suspects it is meant to serve as an assurance that a radical hermeneutics will not (however inadvertently) legitimate the barbarisms of a recent past. But it *is* seriously announced.

There are in fact only two possible strategies by which it might be thought to be defensible as a genuine form of traditionalism. One proves irrelevant, but it might explain the sense of universality Gadamer's claim projects. The other is a genuinely pertinent option, but Gadamer cannot consistently adopt it. By way of the first, the "classical" may signify the whole of what is intelligible at any point at which we reflect on what we should favor as the norms of human life. There is a use for such an idiom. It may signify the "universe of discourse," the "one world" to which everything belongs. It is an idiom that Husserl perceptively explores. As Husserl explains: "The world . . . does not exist as an entity, as an object, but exists with such uniqueness that the plural makes no sense when applied to it. Every plural, and every singular drawn from it, presupposes the world-horizon."[41] The "world" is one, all-inclusive, the universal setting of historical reflection, in the logically vacuous sense in which it has "no number." There can be no "plural" worlds that encompass "everything": "plural worlds," for instance Priestley's and Lavoisier's, which Kuhn considers, are themselves artifacts within the all-encompassing universe of discourse. Nothing can be omitted from it, nothing that could be mentioned. That is its sole virtue. The intelligibility of whatever falls within *that* world is, trivially, then, the source of the "classical," if the "classical" has any viability at all. And yet, of course, Gadamer posits the "classical" within the space of that inclusive world. He does not tell us why it obtains. It is not said to be retrieved "trans-historically," but it is retrieved *across* history as the stable, constant norm it is said to be. It is said to be effective for that inclusive world, coex-tensive with its range, "universal" in that sense. Unfortunately, that is a sense that Gadamer never explains. It remains an utter mystery.[42]

The second option holds that human selves are indeed historically constructed in just the sense in which Gadamer speaks of the "I" and "thou." Human selves or persons are historicized constructions formed from a precultural human nature (biologically specific at least) that cannot take on those meaningful forms (selves) except in terms of the enculturing powers of some particular society's "form of life." Human beings, then, are creatures of divergent, historically variable social traditions; but such traditions are themselves no more than the alternative manifestations of a common (if inchoate) "nature." The principal theory of this sort appears in the forms in which Aristotle's *Nicomachean Ethics* has been revived in our time, most notably perhaps in Alasdair MacIntyre's traditionalism,[43] but also among such diverse theorists as Charles Taylor, Stuart Hampshire, and Martha Nussbaum.

There are two quite obvious difficulties that confront the second option, which are not particularly addressed to any one version of the theory but affect them all adversely: for one, there is no convincing evidence that the diverse moral traditions of the world actually converge toward any comprehensive normative model or any that could be said to be "classical" in the Greek sense; for a second, there is no known philosophical strategy by which a coherent account of the norms of practical life can be compellingly projected from the natural resources of the precultural biological template from which historical traditions emerge or that can be fitted to the most important traditions so as to favor the selection of "classical" values along hermeneutic or historicist lines. There *is* a way of ensuring the desired result, but it involves some form of essentialism, no matter how attenuated. Gadamer offers no grounds for its preferment, and it seems to oppose the thrust of his own constructivist theory. In any case, it requires at some point an account of invariant human nature.

Habermas avoids all such encumbrances at a stroke, for he restricts himself entirely to the question of what may be claimed to be presupposed by the exercise of practical reason in the context of communicative discourse.

FIVE

The Redefinition
of Historicism

I

We are suddenly confronted by a conceptual desert. There simply is no familiar theory of history that abandons the support of all the supposed invariant structures of the world and thought. Somewhere, in every candidate theory that comes to terms with the deep contingencies of change, a certain loss of nerve insinuates into the flux of history some apparently reassuring necessary fixity that makes the flux benign again. Descartes's *Discourse on Method* already points the way in the context of late Renaissance science—on the very threshold of high modernity.

Curiously, there is not much difference, in this rather arch sense, between Descartes's arrest of the threatening chaos of dubitable opinion by way of the fortunate fixity of the *cogito* and W. V. Quine's insistence on the timeless adequacy of an extensional logic for describing and explaining the ephemera of the world. Both detect a conceptual unpleasantness and both provide an antidote. The first (Descartes) chooses an apodictic source of knowledge; and the other (Quine), "only" a formal strategy for regimenting sentences that take truth-values. The first is explicit about the discovery of a certain natural necessity; the other appears to drop every such claim but makes it procedurally impossible to challenge the unique adequacy of his strategy. The first proceeds by the exclusive privilege of a single self-evident proposition. The other obscures, within the engulfing holism of experience, the barest need to legitimate the equally unique privilege of his formal policy. History disappears from the accounts of both.

Ingeniously, Quine assures us that, whatever the impenetrable canopy of the global "analytical hypotheses" of our own experience, there is always in place a syntactically constant linguistic structure that can be neatly imposed on every natural language so as to fit the needs of a canonical science—that experience can never disallow and never better. There is a pertinent difference between Descartes and Quine nevertheless. Descartes everywhere insists on the changeless order of the real world: otherwise, his worries about indubitability would make no sense. History, for Descartes, reduces to nothing more than an external chronicle of change focused on the discovery of the original changeless juncture (the *cogito*) at which world and word are first rightly joined. An "occasional" God has no need of history. By contrast, Quine collapses whatever is unruly in history into the utterly blind holist contingencies of our "analytical hypotheses"—which, as it happens, we can never completely fathom, which might be other than they are, which form the tacit horizon of our understanding, which are entirely unanalyzable, and which yield no "fact of the matter" about themselves.[1] The first seems too lucky to be true; the second, too spare to be fruitful. And yet, miraculously, they converge (from utterly different directions) on "geometrical" reason and the irrelevance of history. Between them, they span nearly four hundred years of the modern world.

The important point in Quine is this: *whatever they are*, our "analytical hypotheses" need never disturb the adequacy of our presumptive physicalism and extentionalism (just those conceptual strategies that a strong unity program "happens" to favor). As Quine has it: "The point is not that we cannot be sure whether the analytical hypothesis [that we use in establishing truth and interlinguistic synonymy, sentence by sentence] is right, but that there is not even, as there was in the case of 'Gavagai' [that is, a particular native-language sentence that, preserving equivalence of truth-value, we translate within the scope of our own analytical hypothesis], an objective matter to be right or wrong about."[2] Still, what we "know" about our "analytical hypotheses" and the world *is* "right" enough to ensure the *normative* preferability of physicalism and extentionalism. Remarkable!

Quine never explains or defends his prejudice: it is inexplicable, as he cheerfully concedes. It is also nowhere explicitly linked to cognitive inquiries. Somewhat unexpectedly, therefore, Quine stands before us as a traditionalist every bit as stubborn and arbitrary as Gadamer, except that he suppresses history whenever it threatens his would-be canon. He insists on the universal adequacy of physicalism and extensionalism as willfully as Gadamer insists on his beloved Hellenism. For example, in a famous passage, Quine is happy to wear his philosophical heart on his published sleeve:

> [Beyond "any temptation to posit peculiar 'intentional objects' of hunting, wanting, and the like"] there remains [says Quine] a thesis of [Franz] Brentano's . . . that is directly relevant to our emerging doubts over the propositional attitudes and other intentional locutions. It is roughly that there is no breaking out of the intentional vocabulary by explaining its members in other terms. Our present reflections are favorable to this thesis. . . . One may accept the Brentano thesis either as showing the indispensability of intentional idioms and the importance of an autonomous science of intention, or as showing the baselessness of intentional idioms and the emptiness of a science of intention. My attitude, unlike Brentano's, is the second. To accept intentional usage at face value is, we saw, to postulate translation relations as somehow objectively valid though indeterminate in principle relative to the totality of speech dispositions. . . . If we are limiting the true and ultimate structure of reality, the canonical scheme for us is the austere scheme that knows no quotation but direct quotation and no propositional attitudes but only the physical constitution and behavior of organisms.[3]

So Quine has a "Cartesian" confidence after all. There also remains an unmentioned third alternative that Quine would never countenance, namely, that the holism of our "analytical hypotheses" can *never* be total, can never be such that there are no ways of testing the relative felicity of alternative scientific practices. (Witness Kuhn, for instance, or, closer to Quine, Pierre Duhem.) The relevant judgment calls on our reflexive powers and historical understanding, which Quine would never admit. And yet, *Quine's* "analytical hypotheses" are little more than thin versions of Wittgenstein's *Lebensformen* and Husserl's plural lifeworlds. All three doctrines present themselves synchronically, so that their historical instability is hardly noticed. They erase the sense of history.

The fact is, it is very difficult to see what shapes a theory of history or gives it an air of conceptual adequacy. If you are persuaded by Descartes or Quine, you cannot be drawn toward Gadamer's sort of history or toward any that is more radical. To say so is to confirm the good sense of so saying. To form an effective argument for a genuinely new theory of history entails reordering the conceptual space in which it is to be received. It can never make its way by mere isolated epiphanies meant to charm us at some chance point in history. It requires massive, new, congruent conceptual connections if it is ever to displace the older theories that have already ingratiated themselves in their own notional neighborhoods. You must make room for a new theory by threatening to raze a bit of the old landscape. We know that we must be ready to legitimate such changes. History demands it. But they cannot be mere creatures of the older canon or the new. They belong to the fluxive process of history itself in which we—who are to judge—are also formed and reformed by similar processes.

The issue is not whether there *are* invariances: there are always "indicative" uniformities, first-order invariances within the apparent world that promise to be as stable as you please—death and taxes, for instance. The point is rather that it is not conceptually necessary to assume that such "indicative" regularities also embody strict epistemic or ontic invariances that cannot, on pain of incoherence or contradiction, be denied. The rejection of legitimative necessities (second-order philosophical necessities) violates no known rule of reason or reality. To concede the point is to stalemate the ancient canon we have traced to our own time. It is on that conceptual footing that a genuinely radical theory of history may be attempted. Otherwise, history will always be able to be recovered as the extrinsic chronicle of local changes relativized (in principle) to some (supposedly) changeless order of things. Hempel's and Popper's and Quine's indifference to history strikes the right note, therefore, for their own particular undertakings. After all, they are devoted to invariance (though not always obviously).

The point is: "indicative" invariances are no more than discerned regularities that are thus far without exception. They are "phenomenal," "first-order," lacking strict necessity, never addressed to full-fledged Kantian-like "possibilities" regarding the invariant structures of knowledge and reality; and even where they appear, they can be instantly relativized to the historical horizon within which they do appear. We may, if we wish, construe their apparent necessity as contingent and blind (though not in the way of the skeptic). This is indeed the option Descartes and Kant and Husserl—and Quine—might have preferred, but they refuse it. Descartes contends that the Evil Demon cannot affect the *cogito*. Kant regards the categories of the understanding as necessarily species-wide, unique, incapable of revision. Husserl believes that transcendental phenomenology finally grasps the apodictic. Only Quine resists the slightest breath of legitimation, though he remains as inflexible as the others, as adamantly opposed to history's penetration of our best claims to know ourselves and the world. It remained for Foucault to reinterpret the a priori explicitly—construed as inseparable from our first-order sciences ("archaelogically," as Foucault says)—as an impenetrable artifact of the same history that enables our particular sciences to form:

> Man's mode of being [says Foucault] as constituted in modern thought enables him to play two roles: he is at the same time at the foundation of all positivities and present, in a way that cannot even be termed privileged, in the elements of empirical things. This fact—it is not a matter here of man's essences in general, but simply of that historical *a priori* which, since the nineteenth century, has served as an almost self-evident ground for our thought.[4]

This is very close to what a legitimation of Quine's program would have had to be, if Quine had been willing to countenance legitimation. But he refuses. Also, what he would have validated (his physicalism and extensionalism) are very far from Foucault's philosophical taste formed in the same era. Still, Foucault manages, without referring to Quine, to capture the sense in which a good deal of contemporary philosophy is a sort of Cartesianism *manqué*.

Foucault goes on to identify the new dilemma of the emergent sense of historicity:

> The more History attempts to transcend its own rootedness in historicity, and the greater the effort it makes to attain, beyond the historical relativity of its origin and its choices, the sphere of universality, the more clearly it bears the marks of its historical birth, and the more evidently there appears through it the history of which it is itself a part (and this, again, is to be found in Spengler and all the philosophers of history); inversely, the more it accepts its relativity, and the more deeply it sinks into the movement it shares with what it is recounting, then the more it tends to the slenderness of the narrative, and all the positive content it attained for itself through the human sciences is dissipated. . . . Man, therefore, never appears in his positivity and that positivity is not immediately limited by the limitlessness of History.[5]

To grasp the point of this is to see at once that legitimative questions remain in place—are definitely still needed—under the condition of historicity, and also, that such questions can never recover the strict necessity or universality claimed by the older canon. Frankly, historicism is a form of relativism applied to the cognitive intransparencies we have already conceded.[6] That is the most radical turn philosophy has taken in our time. It is important to realize that it offers an entirely coherent option. It is also the clue to Foucault's later efforts to fathom a "genealogical" space (beyond the "archaeological").

II

The grandest, almost the first sustained, argument in behalf of invariance (the canon) is Aristotle's—which utterly fails. Its failing will not be judged damaging by its modern champions (physicalists, extensionalists, unity of science theorists). For they suppose that *they* are not committed a priori to any similarly fixed structures. They are mistaken in this, but never mind. The failure of Aristotle's argument is the paradigm failure of all claims of *de re* necessity. To grasp the argument is to grasp that, *thereafter*, every cognate claim can only be a provisional *bet* within the shifting terms of historicized experience. If so, then there is no legitimate basis for Quine's advice when he says he is "limning the true and ultimate structure of reality." Bets are bets, however, artifacts of contingency; and stalemate *here* is victory. For our charge, you remember, is not that there are no seeming invariances of reality or thought, but only that inquiry is not bound to admit, *tout court*, any or all *de re* or *de dicto* necessities. The important argument is the modal one. We can always repudiate first-order necessities at a price.

The irony is that we are yielding to Quine in this. On Quine's account, there cannot be a principled disjunction between analytic and synthetic sentences: modal necessity cannot be more than an artifact of some contingent posit. In this, anachronistically, Quine "follows" Foucault. Also, as Quine goes on to say:

> Curiously, a philosophical tradition does not exist for just such a distinction between necessary and contingent attributes [regarding particular things—as in querying whether, generally, man is rational and/or two-legged]. It lives on in the terms "essence" and "accident," "internal relation" and "external relation." It is a distinction that one attributes to Aristotle. . . . But, however venerable the distinction, it is surely indefensible; and surely then the construction [involving the arithmetic of natural numbers—take for instance a relatively telling example: $X[X > 4]$ is necessary of 9, say] which so smoothly implements it must go by the board.[7]

But if the distinction must fail, then so must Quine's recommendation regarding "the true and ultimate structure of reality." (So also must Aristotle's metaphysics.) Quine cannot have it both ways; and, if he cannot, then it is a foregone conclusion that a purely formal resolution of the puzzles of intentionality and modal operators is quite irrelevant to assessing the (now) ambiguously disjoined *de re* and *de dicto* invariances Quine seems to recommend (that is, those in favor of physicalism and extensionalism), though Quine claims to speak "empirically."

In Aristotle, the issue is more straightforward. One of Aristotle's arguments, in *Metaphysics*, goes as follows:

> If there is nothing apart from individuals [no essences or universals or first principles], there will be no object of thought, but all things will be objects of sense, and there will not be knowledge of anything, unless we say that sensation is knowledge. Further, nothing will be eternal or unmovable; for all perceptible things perish and are in movement. But if there is nothing eternal, neither can there be a process of coming to be; for there must be something that comes to be, i.e. from which something comes to be . . . since nothing can come to be out of that which is not.[8]

Aristotle takes this to mean that any predicative practice would lead to contradiction if, speaking of individual things (primary substances), one violated the rule that "we *must* predicate of every subject [individual substance] the affirmation or negation of every attribute"—which we seemingly do violate in speaking of the "indeterminate" (with respect to essences) or in speaking only of what appears one way or another to the senses.[9] We should (by that violation: that is, the repudiation of excluded middle) inevitably *deny*, of particular things, what (ultimately) cannot merely appear to be true of them or cannot be merely indeterminate regarding them. Aristotle believes that though affirming something's looking thus-and-so under such-and-such circumstances, or denying its looking thus-and-so under these-and-those circumstances, is hardly contradictory, extending the practice to *all* would-be attributes *would* produce the undesirable result: people would "soon find themselves contradicting themselves."[10]

Nevertheless, as we have seen, Quine knowingly "violates" the "canon." Aristotle explicitly remarks that "in general those who say this [sort of thing] do away with substance and essence. For they must say that all attributes are accidents, and that there is no such thing as 'being essentially a man' or 'an animal'"—which Aristotle believes leads directly to self-contradiction.[11] Again, by construing logic *in accord with* his own metaphysics of invariance (and never otherwise), Aristotle concludes that bivalence is necessarily binding on all rational discourse.[12] But he never stops to demonstrate: (1) that the *de re* necessity of his own essentialism *is* strictly necessary, or (2) that excluded middle imposes any necessity *de dicto*, once logic is separated from an essentialist metaphysics, or (3) that logic and *his* (Aristotle's own) metaphysics can never be disjoined. He shows only: (4) that, relative to *his* metaphysics, the principle of excluded middle is indeed a necessary principle. He fails to show that bivalence is a "principle which every one must have [and use] who understands anything." For, even in affirming noncontradiction to be "the most certain of all [principles]," he *interprets* it instantly to entail an essentialism that precludes construing attributes as accidents,[13] which, of course, begs the question raised by (1)–(3). Aristotle never rightly engages the essential challenge to his argument in favor of invariance (which may be found already in Protagoras).[14]

III

We have made an important gain regarding the analysis of history, though it may not seem so. We are moving to define *historicism* in a fresh way. What we have shown is this: (1) all doctrines of necessity *de re* and *de dicto* may be opposed without self-contradiction or incoherence. They are not rationally impossible to reject. Of course, (1) does not address history directly, although it sets a favorable condition on what we might mean by historicism, namely, that the doctrine of historical flux, the denial of strict invariances of reason or reality, need not be self-defeating in any formal sense. [Construe (1) therefore as the minimal form of the doctrine that reality is a flux.]

It is certainly possible to characterize history consistently on the assumption that there must be exceptionless invariances in nature and reason. That *is* the standard view of things, after all: both Aristotle's and the unity of science program's favor it. But if (1) obtains, then philosophy would be delinquent if it confined itself to a conceptual option open to coherent opposition and obviously disputed. Also, as we were warning a moment ago, to define history in a new way is to alter our sense of the surrounding conceptual space in which it is to be made to fit. Admit that, and you will see at a stroke that the strongest version of historicism— whatever it ultimately proves to be—would require that: (2) every concept of nature, reality, essence, attribute, person, thing, process, event, change, state, time, space, cause, purpose, thinking, knowledge, belief, reason, memory, truth, consistency, coherence, principle, rule, norm, value, fact, number, logic, grammar, meaning, reference, identity, context, validity, confirmation, legitimation, justification, category, predicate, name, ideal, description, explanation, evaluation, interpretation, and every similar notion needs to be reconciled—cast in terms of—the flux. Generically, then: *every theory of history formulated in terms of (1) and (2) is a form of historicism.* Nothing could be plainer, though the supporting arguments and the best candidates still elude us.

There is another step that brings us closer to the edge of the solution wanted. Grant the cognitive intransparency of the world and the symbiosis of world and word we have already favored—grant only that—and you will find that conditions (1) and (2) are met most sparely if we admit also: (3) knowledge is an artifact of history.

We are approaching the boldest single conceptual change of our age. (We have seen it dawning already in Foucault.) It appears in many forms; we cannot capture it in a single formula. But if we see that (3) is straightforwardly entailed by (4), namely, (that) persons or human selves are artifacts of contingent social history, we begin to grasp the gathering force of all those conceptual experiments (since Hegel's innovation) that deepen our sense of the historicized nature of every notion that belongs to the space of (2). Put redundantly: every theory of history in accord with (1)–(4) is a strong form of historicism.

For example, Gadamer's account of the "I and thou" is a version of (4) cast in a somewhat Hegelian and Heideggerian mode. Accepting (4), Gadamer is led to abandon (it seems) any serious analysis of (3) along the lines of recovering an appropriate objectivity or science or sense of truth. He has no interest in it, as it happens. This failing—which, we may suppose, alerted Habermas to the subversive possibilities of hermeneutics—may (as it did in Habermas's own case) encourage a hasty retreat back to an apriorist or progressivist assurance; or else, even less acceptably, as in the lurid forms of postmodernism (in the work of Jean-François Lyotard, Luce Irigaray, Richard Rorty), it may simply lead to abandoning all hope of ever formulating a viable and plausible (second-order) *theory* of objectivity. We sense, therefore, the need for a third policy: something between the stubborn restoration of invariant norms and sheer philosophical anarchy. Historicism drifts in all these directions. It has no single form.

Though it will be doubted, there may be no more compelling version of (4) than that associated with Karl Marx's conception of praxis, once Marx's philosophy is separated from the ulterior political uses to which it had been put in the heyday of the Soviet empire and once praxis is disentangled from Marx's own penchant for a strenuous teleologism and objectivism. Be that as it may, Marx (more compellingly than Hegel) has given us a convincing sketch of what, in causal terms, it means to historicize human nature—or at least that part of human nature (the person, the self, the encultured agent) that emerges in different social, cognitive, and active guises in this or that historical age.

In a well-known broadside against Pierre-Joseph Proudhon, for instance, Marx offers the following:

> Monsieur Proudhon has very well grasped the fact that men produce cloth, linen, silks, and it is a great merit on his part to have grasped this small amount! What he has not grasped is that these men, according to their abilities, also produce the social relations amid which they prepare cloth and linen. Still less has he understood that men, who produce their social relations in accordance with their material productivity, also produce ideas, categories, that is to say the abstract ideal expression of these same social relations. Thus the categories are no more eternal than the relations they express. They are historical and transitory products. For M. Proudhon, on the contrary, abstraction, categories are the primordial cause. According to him they, and not men, make history.[15]

It is possible to reclaim what Marx says here (and elsewhere) as clarifying praxis, without implicating in any essential way his own particular reading of history. This is not to disallow an empirical role to his notion of class conflict or its larger bearing on the dialectical process of history. It is rather to say that there is also a generic argument here—memorably instantiated by Marx's own particular conviction and requiring in any case one or another "materialist" reading to get the causal connections right—that may be fitted to views of the historical formation of human agents very different from Marx's own: for instance, the views of Hegel, Nietzsche, Ranke, Dilthey, Weber, Heidegger, Gadamer, and Foucault. That is not our concern. But what may be thus abstracted constitutes Marx's notion of praxis abstracted from his own particular theory of social structure and social process.[16]

What the generic argument entails is what interests us. For, it affirms that effective human agents, not abstract forms, produce goods, and that, in producing goods in socially regularized ways, they produce the effective social relations in which they are and continue to be effective. Furthermore, in this or that particular mode of (material) production (praxis), their ideas, conceptions, categories are naturally formed and focused and have application and effect (horizontally) as the determinate fruit of the reflexive (or ideal) powers of just such productivity. Third, since concepts and categories are merely "historical and transitory products" (rather than "eternal"), and since human agents are distinguished precisely by their capacity to produce and use such concepts in their ongoing labor—even to change their activity and social relations as a result of particular interventions—*they also produce themselves histo-*

ically. They do so in at least two ways: (1) in the sense that their offspring think and behave differently from themselves as a result of their interventions; and (2) because, in their own lifetime, changes in production and technology may (as by the division of social labor) accelerate differences among those differences that mark *them* as the products of an earlier form of social labor.

This is a crude sketch of Marx's immensely plausible theory: in effect, the theory of the *Theses on Feuerbach*. But even in this form, it yields quite powerful corollaries of the items of our earlier tally. Certainly, at least the following additions: (2′) human concepts emerge from and are applied to the world through the *praxis* of historical life; (3′) all conceptual distinctions that service truth-claims are horizonal only, knowledge is bound to its local history, and the independent structures of the world are posits in accord with our historically formed interests and interventions; and (4′) persons (or selves), products of their own *praxis*, lack *natures*, have or are only *histories* (or have historical rather than invariant natures).

These three additions—(2′)–(4′)—begin to fill the lacunae that (1) had earlier obliged us to confront. No doubt, these radical claims will force some further puzzles on our attention. But they no longer threaten to be insuperable. It may in fact be the older canon's turn (invariance's turn) to be conceptually nonplussed: it has nothing to say about these newer themes. There is no sustained attention to the puzzles of individuation, numerical identity, reidentification, reference, and the like, under the condition of radical history, anywhere in the analytic canon—not merely in Aristotle and Kant, but in the unity of science, among Quine's large following, in the whole of current Anglo-American philosophy. For instance, there is no provision anywhere in the canon for the *inherent historicity of reference*. The question does not arise, has never been acknowledged.

We must put the issue aside for the moment. (We shall return to it shortly.) And yet, if the argument be valid, the theory of science requires a strong historicism. There's a large challenge there, you must admit.

IV

We must pick and choose our questions with care. Notice that (2′)–(4′) challenge *de re* and *de dicto* invariances. In doing so, they pose especially difficult questions of coherence for themselves: regarding persons, for instance, whether it is true that any view that denies that referents must exhibit a discernibly changeless nature produces insoluble paradox; and, regarding reference and predication, whether it is true that context-dependent reference fails unless it is eliminable in principle (as by substituting uniquely instantiated predicables), or whether such a substitution can be effected (if the meaning and extension of general predicates remain historicized).

The contest has been brewing through this entire inquiry. It would not be amiss to suppose, therefore, that all questions of a similar sort bearing on the concepts collected at (2) could be answered favorably if the formal features of the use of "person" and the logic of reference and predication could be laid out along the lines being suggested: that is, in the historicized way and without paradoxes. In a sense, they are the contemporary counterparts of Aristotle's objections, in *Metaphysics* Book Gamma, against Protagoras. That's all to the good, for it suggests that we have not abandoned the deep question of the relation between invariance and change.

We may claim in all this that our earlier clue was sound enough: to "demonstrate" the validity of the theory of history being advanced entails preparing the conceptual space into which it must be fitted.

We *are* theorizing about history, therefore. We are attempting to show that history need not be the negligible extrinsic chronicle of ephemera instantiating the more important invariant order of reality—the order that occupies such theories as Hempel's and Popper's, on the one hand,[17] or, by way of an equally objectionable strategy, the order that leads instead to Vico's and Collingwood's theories. We have never really left the original battle.

We may allow ourselves the luxury of a few tangential observations before turning to the contest posed. On the assumption of the intransparency and symbiosis urged—which, after all, dominates nearly every strong philosophical theory at the end of our century—any tendency to recommend an ordered or strongly disjunctive hierarchy of philosophical questions—for example, regarding prioritizing "theories of meaning" over "metaphysics," or the adequacy of certain "models of truth" with respect to the discursive practices of our native language over an analysis of the structure of the "real" world—cannot fail to be conceptually suspicious: very possibly because it affords a way of smuggling cognitive privilege or privileged invariances past the philosophical police. We witnessed this already in Quine's insistence that his own extensionalism was, in effect, neutral to or empirically reconcilable with any and every effort to limn "the true and ultimate structure of reality"—in a way that

never really required the legitimative queries of the philosophical customs office. (Recall what Quine says about intentionality!)

Here may be found an entire twilight world of conceptual recom-
mendations that never quite announce the canon their prejudices aspire
to satisfy. For example, one such account begins in a noticeably dis-
arming way (that is, without any argument) as follows: "There are just
two truth-values—true and false. What are they: mysterious Fregean
objects, properties, relations or correspondence and noncorrespon-
dence? The answer is that it does not matter what they are: there is
nothing essential to them except that there are exactly two of them."[18]
The implication is that this captures an invariance *de dicto*, but it never
actually makes a formal claim. It is, therefore, in avoiding metaphysics
and epistemology, a traditionalism in its soul, but we might never pin it
down. It privileges bivalence in the context of speaking of *any* sector of
the real world. It does not stop to ask whether our picture of that sector
will best support bivalent truth-values, or whether we had better adjust
our picture of the world so that it does; it simply assumes that the
admission of bivalence takes precedence over any account of substantive
inquiry. But once you give up the crisp, invariant, independent reality the
argument has forced us to consider, bivalence cannot but be placed at
risk. Certainly, it can no longer claim to be necessary. There simply *are*
no alethic findings that may be fixed in place without ever examining the
deeper conditions of knowledge and the nature of the world. There can
be no prioritizing of "alethic," "epistemic," and "ontic" questions vis-
à-vis one another: they cannot be disjoined in an intransparent and
symbiotized world. (The grip of the argument begins to tell.)

Again, in the spirit of Quine's objection against a principled distinction between analytic and synthetic truths, one must be prepared to argue
conformably, as Putnam certainly is in reviewing Euclidian geometry and
quantum mechanics more or less as follows:

> I want to begin [says Putnam] by considering a case in which "necessary"
> truths (or rather "truths") turned out to be falsehoods: the case of Euclidian
> geometry. I then want to raise the question: could some of the "necessary
> truths" of logic ever turn out to be false *for empirical reasons*? I shall argue
> that the answer to this question is in the affirmative, and that logic is, in a
> certain sense, a natural science.[19]

Putnam is admirably clear about the point of his maneuver. Against
conventionalisms of every sort (Carnap's in particular), he remarks:
"Those who begin by 'explaining' the truth of the principles of logic and

mathematics in terms of some such notion as 'rule of language' [meaning, provisionally: 'the rules of classical logic' are 'really arbitrary linguistic stipulations' or else 'nonarbitrary stipulations' that we are 'free to adopt' consistently without aiming to provide 'a true description of the world'] end by smuggling in a quite old fashioned and unexplained notion of *aprioricity*."[20] The question Putnam raises and the question we were just insinuating against the unconditional adoption of a bivalent logic oblige us to consider: (1) whether the disjunction, hierarchical ordering, prioritizing of philosophical questions (second-order legitimative questions regarding truth and meaning and knowledge and the like)[21] *are* conceptually supportable in an intransparent and symbiotized world; and (2) whether, in deciding (1), any reasonable finding *can* escape the constraints of historicized experience. Assuming the answer to be no in both cases, we may claim that any philosophical strategy in the twilight zone of history, of the sort in question, is bound to be traditionalist in spirit (that is, philosophically arbitrary about privileged invariances in the context of experience).

This means that we have already indicated something of what a coherent historicist's reading would be like: namely, regarding the link between logic or mathematics and empirical science, that (1) would-be *de dicto* necessities must remain forever open to being shown to be empirically false (on some reasonable interpretation of the world's structure);[22] and, regarding the link between alethic, epistemic, and ontic questions, that (2) bivalence is not inviolable and not invariably suited to every sector of empirical inquiry.[23] Notice that to admit (1) is not to disturb any favored mathematics or logic, only to construe it, wherever interpreted, as subject to unforeseeable horizonal limitation; and that to admit (2) is to make philosophy empirically responsible, where it has ceased to yield synthetic a priori truths.

These are quarrelsome constraints. Certainly, they have been mightily resisted. But the tables have been turned: the alleged invariances of logic, mathematics, methodology, the syntax and semantics of natural language are now at least open to suspicion, obliged to make their own way against the changing evidence of historical experience. Not merely in the sense that particular claims may be false, but in the deeper sense that the would-be universals of rational argument can no longer be disjoined from that argument's intrinsic history: *"applied" argument has no fixed nature, only a history*; or, better, its "nature" is itself historically posited, and changed, as a result of reflecting critically (however intransparently) on what, from time to time, seems best to *take as invariant*. (This is very close to Foucault's thesis.) We may as well say we are extracting the "common" theme shared by such disparate thinkers as Marx and Kuhn and Quine. The force of philosophical argument depends on its exemplars; their instruction depends on how they are interpreted in accord with the consensual praxis of their encompassing society; praxis itself changes historically; and we, historically constituted and reconstituted in the process, search out whatever appear, horizonally, to be the best candidates for universal legitimative work.

Fortunately, the thesis is easy to illustrate, easy to apply dialectically. It calls only for a small aside. Thus, when in a very recent examination of the "logical basis of metaphysics" Michael Dummett (who favors certain alethic invariances and who was mentioned earlier in a related dispute, regarding truth and realism, involving Putnam) weighs the *priority* of analyzing reality over analyzing meaning, or of first analyzing "the *correct* model of meaning, and the *appropriate* notion of truth . . . and hence the logic we *ought* to accept as *governing* [the sentences of some disputed inquiry]" and only *then* going on to pursue metaphysics, we cannot fail to see in this Dummett's effort to assure us that: "We are dealing, after all, with forms of statement which we actually employ and which, with the exception of the statements of mathematics and scientific theory, are familiar to all human beings. Their meanings [he insists] are already known to us. No hidden power centers these meanings on them; they mean what they mean in virtue of the way we use them, and of nothing else."[24] (One can hardly fail to recall Quine's equally gentle urging, all the while he manages to scuttle any appeal to intentionality.)

Dummett means, of course, to recommend against the priority of any "top down" policy, that is, against beginning with metaphysical problems and then "deriving" from their solution the solution to the "meaning-theoretical" questions (of truth and logic) that we need. We should, he says, "approach these problems from the bottom up" rather than *start* with the disagreement between the realist and the various brands of antirealist over the "correct model of meaning."[25] The implication is that the two issues are quite separate and that "metaphysical" questions need not color the (neutral) analysis of the "correct model of meaning."

Dummett's objection to the realist's priorities insists that, in metaphysics: "No knock-out blow has [ever] been delivered. The decision must be given on points; and we do not know how to award points." He goes on to say: "We have to treat the opposing [metaphysical] theses as though their content were quite clear and it were solely a matter of deciding which is true; whereas . . . the principal difficulty is that, while one or another of the competing pictures may appear compelling, we have no way to explain in nonpictorial terms what accepting it amounts to."[26] He all but declares that there are no comparable difficulties confronting the discovery of "the correct model of meaning":

> My contention is that a theory of meaning does have metaphysical consequences, whether we downplay them as pictures or accord them the status of theses, but we must attend to the meaning-theory *first*, and construct our metaphysics in accordance with it, rather than first enunciating metaphysical assumptions and then attempting to draw from them conclusions about the theory of meaning.[27]

The view adopted here is that there is no such choice to make: there is no principled disjunction between metaphysics and meaning-theory. The insinuation that there is is nothing but an incipient traditionalism once again (or a form of straightforward cognitive privilege). Also, the effect of Dummett's local strategy should not be lost: certain lines of speculation will seem alien and inapt if we agree to be initially led by so-called "meaning-theoretical" priorities. On the argument here favored, prioritizing the analysis of meaning over reality is simply a way of favoring certain invariances of logic that Dummett is too coy to advocate in a full-blooded way (that is, "metaphysically"). It explains for instance why his own departure from classical logic—in recommending against a strict bivalence—does not also reach to questioning *tertium non datur* (that is, the principle, not the mere theorem).

We cannot tarry over the point, but it is important enough to identify. Dummett's intuitionistic ("antirealist") objections to bivalence are *principled* objections, concerned, that is, to question the policy of adopting a bivalent logic for seemingly well-formed statements independently of whether they are decidable or not. He is famous of course for his objection. But, having decided that, he resists every effort to raise the same sort of principled question about the policy of *tertium non datur*; hence, he treats the would-be constraint—that a well-formed statement, once shown to be decidable, cannot be neither true nor false—as a *theorem* in (an antecedently adopted) two-valued logic rather than an independent *principle* regarding an initial free choice of truth-values. By this, he rejects an obvious option, namely, that we may refuse to admit that the falsity of (some proposition) *p is* equivalent to the truth of not-*p*.[28] The matter is really extraordinarily important but so skillfully papered over that it is scarcely noticed.

It is true that Dummett briefly entertains the following possibility—which he cannot reconcile with his own philosophical strategy: "Why should the past not change after our consciousness has travelled through it, and why should not the future now be in a different state from that in which it will be when our consciousness arrives at it? That supposition [he says] undermines the whole picture. For, if the past can change, what has its condition *now* to do with the truth or falsity of what we say about it?"[29] But he does not linger over the complexities of history, and he assigns the option to a meaning-theory misled by an untenable metaphysics.

Dummett has, in this, not served us as well as he might: for, in formulating this particular view of the past and future (the one he rejects), he pretends it is entirely a *realist* option, that is, one that his own "bottom-up" strategy rightly displaces. Whereas the truth is that the same option can be formulated in a way that does not admit the disjunction between metaphysics and meaning-theory at all. All we need suppose is this: that, in any ongoing inquiry of history, the *historical* past, validly characterized at some time t, may *have changed* when characterized at some later t'—without ever intruding the "realist's" distinction between "the objective correctness of an assertion [regarding the way the world is apart from any human intervention]—its truth—and its [mere] subjective justification, the evidence possessed by the speaker."[30] In effect, the puzzle may be posed *for* Dummett's "antirealist"—or, simply, without reference to the quarrel Dummett poses. Dummett's cursory dismissal of the option, which we intend to take very seriously, betrays a blindness regarding how reality may be said to be structured, and hence a blindness about the possible options of meaning-theory itself.

Put more grandly: Dummett believes there is an invariant "meaning-theory" anyone speaking as we do will tend to grasp, but the usual "metaphysics" is not similarly grounded. In this, he supposes that he sides with Wittgenstein, thinking of the first as tantamount to a "form of life" and thinking of the second as a dubiously idle use of language. If that *is* Wittgenstein's view, then Wittgenstein is himself a traditionalist. In any case, there is no reason to suppose that it is not at least as coherent to say, and more reasonable to believe, that a "form of life" is subject (however imperceptibly) to the drift of historical change. But if that is so, then there can be no secure invariance in "meaning-theories" and there can be no principled disjunction between "meaning-theories" and "metaphysics."

V

We must return, however, to our earlier questions: you remember they had to do with treating reference and predication in historicist terms.

Consider reference a little more closely. There is good reason to believe that Bertrand Russell, in his celebrated paper "On Denoting," failed to distinguish satisfactorily between denoting and referring, between a certain use of terms (to designate this or that particular thing) and a certain use of sentences (affirming something or other about something or other).[31] Nevertheless, an ulterior intuition (more Quine's than Russell's) might still be correct: that is, that, *if* all definite descriptions could be reduced to sets of general predicates, and *if* such predicates (those replacing effective definite descriptions or proper names) could be shown to be uniquely instantiated (if instantiated at all), then both definite descriptions and proper names and referential devices could be completely retired from grammatical service. An "ideal" language would then eliminate both. The benefit would be quite stunning: *reference would in principle be entirely context-free* (entirely free of historical encumbrance).

Unfortunately, Russell's (as well as Quine's) proposal proves unfeasible when viewed in a cognitively operative way. It is certainly conceivable that, for *any* particular thing we care to designate, there *is* some general predicate it uniquely instantiates. That is the point of Quine's "improvement" over Russell's account, of course. (Russell was simply too sanguine about "knowledge by acquaintance.") Quine converts proper names ("Pegasus" and "Socrates") into general predicates ("pegasizing" and "socratizing," say), which exhibit "divided reference": that is, each, as "a general term," "is true of each, severally, of any number of objects."[32] Quine reparses proper names and other singular terms as general terms, intending to retire their referential use. They now play (in Quine's "improved" language) an entirely predicative role. The maneuver is a famous one:

> Our ill-starred previous suggestion of "$(\exists x)(x = \text{Pegasus})$," as a paraphrase of "Pegasus exists," comes into its own when "$x = \text{Pegasus}$" is reparsed as "x is Pegasus" with "Pegasus" as a general term. "Pegasus exists" becomes "$(\exists x)(x \text{ is Pegasus})$," and straightforwardly false; "Socrates exists" becomes "$(\exists x) (x \text{ is Socrates})$," with "Socrates" as general term, and probably true (with timeless "is," of course). "Socrates" is now a general term, though true of, as it happens, just one object; "Pegasus" is now a general term which, like "centaur," is true of no objects. The position of "Pegasus" and "Socrates"

in "$(\exists x)(x$ is Pegasus$)$" and "$(\exists x)(x$ is Socrates$)$" is now certainly inaccessible
to variables and certainly no purely referential position, but only because it
is simply no position for a singular term; "x is Pegasus" and "x is Socrates"
now have the form of "x is round."[33]

This is a very pretty move, but it utterly fails. The fact is that Leibniz had
long ago considered the matter and decided that, although there was no
logical objection against there being two distinct universes in which, for
any general predicate, there were two numerically distinct particulars
that might instantiate that predicate (or predicable), one particular in
each universe, a benevolent God would not have allowed it. Setting aside
Leibniz's somewhat purple style, we may admit that it remains true
enough that no human being (as opposed to God) could possibly know
that, for any reparsed such name, every particular thing open to reference
by the proper use of its proper name could be uniquely designated by
some substituted general term. Only a human population capable, in
real-world terms, of knowing everything that fills the world could possibly know whether, say, "socratizing" was "true of, as it happens, just
one object."

Quine shows us only what the paraphrastic program would look like
if it could succeed; he has nothing to say about *whether* it succeeds in
any operational sense, and he has no interest in the matter. But, and this
is decisive, there's no point to the program if it can't succeed, since
reference is an intentional speech act *for* singling out just that about
which we mean to affirm this or that. The upshot is that reference, when
cognitively construed, cannot be retired from human discourse. Among
natural languages, it is ineliminably context-bound, subject to the consensual practices of historical societies. (Hopefully, you will see that the
difficulty affects Dummett's argument as well.)

No doubt you will have realized that the entire pretension of the
strong unity of science program entails the success of being able, in
principle, to retire reference by way of some such paraphrastic program
as that of Russell (who supposes he could retreat to the use of "logically
proper names")[34] or that of Quine. To have failed in this is tantamount
to being incapable of ever arriving at strict nomological invariances.
For, on the unity view, the laws of nature must be context-free to be
genuinely invariant; but if, granting what we have just said about reference, laws *are* empirically confirmed, they cannot then be context-
free.[35] Furthermore, the trivializing notion of history we were sketching
a moment ago (the one concerned with ephemera related to strict invariances, in the uncomplimentary sense Hempel and Popper favor in

their different ways) is now very much on the run. For its distinctive charm relies entirely on the eliminability of context in scientific discourse. However, the notion of history gains an advantage here, for *science* is now beginning to take shape (via the problem of reference at least) as a theory indissolubly narratized in accord with human interests, in and only in the context in which particular persons live and pursue such interests. That, of course, is very close to the essential theme of Marx's view of praxis.

The defeat of Russell's and Quine's paraphrastic programs need not invite the question of history of course, but it affects the fortunes of any would-be theory of history nonetheless. Every notion of history that would elude models of the sort Hempel and Popper favor requires the failure of just such programs as Quine's.

Context is merely an economy notion in the unity program's view of the world: we are said to identify things "in context" because, although we can always, in principle, fill in the uniquely designating predicates we require, it's simply too strenuous to do so in every case. But if the unity proposal proved impossible in real time, we should have to admit that reference suffered from an incurable logical informality. We could not then actually *individuate, identify, reidentify in altered circumstances, or successfully refer to, this or that, without composing some narrative history* (or suitable clue about such a history) in which, in a "story-relative" way,[36] we linked whatever we cared to predicate of anything to the fortunes of our own identity, itself similarly linked (in a story-relative way) to the referential practices of other members of our society.

This modest admission bears an enormous message of its own: *reference*, it says, *is always and already a historical event—in the historicist's sense*. But if so, and if language is ineliminably referential, then the languaged life of human beings cannot be properly characterized in any but historicist terms. Q.E.D.

The tale becomes denser when we turn from reference to predication, but the verdict is the same. We need to remind ourselves that we are merely sampling the puzzles associated with the concepts collected at (2), above. Even so, it is unlikely that we could have hit on any puzzles more central than those of reference and predication. If we now show how difficult it is to deny that predication is intrinsically historicized, the argument needed will have been won. We should then have been able to show, *en passant*, not only that a detailed historicism along the lines of (1)–(4), tallied above—including (2′)–(4′)—was entirely coherent, but also that no full-blooded account of reference and predication can rightly escape being cast in historicist terms. That would disqualify nearly every well-known theory of language, from Gottlob Frege's to Saul Kripke's. The extraordinary thing is that the prospect is never seriously broached by authors who subscribe to the canon (the context-free view of reference).

VI

The puzzle of predication, like that of reference, though for rather different reasons, has been the preserve of theorists committed to the invariances of nature and/or thought. The medieval controversy about universals could not be more instructive. (It's worth noting that Quine never discusses the matter.)[37] But the scandal remains that the grand theories of realism (whether Platonist or Aristotelian) and nominalism (or conceptualism) are utterly unworkable—in the same cognitive or operational sense we pressed a moment ago against would-be solutions of the puzzle of reference.

Platonism is completely unhelpful in the plain sense that the eternal Forms are meant to ensure that there are real similarities that may be *assigned* to plural referents. The Forms themselves could only be operative in a cognitive way if *we* were able to recover them criterially. But there is no account of how to do that in Plato (or in Aristotle)—or, for that matter, in Jerry Fodor's or Noam Chomsky's or Jerrold Katz's much more up-to-date Platonisms (or "rationalisms," as they are inclined to say: "innatisms" or "nativisms"). Fodor is a self-confessed Platonist, and Chomsky is at least an implicit Platonist, in the sense that the conceptual and grammatical universals we putatively use in thought and speech, even those we learn in a contingent culture, are ultimately based on some genetically hardwired "structures" subtending pertinent "competences." Jerrold Katz has offered a particularly unguarded and succinct formulation of the new Platonism:

> The rationalist hypothesis claims that the language acquisition device contains a stock of innate ideas that jointly specify the *necessary* forms of language (realized in any actual natural language) and thus the *necessary* form of a speaker's internal representation of the rules of his language. But no rationalist has given a precise formulation of these innate ideas, or an exact account of the process by which abstract and particular concepts are created from this intersection of innate conceptual forms and sensory stimulation. Thus, one might even say that there is no definite rationalist hypothesis, but just a general notion about the character of such a hypothesis.[38]

Nothing produced since the appearance of this statement in the late sixties requires or invites the least adjustment. (Without prejudice: Katz's formulation serves Fodor's and Chomsky's as well as any.) Put another way, Chomsky and Fodor (and others) have been led to Platonism or rationalism chiefly in order to account (by way of an "invariant condition")[39] *for* the acquisition of natural language: they have *never* attempted to solve the problem of universals; they insist only that it must be solved in an innatist way.

Fodor is more combative than Katz—but, finally, he achieves little more (very little more) in the way of explaining predicables: "I'll argue not only that there is no learning theory but that in certain senses there certainly *couldn't be*; the very *idea* of concept learning is, I think, confused. . . . As far as I know, nobody except the nativists has addressed the question of how the concept *miv* [that is, on Fodor's invention, *red and square*] is acquired, and what they have said is that it *isn't* acquired."[40]

Consider, to fix our ideas, a specimen passage from Fodor's well-known account comparing the "ontogeny" of the complex concept TRIANGLE on empiricist and rationalist grounds:

> An Empiricist might give the following ontogeny for the concept TRIANGLE. Primitive concepts of line and angle are available as the causal consequence of sensory stimulation. The concept TRIANGLE is a logical construct out of these primitive concepts. Learning the concept TRIANGLE is a matter of confirming some such hypothesis as *the concept TRIANGLE is the construct of something which is* . . . where the blank is filled by something tantamount to a definition of "triangle." Whereas, the nativist story might go like this: there are trigger stimuli sufficient to occasion the availability of such concepts as LINE and ANGLE: and there are *also* trigger stimuli sufficient to occasion the availability of such concepts as TRIANGLE. Insofar as one acquires the concept TRIANGLE "from experience," one normally does so as a consequence of being exposed to triggering stimuli of this latter kind. It may be that the concept TRIANGLE can be viewed as a logical construct out of the concepts LINE and ANGLE, but even if it is, *performing* the construction (e.g. confirming a hypothesis that exhibits the structure of the concept) is not part of the learning of the concept.[41]

Apart from the shocking realization that the advances of cognitive psychology may come to no more than this, we cannot ignore the plain fact that Fodor's account, surely as well informed as any, begs the entire question of general concepts (universals). Fodor has no operative notion of what a concept is, in terms of "similarities," "resemblances," "qualitative identities," or the like, or how they work: they are only presupposed ("triggered") in the generation of more complex concepts whose own uniformities ("divided reference," in Quine's idiom) are also merely presupposed.

You will find the same insistence regarding the unavoidability of an invariant innate structure of language in Chomsky's many accounts. For instance, relatively recently, he has concluded: "In short, the language faculty [in particular, UG: the universal grammar said to underlie all natural languages] appears to be, at its core, a computational system that is rich and *narrowly constrained in structure and rigid in its essential operations*, nothing at all like a complex of dispositions or a system of habits and analogies. This conclusion seems reasonably well established and has been given considerable substance; there is no known alternative that even begins to deal with the actual facts and language, and empirically meaningful debate takes place largely within the framework of these assumptions."[42] But, of course, the conclusion is entirely premature, since, for one thing, Chomsky has no theory of conceptual similarity at all, *or of its detection*; and, for another, without the benefit of at least the rudiments of such a theory, he has no way of justifying his notorious claim that "there is no known alternative" to his own theory.

There is, however, a still more decisive consideration. It's this: as far as cognitive acts are concerned—the *use* of language to make truth-claims, the *ascription* of predicables to reidentified particulars, the *recognition* of the stable meanings of what is said—the quarrel between empiricists and rationalists is completely question-begging and the quarrel between realists and nominalists (about universals), a complete disaster (that is, impossible to resolve). There's the scandal. Theorists of the platonizing sort insist that human language, human thought, human culture, human history are subject to invariant constraints of the same strictness said to obtain, nomologically, in physical nature. Indeed, Chomsky thinks of himself as a biologist mapping the rigid genetic functioning of the origin of language.[43] But these matters make no sense—as yet—*at* the naive level at which humans first accomplish what they are said to be able to do as the deliberate agents they are. The reason is this: theories of the sort just sampled eliminate or ignore completely *context, history, tradition, practice*; and yet, whatever the division between innate and learned skills, the linguistic aptitude of human agents must surely work through their having internalized the requisite *acquired* criteria and cues. Remember how Fodor speaks of "triggered" responses even in the nativist's model. What are those "trigger stimuli," seeing that language is not in any obvious way a mere physical force? Fodor never explains. No one rightly has.

This draws us on a little further. Empiricism is a most impoverished theory if it supposes that culturally complex concepts can be derived from something like simple Lockean ideas. There's no reason to believe that that could possibly work. Nativism or Rationalism, however, is utterly lacking in instruction about the same problem; for, wherever it cannot show a simple derivation (say: SQUARE from EQUILATERAL and RIGHT ANGLE), it simply makes the complex concept innate! Also, these are hothouse cases at best: they cannot be viewed in terms of any actual society's form of life—or, for that matter, any professional practice. They lack entirely the sense of contextual relevance one finds in Kuhn's and Wittgenstein's—and Marx's—cases. The problem is the same one finds in explaining the generalizing power of instinct-driven insects, except of course for the small complication that the acquisition of a particular historical language cannot be suitably characterized as instinctual. The point is this: the cognitive function of a general *predicate* must, on the argument, correspond to the cognized *predicable* that it designates; but that has nowhere been explained.[44]

Platonism fails because, if it does not generate the Third Man problem (the infinite regress of Forms), it does generate—and fails to meet—the question of just what, *operatively*, the Forms contribute to actual cognitional acts. Nominalism fails because, although it disallows real invariances ("real" universals), it ignores completely the Platonist's question, namely, how it is that humans actually manage to *apply* "the same term" smoothly, spontaneously, effectively, to specimen cases that were never included in the exemplars through which those terms were first introduced. The nominalist is so much occupied with defeating the Platonist (or realist) that he neglects to outfit his own account with the required rigging. In any case, if he succeeded, he would have defeated himself, for the smooth continued application of any invented general term beyond its first coinage cannot possibly depend on the mere act of naming. One sees this, for instance, in the great glee with which Nelson Goodman (that redoubtable nominalist of our day) summarizes his own account of predicative similarity: "As it occurs in philosophy [he says] similarity tends under analysis either to vanish entirely or to require for its explanation just what it purports to explain."[45] Nothing more need be said on that score. The nominalist pretty well admits his bankruptcy (it is everyman's); but, like the inexplicable protagonist of *The Jew of Malta*, he delights in his own self-destruction. We must look elsewhere.

VII

A more promising, a very well-known, beginning has been made by Eleanor Rosch, who has, also, considerable doubts about its adequacy. She and her associates have conducted empirical research into "the co-occurrence of attributes in the most common taxonomies of biological and man-made objects in our own culture."[46]

The constraints on classification Rosch imposes are well worth reviewing. For one thing, she selects taxonomies in actual use in "our own culture." She does not consider the historical or institutional or interest-relative nature of the actual forms of enculturation or its bearing on discerning uniformities that yield a "taxonomy": she features the product rather than the process, so to say.

Second, she studies "*taxonomies.*" On her account, a taxonomy "is a system by which categories are related to one another by means of class inclusion. . . . Each category within a taxonomy is entirely included within one other category (unless it is the highest level category) but is not exhaustive of that more inclusive category."[47] (By category, Rosch means "a number of objects that are considered equivalent [that is, equal as members of that category].")[48] So she confines her research to rather special ways of ordering categories; strict class inclusion is, you must admit, a most strenuous and unusual constraint—not really common at all in ordinary usage. Although she examines both the classification of biological species and that of familiar household furniture, she does not examine relatively free-floating categories: for instance, those only loosely bound in terms of common professional and cultural interests, transient but effective categories—those lacking altogether any underlying presumption favoring nomological invariance, or lacking a strong match between the distributed functions of a set of related articles and a well-entrenched overall (social) sense of a rational plan governing their use (as in outfitting a house with appropriate furniture).

For example, Rosch does not consider predicables like *period styles in painting* or *ethnic stereotypes and prejudices* or *mutual characterizations among opposing political factions.* These are normally missing from most "serious" attempts to understand the structure of categories, concepts, predicables. Nevertheless, it may be argued, such categories yield the most instructive—and the most strategic—exemplars. They are clearly both historicized as to their content and explicable only in terms of our understanding of how the process of history effectuates their regular use. They are categories that depend on some process of *relatively transient social entrenchment*; but it is hard to discern such a process in the use of distinctions of simple sensory qualities (colors, for instance) or taxonomic distinctions that are so well entrenched that we have lost sight of their original social source (cats and dogs, for instance) or functional distinctions that are strongly regularized (commercially manufactured furniture, for instance). In short, Rosch's choice of categories unwittingly obscures the very process that might have accounted for recognizing "similarities" in a way that bears on the solution of the ancient problem of universals.

There is reason to believe that Rosch's taxonomic categories are actually derived from more historicized, less regular categories (like those just mentioned) by "erasing" (doubtless for cause) the sense of their particular history. They become so standardized that seemingly plausible explanations of their perceived regularity as "products" (the perception of "natural kinds" or strong exemplars, say) are nearly artifacts of their having been favored again and again for "strategic" study.

Rosch rounds out her account by advancing

> two general and basic principles . . . for the formation of categories: The first has to do with the function of category systems and asserts that the task of category systems is to provide maximum information with the least cognitive effort; the second has to do with the structure of the information so provided and asserts that the perceived world comes as structured information rather than as arbitrary or unpredictable attributes.[49]

The notion of "maximum information" intended here is obviously served best by something like the unity of science model—or, some well-entrenched conception of rational production or tradition-bound behavior *within the terms of reference of one's own culture.* There is no other sense in which, say, the ordering of period styles in the visual arts could possibly yield "maximal information," though, no doubt, the information stored in such a schema (hardly a "taxonomy") must be high enough to justify its continued use. Rosch's principle is specifically intended to serve a realist science, one with very strong nomological intuitions.[50]

So Rosch orients us in a promising direction—but by default. She helps us see what is lacking in all these classificatory studies favoring a strong invariance—hence, what makes Marx's conception of praxis (strengthened now by what may be drawn as well from Wittgenstein's forms of life, from Kuhn's paradigm shifts, possibly from Gadamer's *wirkungsgeschichtliches Bewusstsein*, certainly from Foucault's *epistemes*) so much closer to the mark.

We may now collect the intended lesson by comparing, very briefly, two treatments of vagueness and indeterminacy regarding predicables: one, by Michael Dummett; the other, by that remarkable American talent, Charles Sanders Peirce (if we but discount Peirce's curious progressivism.) What they say is brief enough. (Bear in mind Dummett's confidence in "meaning-theories.")

Dummett says the following about "vague predicates":

> Let us suppose that we wish to give a semantic theory for a language which, like all natural languages, contains vague expressions, including vague predicates. Some people think that some of the laws of classical logic, in particular the law of excluded middle, must fail in such a language, but there is at least one plausible view according to which they would not. For every vague predicate, for instance "red," we may consider the relation which a given predicate, say, "rouge," will have to it when "rouge" is what I shall call an *acceptable sharpening* of "red": "rouge" is an acceptable sharpening of "red" if (i) "rouge" is a predicate with a quite determinate application, (ii) everything that is definitely red is rouge, (iii) nothing that is definitely not red is rouge, and (iv) everything that more nearly matches something that is definitely red than some given thing that is rouge is itself rouge. The last clause says that anything that is redder than rouge is rouge. . . . [W]e now say that a sentence of the language is true if it would come out true under replacement of its vague predicates by their sharpenings in accordance with *any* acceptable system of sharpenings [that is, in accordance with which, say, "we should not want simultaneously to admit sharpenings 'rouge' and 'rose' of 'red' and 'pink,' respectively, which left things that we should normally say were on the borderline between red and pink as neither rouge nor rose"].[51]

This is very neatly put and doubtless reasonable. It also preserves excluded middle. But it does not address the question of "acceptable sharpening" as a process, but only as a "product," a fait accompli. So, for instance, it does not address the question of the vagueness or indeterminacy *of* "rouge" *in* the context in which it serves *as* a "sharpening" of "red." Notice that Dummett stipulates that "rouge" has "a quite determinate application." Does he mean that there is no residual vagueness in "rouge" used there? Is that possible—assuming intransparency and symbiosis? He does not say.

Consider, now, the following remarks by Peirce:

> A sign is objectively *general*, in so far as, leaving its effective interpretation indeterminate, it surrenders to the interpreter the right of completing the determination for himself. "Man is mortal," "Which man?" "Any man you like." A sign is objectively *vague*, in so far as, leaving its interpretation more or less indeterminate, it reserves for some other possible sign or experience the function of completing the determination. "This month," says the

almanac-oracle, "a great event is to happen." "What event?" "Oh, we shall see. The almanac doesn't tell that." The *general* might be defined as that to which the principle of excluded middle does not apply. A triangle in general is not isosceles nor equilateral, nor is a triangle in general scalene. The *vague* might be defined as that to which the principle of contradiction does not apply. For it is false neither that an animal (in a vague sense) is male, nor that an animal is female.[52]

Two qualifications (by Peirce himself) must be entered here (somewhat at the risk of oversimplifying Peirce's immensely complicated theory). First, "no cognition of ours is absolutely determinate";[53] *in* any determination (as by Dummett's "acceptable sharpening," say), *some* residual indeterminacy always remains. And second, any determination of truth and reality, in finite contexts, is always merely "virtual"; "perfect" determination, for Peirce, obtains only at the end of an infinite inquiry.[54]

Peirce is far more attuned to the *process* of "sharpening" vague predicates than Dummett; Dummett considers only the significance of some already accomplished "sharpening" (the *product*, so to say).

In a world that is already both intransparent and symbiotized—a world in which neither a classic realism nor nominalism proves convincing—Peirce's bold admission of *the inherent indeterminacy of real predicables* is responsive in a way Dummett's is not. Peirce identifies—by way of the triadic structure of "signs," by endlessly "interpreting" the symbiotized world in a way that yields only relatively "sharpened" ("progressive") signs—the essential social process by which predicative similarities become relatively entrenched through our cognitive interventions. *Predicative similarities become entrenched in that they are essentially socially remembered "products" of our interpretive "sharpening" of the predicative indeterminacies we encounter. Their* precision corresponds to the precision of our consensual recollection of Intentional (interpretive) interventions. The effective generality of predicates, the discernible generality of predicables, is a cultural and historical achievement.

It is as if Marx's thesis, that thinking is a form of praxis, provided a ready-made *causal* account of just how to link (1) what Peirce isolates as the *logic* of generality and vagueness, (2) what Gadamer isolates as the *historical flux* of significant meanings, and (3) what Wittgenstein isolates as the *dialectical* work of the natural societies to which we belong (in which rulelike practices are at once habituating and hospitable to improvisation).[55] We are helped thereby to construct a fresh theory of predicative generality. In short, Peirce's theme of the *determinable in-*

determinacy of real predicables is both the enabling common theme in Marx, Gadamer, Wittgenstein (and Foucault and others) and the minimal clue to the solution of the ancient problem of universals. But it makes no sense if disconnected from a robust historicism, which the ancient world never grasped.

We cannot hope to construct a full-fledged theory of universals here. There's no need for it in any case. But, having scrupled to speculate about why a mere realism regarding universals (the theme of canonical invariances) cannot but fail, we are perhaps entitled to hurry on to the novel lesson that still remains implicit. (Without it, after all, we should never collect its important bearing on the theory of history, or even grasp the point of an otherwise tangential argument.)

The point is this: *there are no universals that are separable from the narrative memory of a viable society*, that is, regarding how, within its own praxis, a society has marked its exemplars, used and extended its general terms to new cases, gradually replaced its favored specimens over time, sensed its shifting borderline and indisputable applications, and formed a serial picture of the apparent direction of and systematic interrelationships among all such predicative lines. (That's what Dummett obscures with his talk of "red" and "rouge.")

That's to say: *a general term has application only in a historicized context*; either it serves antecedently closed *sets* of instantiating exemplars—in which case it is utterly irrelevant to explaining the fluency of natural languages (*contra* nominalism); or else it serves our use of a socially entrenched but open-ended *kind*, for which new instantiations are always at consensual risk—in which case it is, irretrievably, logically informal (not a standard realism or conceptualism at all). It was Peirce's distinction to have formulated a deviant "realism" that captured this open-ended symbiosis. It was Marx's distinction to have sketched a plausible model of the process of social causation that could embody such a (Peircean-like) realism.[56] And it remains Gadamer's distinction to have isolated, however abstractly, the historical process (*Horizontverschmelzung*)[57] by which any pertinently narratized account of effective predication preserves a holist sense of the "realism" required.

The theorizing convergence of Marx and Peirce and Gadamer is fanciful, of course. But the deeper claim, namely, that no viable theory of reference or predication can be disjoined from an encompassing historicism, is not meant to be a mere fancy at all. It is an essential part of the explanation of the structure of general terms—one that could not have been formulated without attending to the metaphysics of history.

That this last option is not recognized at all in the canon regarding universals is an unintended proof of the profound vacuity of so much of official philosophy.

In any case, if we agree that neither reference nor predication is intelligible except in terms of a society's narratized memory of how its aggregated speech acts have been consensually supported and adjusted to a changing praxis, a very important additional benefit falls out as an instant corollary. For, if the principled discursive functions of natural language are effective only as used by languaged agents who remember (by a division of social labor) how their language *has been used* and are competent enough to judge how that language *may be acceptably extended*, then it cannot be incoherent to claim that persons (and other cultural phenomena) *have only histories rather than natures*—have "natures" as a direct function of a social, narratized memory of how they themselves have been identified and could be reidentified.

We argued earlier that reference must be narratized in order to work at all: which means, of course, that we can never rely on any strictly unique attributes in things. But if so, then, by parity of reasoning, the identification and reidentification of persons cannot rely on any comparable fixity; and if that is so, then it cannot be incoherent (for that reason alone) to concede that the "natures" of persons may change—in that their histories may change. (Neither Aristotelian essences nor haecceities will do, you see.) The solution to the problem of numerical identity, then, joined to that regarding reference and predication—and, of course, the choice of the "correct" model of truth and logic fitted to the different sectors of the world—confirms how difficult it is to resist historicism under the global conditions of intransparency and symbiosis.

SIX

Toward Radical History

I

We have turned an important corner in the argument. We have been able to show—or to take for granted, where the matter can hardly be contested—that certain heterodox notions are not in the least incoherent or self-contradictory or self-defeating. We have earned the right to proceed beyond those notions and to build upon them. They remain contested all right, but they can no longer be considered seriously paradoxical: these include, for example, the notions (1) that reference and predication are inherently historicized; (2) that individuation and reidentification are ineliminably context-bound and logically informal; (3) that predicative similarity is a function of the consensual practices of viable societies and cannot be confirmed in any more reliable way; (4) that theoretical discourse is inseparable from a given society's praxis, through which it fixes effective reference and predication; (5) that the rational structure of science is inseparable from its history; (6) that numerically distinct referents may be successfully individuated and identified though they lack fixed natures and have (or "are") only histories; (7) that the "nature" of such referents may change, or (as with selves) may be changed reflexively, in altering their histories, without adversely affecting their numerical identity; (8) that the identity of individuated things persisting through change depends in all instances on a society's narratized memory of how it has individuated and identified such referents at earlier times; (9) that bivalence and alternative logics are open to empirical choice on the basis

of fitting the distinctive judgments a given domain can effectively support; (10) that all interpreted *de re* and *de dicto* necessities may be
opposed without self-contradiction; (11) that the structure of human
thought and reason and logic are, in a measure, artifacts of a society's
linguistic history; (12) that human persons or selves are social constructions that emerge within the symbiotized natural world and a society's
historical and linguistic traditions; and (13) that all formerly affirmed
invariances bearing on the foregoing and related distinctions hold only
within the tacit horizon of a given society's conceptual imagination.

Surely, this tally defines an absolutely breathtaking vista that goes
utterly contrary to the "canon" (both ancient and modern) that claims
that the denial of the real invariances of thought and reality yields only
contradiction and insuperable paradox. Not only are (1)–(13) individually coherent, they are coherent when taken together. They afford a
foundation, therefore, for a novel theory of history. Very nearly every
prominent such theory, certainly every theory cast as canonical or compatible with the standard objectives of science, opposes some significant
subset of (1)–(13). There is no developed theory of history that fits the
entire set of (1)–(13). *And that is just what we are after!* We may claim,
therefore, that any theory in accord with (1)–(13) counts as a *radical
history*. Histories of the sorts already canvassed we may call *canonical*.
(They are hardly uniform among themselves.) What, we may ask, will
a radical history require?

One set of considerations returns us to an issue already broached. We
had noticed, for instance, reflecting on Hempel and Gadamer, that not
only were their conceptions of history opposed to one another in methodological terms, but each defined the scope of history in an entirely
different way. For Hempel, anything might be assigned a history that
simply persisted through physical time. Hempel impoverished history
because (to repeat a point already gained), he subscribed to the empirical
adequacy of physicalism, and because (for him) a genuine science favored
descriptions and explanations that fell under nomologically invariant
universals. History proved, on the reading, to be no more than a heuristic
concern of investigators who rightly centered their energies (*regarding
the same phenomena*) in ways that waived altogether any abiding interest
in history. History contributes nothing essential in the way of knowledge. History is the play of a certain *extrinsic* interest we take in things,
which, rightly understood, may be satisfactorily described in ahistorical
terms. On Hempel's view, anything has a history because history counts
for so little.

For Gadamer, however, the "merely" physical world has no history at all in that sense in which the human world is intrinsically historicized. History belongs to the human world, in that man belongs to history. The formula is the pivot of Gadamer's own version of radical history; it defines the sense in which he opposes the interpretive work of Schleiermacher and Dilthey.[1] Gadamer is convinced that Dilthey failed to free himself from the empiricist model of individualistic psychology that John Stuart Mill had favored in his *Logic*—just where Mill distinguishes between the physical and "moral" sciences (which, textually, first invited the use of the opposed terms "*Naturwissenschaften*" and "*Geisteswissenschaften*"). Dilthey failed to go beyond the ahistorical conception of reason and sensibility and intention in Kant (despite having criticized Kant). The conjunction of these two elements (Gadamer feels) leads Dilthey into the hands of the Millians in framing the contrast between the two sorts of "science."[2] The result is, Dilthey relies too heavily on the example of the physical sciences *in* formulating his own sense of the rigor of the human sciences. This is also part of the motivation of the "radical" hermeneutics Heidegger introduces, which, greatly dampened metaphysically, Gadamer espouses.

II

The philosophical record confirms the prescience of Gadamer's judgment—which is not yet to endorse his conception of history. An empiricist theory of history and the human sciences was bound to develop along broadly Millian lines in general agreement with the spirit of the unity canon but in a way that would resist Hempel's extreme reductionism. It was bound to admit the "difference" between the two sorts of science: the presence or absence of intentional phenomena; but, it would argue, *that* difference is entirely benign as far as science is concerned, and so it would apply inductive procedures to the human sciences without first adjusting them to reductive physicalism.

There is, actually, one extraordinarily fierce incarnation of this Millian notion: Adolf Grünbaum's *The Foundations of Psychoanalysis*. It supposes that intentionality poses no procedural difficulty for the "unity" treatment of the human sciences. Thus, Grünbaum chides Paul Ricoeur's well-known irenic attempt to combine causal and hermeneutic elements in the human sciences—invoking instead the Millian model:

> Ricoeur evidently recognized [says Grünbaum] that psychoanalytic explanations are both *causal* and are intended to illuminate various sorts of be-

havior. If so, then their validation, if any, will have to be of a kind *appropriate* to these avowed features. But how does Ricoeur envision the appraisal of the psychoanalytic codification of a purported causal connection? As I shall argue in Part II of this book, the demonstration of the *causal* relevance of various sorts of repressions cannot be effected by such clinical methods as free association, which are endemic to the Freudian enterprise. Instead, the establishment of a causal connection in psychoanalysis, no less than in "academic psychology" or medicine, has to rely on modes of inquiry that were refined from time-honored canons of causal inference pioneered by Francis Bacon and John Stuart Mill.[3]

Here, the sense is that hermeneutic complications do not require any departure from the usual inductivism, or any distinctive logical preparation of the initial data to permit induction to take hold.

Grünbaum adduces some interesting evidence to show that, among his methodological quarrels with opponents, Freud did indeed favor a Millian-like inductivism, for instance against Leopold Löwenfeld.[4] And we know that, under the influence of Fliess and others, Freud was strongly attracted to an inductivism of Helmholtz's sort, by no means simply in tow to a reductive physicalism.[5] Still, as it stands, that is no more than gossip.

The point at stake is *not* to trash inductivism or a Millian treatment of psychoanalysis (or of any of the other human sciences) but to isolate what would be needed if psychoanalysis (suitably disciplined) were to be tested inductively. The strange thing is that there is no discussion of the question in Grünbaum's account—no discussion at all of the methodological peculiarity *of* the human sciences bearing on whether an inductivist model is suitable or not, no argument to the effect that it is *not* methodologically peculiar. It may be true that Ricoeur and Gadamer are naive about induction and inductivism (Grünbaum adds Habermas's name for good measure); but, for his own part, Grünbaum utterly neglects to address the standard difficulties of applying inductive procedures to hermeneutic materials (reports of dreams, associations of ideas, autobiographical narratives, dialogue, clinically interpreted behavior, and the like); and he has almost nothing to say about the metaphysics of history (say, along the lines Gadamer explores), except to discount the need for a reductive physicalism. (We shall return to Grünbaum's remarks on history.)

We cannot discount an inductive treatment of psychoanalytic claims (*pace* Habermas and Ricoeur—and Popper, for that matter); but there is no need to. What we need to know is just *how* induction works when applied to intentional materials. The answer is entirely straightforward:

it bears directly on the nature of the *predicates* favored in the human sciences. The issue ramifies, of course, in the direction of questions about causality, explanation, understanding, and, most interestingly, about the relationship between physical and historical time. We shall have to content ourselves with two issues only—predicates and time—but they will serve us well enough.

About predicates, one consideration is decisive: the pertinent terms are not only inten*t*ional, they are also inten*s*ionally problematic. Grünbaum considers very briefly the question whether reasons are causes and concludes both that reasons *can* be causes and that Freud believed that explanation by reasons was a species of explanation by causes.[6] Fine. But even if the argument were successful (it is a good deal more problematic than Grünbaum acknowledges), it would still *presuppose* a favorable analysis of the pertinent predicates—which he nowhere supplies. For instance, if causality behaved in an extensional way, as Donald Davidson supposes,[7] then the intensional complexity of psychoanalytic phenomena could not be safely ignored. For Davidson, of course, may be shown to be both equivocal and unclear—probably also inconsistent—in admitting that intentional events (the mental) *are* causally efficacious and *do not* behave extensionally. (This is the crux of the inconsistent triad of his well-known doctrine of anomalous monism.)[8]

When Grünbaum considers inten*t*ional ascriptions in Freud's work, he confines himself entirely to an explicit, quite delimited psychological reading of "intentions"—that is, a reading regarding what agents consciously intend (or even unconsciously intend). He never mentions Brentano's notion of intentionality—which Freud was well aware of, and which bears inexorably on the methodological questions *Grünbaum* strenuously airs; he moves only to discount a certain reading of intentions in terms of the cause of acts or actions.[9]

But that won't do at all. For it is just possible that the logical features of the predicates in question harbor a difficulty that makes inductivism inapplicable, or applicable only if very severely constrained: constrained perhaps in such a way as to disallow the possibility of discovering nomological universals (in the sense Grünbaum shares with Hempel). That prospect deserves an inning, if for no other reason than that *that* may well be part of the "hermeneuticist's" complaint against the unity of science. But more than that, it raises an essential question about the defense of the inductivist's conception of psychoanalysis. So, Grünbaum's account is deficient at best, for the unity theorist supposes that the laws of nature behave in a thoroughly extensional way.[10]

Two further charges may be trotted out. We cannot discuss them in Grünbaum's company, because Grünbaum does not address them. Perhaps he believes they do not affect the issue. Leave it at that. But if what is common to the extension of general predicates is (as we have seen) a function of a society's narrative sense of its own history of usage, then the logical peculiarity of intentional predicates is bound to be more troublesome than that of its nonintentional cousins. On the argument, the *use* of all predicates is "Intentional" (in a profound sense Brentano does not air) in that that use is subtended by the institutionalized practices (traditions, forms of life) of a particular society. There is a deep informality, then, that affects even the designation of common sensory qualities ("red," say, in the sense Dummett slights).

The Intentional enters the story in two ways: in one, it bears on the extension of all predicates; in the other, it concerns a special subset of predicates that designate the features of collective cultural life—just the ones for instance that reflect the details of a society's self-understanding (as in psychoanalysis). Together, their admission points to the radical possibilities entailed in historicizing reason and knowledge. The point at stake is that "Intentional" properties engage societally and historically consensual distinctions regarding significative, semiotic, and related functions that go beyond (but also include) the psychological and individualized notions associated with Brentano and Husserl. The familiar "intentional" distinctions *are* indeed reviewed (informally, it is true) by Ricoeur and Gadamer; but they are nowhere mentioned in Grünbaum. The double complexity of the Intentional cannot fail to affect every inductivism, falsificationism, or other formal methodologies.

Beyond that, the following argument seems very strong indeed: first of all, *intensionally complex predicates* cannot be discerned in any simple way, they must be correctly *interpreted* to be said to be multiply *instantiated* at all; second, the validity of such interpretation depends on *noncausal* considerations regarding the fit between interpretation and the practices that subtend them; third, the validity of any claims of causal regularity involving intensionally complex intentional predicates (that is, "Intentional" predicates—Ricoeur's question)[11] already presupposes the confirmation of a valid interpretation; fourth, intentional predicates are "functional" predicates, in at least the sense that they are cross-category distinctions answering to salient human interests—*for which*, either necessarily or very probably (on any familiar view), there are no strict nomological invariances to be had (invariances answering to "natural kinds");[12] fifth, it is an open question whether, for "functional" or intentional attributes, there could be any inductive procedures for assigning uniquely correct interpretations, or for legitimating subsequent inductions on phenomena thus extensionally regularized; and sixth, an inductivist reading of psychoanalysis (say), that ignores the fact that the actual language of psychoanalysis is too informal to support covering laws directly, begs the deeper question of whether, in principle, there *are*, any pertinent such laws to be had or approximated at all.[13] Q.E.D. For example, it was a great worry of Herbert Feigl's that the "many-many" problem might prove insoluble. What Feigl meant was this: any physical movement of the body might convey indefinitely many different kinds of significant actions; any significant action might be conveyed by indefinitely many different kinds of bodily movement; and there can be no rule or algorithm for correlating the two.[14]

Now, if an argument of this sort were effective, there would be good reason to insist on the fundamental difference between the natural and human sciences—without yet invoking any hermeneutic doubts about causality in the human sphere or about the bare eligibility of induction. What would be needed would be an acknowledgment: (1) that the use of induction must always be constrained by prior interpretive considerations; and (2) that, wherever physicalism was not successfully invoked or presupposed (or a similar-minded reduction along "informational" lines),[15] the inducti*vist's* claim and practice would be entirely pointless.

III

There is another question that these reflections bring into view. They concern the meaning and "metaphysics" of understanding (or *Verstehen*), in the sense Dilthey features—and that Ricoeur and Gadamer (and even Habermas and Apel) share (or concede). The least clue is clear enough: on the admission of Dilthey's general distinction, induction cannot be invoked "objectively" in the human sciences in the same sense, procedurally, in which it is invoked in the natural sciences. It cannot, simply because the relevant predicates pose a difficulty that, on the argument, does not arise in the physical sciences. This, of course, is not to disallow the use (or the "objective" use) of induction in the human sciences. The fact is that the Intentional predicates of the human sciences are applied only in *verstehende* ways, even when they are applied observationally. The human sciences are inherently reflexive, problematically consensual, self-interpretive. This is *not* true of the physical sciences, in the sense that the ostensible "objects" of the physical sciences lack intentional attributes.

It is true enough that any ascription (any ascrib*ing* of properties) entails Intentional complications on the cognizer's part. On the most strenuous reading, this would mean that the physical sciences were also infected in the *verstehende* way—which would, in principle, profoundly affect the fortunes of induction. It is also true that the same reflexive concerns arise when *verstehende* predicates are applied to alien cultures. (This is the deep lesson of that splendid piece of rock, the Rosetta Stone.)[16] Causality, objectivity, the use of induction are hardly ruled out; but this single consideration (reflexivity: the identity of "subject" and "object" in regard to the "meanings" and Intentional significance of cultural phenomena) certainly must color the methodological analogy between the natural and human sciences.

Once this is admitted, it is but a step to the deeper metaphysical questions Gadamer raises about the hermeneutic complexity of human existence and the bearing of that complexity on the human sciences. (*We* may add: *and* its bearing on the natural sciences.) Also, to admit the point is to honor the conceptual concerns of Gadamer and Ricoeur (and Habermas and Apel and others) well beyond anything Grünbaum concedes. So Grünbaum's reasonable complaint against the "hermeneuticists" harbors a form of self-defeat as well. To appreciate the full force of this, we must consider what Grünbaum actually says about scientific laws, time, and history.

But before turning to these matters, consider what Gadamer says about the human sciences. It will help balance accounts, because there are errors of omission (and commission) on both sides of the philosophical ledger. Gadamer claims, at the very start of *Truth and Method*, that "The experience of the socio-historical world cannot be raised to a science by the inductive procedures of the natural sciences."[17] For instance, in his criticism of Mill's influence on German-language efforts in the emerging *Geisteswissenschaften*, he argues against the exclusive use of the "inductive method." He also asserts that the "ideal" of historical knowledge and the human sciences is "to understand the phenomenon [in question] in its unique and historical concreteness"—hence, in a way that cannot be achieved inductively at all.[18] In this, Gadamer sides completely with Dilthey, whom he nevertheless criticizes for his psychologism (which is itself not nearly as simpleminded as Gadamer alleges) and for his sympathies regarding the exemplary status of the physical sciences (which obviously enabled Dilthey to make his point effectively).

But Dilthey had argued for a very strong disjunction between the human and the natural worlds and, coordinately, for a very strong disjunction between *Erklären* (explanation in the "positivist" mode of the physical sciences) and *Verstehen* (understanding in the hermeneutic sense). It is only in the generous work of a thinker like Paul Ricoeur that one finds an attempt to correct the conceptual extravagance of Dilthey's disjunction in order to demonstrate (no easy matter) the ineluctable sense in which, *in* the hermeneutic context, *inductive* (*erklärende*) considerations cannot be avoided.[19] Ricoeur's very reasonable adjustment rests on two considerations: first, that the modeling of explanation is, by this time, displaced from an exclusive reliance on the exemplary work of the natural sciences to the resources of natural language (common to the natural and human sciences); and, second, that the interpretive work of hermeneutic understanding has long ago been removed from the merely psychological notion (Dilthey somewhat ambivalently favors) to the fully cultural and societal notion.[20] Ricoeur's effort effectively recovers (ironically, as it turns out) a proper niche for *Grünbaum's* inductivist treatment of psychoanalysis; at the same time, it confirms what we were just saying about Grünbaum's having neglected to consider the special (hermeneutic) conditions under which induction functions in the human sciences. In a word, Ricoeur's proposal requires a melding of the hermeneutic and the inductive.

Now, it is precisely at this point that Gadamer's more important reflections come into play—just the ones that a theory of radical history would be obliged to accommodate:

> True historical thinking must take account of its own historicality. . . . The true historical object [says Gadamer] is not an object at all, but the unity of the one and the other [the "object" understood and the "subject" who understands it], a relationship in which exist both the reality of history and the reality of historical understanding. A proper hermeneutics would have to demonstrate the effectivity of history within understanding itself. I shall refer to this [he adds] as "effective history." Understanding is, essentially, an effective-historical relation [*wirkungsgeschichtliches Bewusstsein*].[21]

This may be Gadamer's finest piece of analysis. It introduces a constraint on human understanding that may be said to be "metaphysical" rather than merely epistemological—in the sense that admitting it entails admitting: (1) the impossibility (in principle) of completely fathoming the preformative conditions enbedded in understanding and interpreting cultural phenomena; and (2) that condition's being an ingredient in the deepest sense in human existence and inquiry.

Human beings "belong" to history (as Gadamer argues): they have only histories (not "natures"), or they "are" histories (as we were saying earlier on).[22] If so, then (as Gadamer also insists) Habermas's attempt to recover an *objectivity* regarding the norms of rational communication is transparently doomed to fail.[23] It works only by pretending to escape the hermeneutic encumbrance. It privileges "reason" somehow, denies that it is inherently prejudiced in the horizonal sense, all the while it argues from the bowels of history itself. In short, it is naively progressivist. It is not so much that it draws an illicit analogy between the rigor of the human and natural sciences as that it fails to concede that all forms of critical inquiry are generically historicized.

The irony is that Habermas and Grünbaum noticeably converge here. It follows that, for his part, Grünbaum completely misunderstands the thrust of Gadamer's (and Ricoeur's) concerns, possibly because of his preoccupation with Habermas (who is hardly a reliable hermeneut). Grünbaum completely fails to perceive the ubiquity of the hermeneutic complication. This brings us back to the conclusion we reached earlier by way of an analysis of intentional (or Intentional) predicates.

IV

There is more to be drawn from Gadamer's account. For one thing, it provides a very neat *reductio* of the historical methodology of classical historicism, as practiced for instance by Leopold von Ranke. (Bear in mind that what we earlier supported as "historicism" is entirely different from "classical historicism.") Ranke represents the beginning of a hermeneutic objectivism in history, in rebellion against Hegel's notion of a single all-encompassing world history. The clues, in Ranke, are quite telling against the "Hegelian" notion; although, ironically, Hegel's "totalizing" of history actually preserves a more radical sense of cognitive contingency (of the sort Gadamer favors) than does Ranke's more modest investigation of the documentary deliverances of the *Volkgeist* of particular societies. (Of course, Gadamer consciously favors Hegel here.)

In any case, the clues (in Ranke) are these. First, "history admittedly can never have the unity of a philosophical system; but history is not without inner connection."[24] Second, "since there is much that we do not know, how are we to understand the causal nexus everywhere, not to mention getting to the bottom of the essence of totality? I consider it impossible [says Ranke] to solve this problem entirely. God alone knows world history. We recognize the contradictions—'the harmonies,' as an Indian poet says, 'known to the Gods, but unknown to men'; we can only divine, only approach from a distance. But there exists clearly for us a unity, a progression, a development."[25]

Ranke is both a progressivist and a traditionalist of sorts—victimized by the same logical impasse he rightly notes in Hegel (that is, *in* the conventional, perhaps fictitious, Hegel who takes his own history as actually revealing the *Weltgeist*'s progressive self-discovery). It is at this point that Gadamer correctly remarks: "The naiveté of so-called historicism consists in the fact that it does not undertake (a) reflection [on the hermeneutic conditions of understanding], and in trusting to its own methodological approach forgets it own historicality."[26] Gadamer defeats Ranke (and the classical historicists) therefore in exactly the same way he defeats Habermas—and, by implication, Grünbaum as well. None of these theorists (Grünbaum, Habermas, Ranke) gives evidence of fully grasping the bearing of the very historicity of their own attempts at objective history upon the objectivity of what they claim.

There is a second benefit in Gadamer's argument. It leads us to see the strategic importance of Heidegger's recovery of the notion of the "fore-structuring" of understanding—in *Being and Time*. It is not unreasonable to suppose that Heidegger sets Hegel up as his paper opponent, as he discusses the radical *"Temporalität"* of *Dasein*'s unique mode of existence (vis-à-vis the "care" of *Sein*). But the fact remains that it was Heidegger's sense of this preformative or forestructuring constraint in the "ontology" of *Dasein* (which no objectivist "metaphysics" could explicitly discern) that led Gadamer to radicalize his own reading of hermeneutics—against the romantic hermeneuts, against the increasingly Kantianized objectivism of Ranke, J. G. Droysen, and Dilthey—applied equally to history, interpretation, science, and self-understanding. (This confirms, of course, the arbitrariness with which Grünbaum urges his inductivist reading of psychoanalysis and his insistence on Freud's contribution to such a reading.)[27]

We need an extra moment or so to clarify Heidegger's important role in the development of the theory of history. (It cannot be pursued without misgiving: Heidegger's language is so often impenetrable. But it offers an important lesson nevertheless.) Heidegger is appealingly direct in the opening words of *Being and Time*. He says there that he means to "raise anew *the question of the meaning of Being.*" "Our provisional aim," he adds, "is the Interpretation of *time* as the possible horizon for any understanding whatsoever of Being."[28]

There's no doubt that this is the very vision Heidegger later so slyly dissolves in the notorious *Letter on Humanism* (the famous *Kehre*). But, from another point of view, it is also meant to oppose what Heidegger takes to be Hegel's illicit notion of world history as the unified process of *Geist*'s self-understanding through time. (Notoriously, Heidegger's remarks are difficult to fathom, but we dare not forsake the pilgrimage. Have courage.) First, then, Heidegger is entirely explicit about the opposition between his treatment of *Dasein* and Hegel's account of *spirit* (or *Geist*), particularly as it appears in the *Phenomenology of Spirit*:

> Our existential analytic of Dasein, on the contrary [that is, contrary to the Hegel of the *Phenomenology*], starts [Heidegger says] with the "concretion" of factically thrown existence itself in order to unveil temporality as that which primordially makes such existence possible. "Spirit" does not first fall into time [as he interprets Hegel as saying], but it *exists* as the primordial *temporalizing* of temporality. Temporality temporalizes world-time, within the horizon of which "history" can "appear" as historicizing within-time. But factical existence "falls" as falling *from* primordial, authentic, temporality.[29]

It would certainly be easy enough to become completely befuddled by this immense verbiage. What it apparently means is this: (1) Being, that which is real in nature or in thought, insofar as it may be assigned intelligible features, is dependent on an ("ontological") precondition (*Dasein*'s "care" with respect to *Sein*) that cannot be discerned in any ordinary (any "objective") cognitive way; (2) the "condition" must be postulated as existentially and ontologically prior to the work of any particular science or rational inquiry, because the very presumption of a cognitional relationship between a subject and a world is already a piece of that originating "temporality" (manifested as a particular history)—a condition, therefore, that precedes whatever *cognitive* source science may be said to issue from; and (3) that postulated precondition— the supposed "relation" between *Dasein* and *Sein*—signifies only that discursive truth-claims are themselves historicized, radically dependent on the preformative forces of history that discursive history can never completely fathom. (One can perhaps see already the remarkable simplification of Heidegger that Gadamer effected.)

Perhaps the following may serve to confirm this reading:

> Truth, understood in the most primordial sense, belongs to the basic constitution of Dasein. The term signifies an *existentiale*. . . . Dasein, as consti-

tuted by disclosedness, is essentially in the truth. Disclosedness is a kind of Being which is essential to Dasein. *"There is" truth only in so far as Dasein is and so long as Dasein is.* Entities are uncovered only *when* Dasein *is*; and only as long as Dasein *is*, are they disclosed. Newton's laws, the principle of contradiction, any truth whatever—these are true only as long as Dasein *is*. Before there was any Dasein, there was no truth; nor will there be any after Dasein is no more. For in such a case truth as disclosedness, uncovering, and uncoveredness, *cannot* be.[30]

You may well ask what the point of this extraordinary maneuver could possibly be. It serves at least two purposes: in one, it signifies that *history cannot be external to whatever we posit as reality*—which Heidegger realizes opposes Aristotle, the medieval philosophers, Descartes, and Kant; in the other, it signifies that *the linkage between any assigned history of human inquiry and the objective structure of the world it claims to know cannot be construed as a series of discernibly progressive stages internal to the life (and thought) of some all-encompassing Reality (Geist)*—hence, contrary to Hegel's optimistic account of objectivity, as Heidegger understands him.[31]

Heidegger believes that there are only two large strategies by which to link history and invariant Being cognitively. Both fail if we take history (or, better, "temporality") to be radically open, not subject to any fixed invariant order (or telos) at all. Heidegger pays his compliments to Hegel for having invented an ingenious alternative to the ancient conception (which equates the fixed, the intelligible, and the real); but he believes Hegel ultimately cheats, because (he supposes) Hegel construes the process of historical "becoming" as the ordered, progressive, "rigged" actualization *of* an ulterior "Being"—already (always) "there," somehow set to become manifest *in* time:

> The essence of spirit is the *concept.* By this Hegel understands not the universal which is intuited in a genus as the form of something thought, but rather the form of the very thinking which thinks itself: the conceiving of *oneself—as the grasping* of the not-I. Inasmuch as the grasping of the *not*-I presents a differentiation, there lies in the pure concept, as the grasping of *this* differentiation, a differentiation of the difference. Thus Hegel can define the essence of the spirit formally and apophantically as the negation of a negation. . . . This negating of the negation is both that which is "absolutely restless" in the spirit and also its *self-manifestation*, which belongs to its essence. The "progression" of the spirit which actualizes itself in history, carries with it "a principle of exclusion." In this exclusion, however, that which is excluded does not get detached from the spirit; it gets surmounted. . . . In its development spirit aims "to reach its own concept."[32]

There is, therefore, a sense (Heidegger thinks) in which Hegelian history remains telically controlled by the real end of time present in every moment of history; in that sense, "temporality" (*Temporalität*) is a sham.

There are two distinct themes here: first, "temporality," the existential condition of *Dasein* (as distinct from the condition of human persons, who, of course, "instantiate" *Dasein*—though not merely ontically, in the usual sense proper to "natural kinds") is radically open, so that no telos (which may appear in human histories) belongs to the "ontological" structures of Being disclosed to *Dasein*; second, Hegel's thesis, namely, the thesis that history is the unfolding career of the World-Spirit, makes no sense unless the particular historical events are already endowed with the essential telic significance of *that* total encompassing career. That is why Heidegger regards Hegel's theory as a sham, as well as why he takes his own solution to be superior.

It's possible that Heidegger misreads Hegel; although what he says is extremely close to the seeming sense of certain passages of the *Phenomenology*.[33] On the other hand, Alexandre Kojève, glossing, as he says, "the Second Stage of the Second Section of the Second Part of Chapter VIII" of the *Phenomenology*, remarks that the opening words—"*Time* is the *Concept* itself, which is *there* [in empirical existence]"—declares that the following "is Hegel's position": "the Concept *is* Time, and hence is *related* neither to Eternity nor to Time."[34] Kojève's reading makes the *Phenomenology* looks like an instructive irony, the sketch of what a totalized or eternal vision of the whole of reality would look like to a creature (man) caught in the finite indeterminacies of inquiring—*in human time*. On that reading, Heidegger and Hegel simply view the same radical contingency from opposite perches; the same theme of radical history emerges from their respective florid inventions. On a literal reading of Kojève, Hegel appears to have been justly criticized by Heidegger. (Kojève is not an altogether independent judge.)

Clearly, Gadamer draws his account more from Heidegger than from Hegel. But if the heuristic reading is correct, then Hegel has unmistakably urged the late modern theme of the flux of history. Also, of course, Kojève's reading subverts Ranke's unsympathetic reading of Hegel— which the insoluble paradox of classical historicism would have obliged us to abandon in any case. For what Heidegger and Hegel discovered— Heidegger, because of Hegel—is the puzzle of radical time, the time of flux: that is, that to specify *its* nature is to violate that "nature," to pretend to fix the unconditional openness of time or flux. (That is what the doctrine of history's telos comes to.) Heidegger is surely caught in his own dilemma here; Hegel, possibly not. For Heidegger does not quite admit that the "ontological" aspect of the priority of *Dasein*'s "relation" to *Sein* is itself (like the histories that presuppose that "relation") no more than a late artifact of a human mind speculating, in its own time, about the nature of historical time. (Here, we begin to approach Foucault's question.)

In any case, to put matters a little more trimly: Heidegger clarifies the sense in which, if history is genuinely open to the future, there cannot be any discernible anticipation of the final telos of history *in* any of its passing moments, as we live forward in time. Heidegger may well have misinterpreted Hegel, if Hegel had meant (in the *Phenomenology*) to hold that, since history *is* telic in the narrative sense, the imposition of history's telos is necessarily retrospective and retroactive—that is, interpretive but not "there" in any realist sense. This returns us of course to the naive conjectures of Peirce and Popper and Putnam and Kuhn.

V

We may turn back, now, to the topics mentioned before this last detour: particularly, to time and history in Grünbaum's account of science. The fact is that Grünbaum's argument in favor of the unity conception is quite startling, quite heterodox (or so it seems). Yet it has raised no eyebrows among his own supporters. His essential statement runs as follows:

> The physical theory of classical electrodynamics will now enable me to show that Habermas and Gadamer have drawn a *pseudo*contrast between the nomothetic and human sciences. For that major physical theory features laws that embody a far more fundamental dependence on the history and/or context of the object of knowledge than was ever contemplated in even the most exhaustive of psychoanalytic explanatory narratives or in any recapitulation of human history.[35]

Allow Grünbaum's extravagance for the sake of the issue: he could hardly suppose that Gadamer's remarks on history (cast in the Heideggerean spirit we've just reviewed) are paler or less fundamental than his own. But let that pass.

The decisive consideration is this: *time* (therefore *history* and *context*) is treated univocally in Grünbaum's references to the natural and human sciences. It is clearly not similarly treated among the "hermeneuticists"— unless in the sly sense that physical time is itself no more than a heuristic restriction made within the encompassing time of human history. (One could easily read Heidegger this way.) Hence, when Grünbaum tenders his comparison, we are directed to understand the phrase, a "dependence on the history and/or context of the object of knowledge," in a sense *first* fixed for the work of classical electrodynamics and only then applied to history and psychoanalysis—that is, fixed and applied in firmly extensional terms.

Grünbaum asks us to consider the behavior of an "electrically charged particle having an arbitrary velocity and acceleration" and the laws "governing the electric and magnetic fields produced by this point charge throughout space at any one fixed time t." He rests his case on the fact that the electric and magnetic fields at any time and at any space point "depend on the position, velocity, and acceleration that the charge had at an earlier time t_0." And he interprets the meaning of all this in the following way:

> It follows [he says] that at *any one instant t*, the electric and magnetic fields produced throughout infinite space by a charge moving with arbitrary acceleration depend on its own PARTICULAR ENTIRE INFINITE PAST KINEMATIC HISTORY! . . . Though the individual histories of each of two or more charged particles can be very different indeed, the electrodynamic laws accommodate these differences while remaining general. . . . As against Habermas, I submit that these electrodynamic laws exhibit context-dependence with a vengeance by making the field produced by a charge for any one time dependent on the particular infinite past history of the charge. And, to the detriment of Gadamer, these laws are based on replicable experiments but resoundingly belie his thesis that "no place can be left for the historicality of experience in science."[36]

This is very nearly the whole of Grünbaum's argument. But it surely signifies that either he has no grasp of what history and historical time mean to his own dear "hermeneuticists," or else he supposes that what they say about them is no more than a rhetorical flourish with regard to physical time and natural change (taken in his own sense). The first reading is scandalous; the second, impossible.

There's no difficulty in settling the matter. Grünbaum certainly assumes that the laws of electrodynamics behave in a thoroughly extensional way. Consequently, what he denominates as time, history, context—*which enter into the formulation of those laws*—must also behave extensionally. But, for one thing, according to the tradition we have lightly reviewed, the one concerned with intentionality and the meaning of radical history, that is just what time, history, and context do *not* do;

and, for a second, Grünbaum's insistence here is no more than the mate of what he failed to consider in applying inductivism to the predicables of psychoanalysis. We may now add that what Grünbaum treats as "context-dependence" is just what the unity movement ordinarily means by context-independence! In fact, Grünbaum presses his reading of the context-dependence of physical laws against *Habermas's* insistence on the canonical view—that is, the view that physical laws *are* indeed context-independent. This yields a marvelous irony and confusion.[37]

It is impossible to ignore these dispiriting quarrels: they are an inseparable part of the field. Nevertheless, there is a strategic question that may help us get clear of these entanglements. Are the *time* of history and the physical sciences the same? If not, how are they related? Of course, the quarrels we've been reviewing are bound to infect this matter as well. But there's still a gain in the offing.

Consider that, among physicists, it is a matter of some debate as to whether time is isotropic or anisotropic, that is, whether time is intrinsically directional. Some philosophers, Paul Horwich for instance, argue that "time is in fact isotropic: its two directions [toward the past and toward the future] are intrinsically the same."[38] Other theorists, among them Grünbaum, whom Horwich opposes, contend that time is anisotropic, primarily because, *de facto*, "the temporal inverses of [certain] processes always (or nearly always) fail to occur, whatever the reason for that failure!"[39] Horwich does not look at the matter in the same way, so he is disinclined to decide the question by reference to the time-asymmetric property of particular laws or the time-asymmetric features of the actual "states of the world."[40]

The matter is certainly vexed; and, in a way, it (that is, the technical puzzles about time in certain physical theories) is (are) not really our concern. Grünbaum cites the opinion of E. T. Jaynes (which Jaynes associates with the views of E. P. Wigner), to the effect that entropy "is an anthropomorphic concept"; Grünbaum himself opposes the thesis in certain contexts of classical statistical mechanics, but without abandoning anisotropy.[41] These issues are hardly settled in current physics, not even the question of time reversal, which apparently exercised Einstein on occasion[42] (and remains, in a sense, implicit in the theory of tachyons). But certainly time, *in the human setting*, whether construed physically or historically (leaving that distinction unsolved for the moment), *is* treated as directional: partly for the reasons Grünbaum adduces, partly for the reason that conscious human life is profoundly prospective, intentional, purposive, committed and interpreted in telic terms. The difficulty of these questions is also partly due to the very idea of *the persistence of particular things* (viewed either in accord with human perception or in accord with how things "must" be). Physics does not quite settle these matters; it tends instead to presuppose their resolution. Things appear to require a sense of some real time internal to their being and persistence, that countenances change (persistence at least) as they remain whatever they are ("the same").[43]

In the human setting, then, *the past*, we say, *is surely irreversible*; that is, it cannot be undone. Still, we must be careful. An egg cracked at time t cannot have been uncracked at t, when viewed at $t+k$; but perhaps technology could have made it whole again. A murder consummated at t entails that the victim cannot have been alive at t, when viewed at any later $t+k$; but perhaps a retrospective interpretation (a successful court appeal), at $t+k$, *can alter the past without reversing time*. How's that? you say. One hurries to oppose the monstrous suggestion. For, if it is rightly judged, at $t+k$, that what appeared, at t, to be a murder was not a murder at t (though it did indeed entail a death at t, which cannot be reversed), the change in *judgment* or *interpretation* (we are inclined to say) does not alter the past in any way. (It alters the judgment.) Is that always so? Is it always true that a change in judgment or interpretation about the past does not alter *the past*? Could it possibly be true that, *sometimes*, an interpretation of the past *alters the past without reversing time, without undoing the physical past*? The surprising answer is: (1) it is at least a coherent view; and (2) it may also be a reasonable view. We cannot yet decide the matter. But suddenly we see a new and deeper inning for theories of Gadamer's sort. Nothing in Grünbaum's account can help us here.

VI

The threat of paradox is also the opportunity to surmount it. Everything so far gained is admittedly risked on the new gamble. We have turned a corner, we said; but now, we must either fall back (more permanently) to something like the "canonical" view we've been tracing through the unity movement, or else move forward to ensure elements of what we have been dubbing "radical history." The paradox just posed is the gate through which the camel passes.

Everything depends on what we mean by saying that the past is irreversible. Does that mean that the *past qua past* cannot acquire properties beyond what it intrinsically possessed at the time it was "com-

pleted" as "the" past (that is, apart from extrinsic, *relational* accretions)?
That is Arthur Danto's theory: the historical past, which is identical with
the physical past, is and can be "changed" only in the sense that the full
significance of *any* event cannot be known at the moment it occurs; no
"ideal chronicler" could possibly complete its history therefore, for its
history includes the extrinsically relational accretions that the original
completed event acquires as historians reflect on it through the passage
of time.[44] On Danto's view, history changes, precisely because the past
cannot change. In this regard, Danto's theory is congenial to the presumptions of physicalism, though it is not itself straightforwardly committed to physicalism.

Part of the answer to the question just posed depends, then, on the
irreversibility of *time* and the unalterability (or alterability) of the *past*;
part depends on the irreversibility (or reversibility) of actual *"states of
the world"* (in Horwich's phrase); and part depends on the alterability
of *histories*. These are quite different options.

We have not yet said what a history is; but if we take Gadamer and
Grünbaum as advocates of prominent theories of history, it is clear
enough that there is a great difference in the views of those who favor
the unity conception and those who oppose it. (Notice that the opponents of the unity thesis need not support the bifurcation of the sciences.
They may treat the physical sciences *as* human sciences!) In any case, we
cannot suppose that the conceptual analyses of time and states of the
world and histories necessarily run in tandem.

If we concede that physical time is irreversible, then it is surely true
that any event E that occurs at t cannot *have been undone* at $t+k$; but
the "state of the world" that would then have obtained (answering to
a general predicate) might well be reversed. Also, the concession says
nothing about what *is to count* as such an event or state of the world.
Reductive physicalism would make short shrift of this small caveat, it's
true: *every* event would then be a physical event—taken token-wise.[45]
Yet physicalism is hardly obviously true, or even reasonable. If it were
false or unproved or unprovable, there might well be events (or states of
the world) more complex than physical events and physical states; and
they might not be irreversible or unalterable *in the same sense* in which
physical time and the physical past are. Mark this distinction carefully;
it's all the "radical" view of history requires.

Here, then, is our fresh option: *history* (*and* the historical past) need
not be "finished" or "closed"—in the sense in which *the physical past
is closed* (or is past or has passed or is gone or is no more). It's a matter

entirely different from that of the reversibility of states of the world. *History need not be the mere passage—or the mere chronicle of the passage—of physical time.* Historical time need not be identical with physical time. (A great deal, you see, depends on the prospects of physicalism.)[46]

The argument so far deployed shows at a glance that the irreversibility of physical time entails nothing about the reversibility or irreversibility of states of the world—*no matter what our theory of history may be.* Think of changes in a gambler's luck. Perhaps scrambled eggs cannot be unscrambled; but buildings (once built) can be torn down and rebuilt, without in the least affecting the directionality of time. So we have made a small gain. It is in fact a greater gain than might be supposed, but its secret is still to be told. For, *if* history is irreversible and unalterable *because* physical time is irreversible, *then it is* no more than the chronicle (or passage) *of physical time.*

It's not the irreversibility of time that matters: it's the conceptual link between physical time and history, the link between the passage of time and the nature of the historical past. But *that* connection (the one favored by the unity program) is not a necessary one; it can be coherently denied—even plausibly denied. It is, however, the mark of the "canonical" view: that is, the view that physical and historical time are the same or that the second is completely determined by the first.

On that account of history, one need not be a physicalist: one may simply eschew metaphysics altogether. It would be enough to hold that the irreversibility of *history* was entailed by the irreversibility of *physical time.* Many believe this, but it is hardly a necessary truth. The elaboration of this option is just the theme of Arthur Danto's theory, which is noticeably marked by a general sympathy for the themes of the unity of science (without actually favoring reductionism), by its avoidance of the deeper questions of the metaphysics of history and historical phenomena, and by its treating narrative histories as merely *adding* extrinsically (relationally) to the meaning of the historical past. Symptomatically, Danto never directly addresses the essential question of what it means, conceptually, *to* interpret phenomena historically in the first place, or what it *is* to be a historical past.[47]

History and the passage of time need not be the same for the canonical theorist; but if they are not, history cannot be anything but a narrative construction extrinsically imposed on the passage of physical time. This is the heart of Hempel's and Popper's and Grünbaum's conceptions of history. So history may be coherently impoverished: merely adopt the

rule that the irreversibility and unalterability of history is entirely determined by the irreversibility of physical time. Call that *the principle of
canonical history;* it defines the sense in which the *past* (*not* history) is
finished, closed, no longer "actual," no longer effective in the actual
world. (That view may well be incoherent—on any theory of history—*if*
the bare persistence of things entails *their* causal contribution to their
own continuing persistence. The causal role of *anything else* will then
either be inadequate or, if defined as adequate, it will also be distinctly
alien to our intuitions about the familiar world.)[48]

Now, the canonical conception is remarkably easy to oppose: (1) by
denying that history is the mere chronicle (or passage) of physical time;
and/or (2) by denying that physical time and historical time are one and
the same; and/or (3) by denying that the physical past and the historical
past are one and the same. These options are marvelously generous. The
first (1) is the pivot on which to go beyond Hempel's cramped view of
the canon, but not beyond the canon itself. [Perhaps Grünbaum favors
(1).] For, on Hempel's view, history is no more than a mere intrusion,
a heuristic interlude of some sort in the serious business of describing and
explaining the events of the natural world under covering laws. Give up
that physicalism or let the metaphysics go, honor the robustness of the
human interests that require history, and you will have salvaged history
as something more than a mere chronicle of the passage of physical time.
(The reality of history—historical realism—would remain doubtful,
however.) But if it were reconciled with the canon, two further limitations would still mark its interpretive work: (1) it would remain extrinsic
to the course of physical time and to the real structure of actual events;
and (2) its narrative claims would never take truth-values except in terms
of merely of being in accord with the chronicle of physical time (that is,
solely in terms of compatibility).

We noticed a moment ago that the canonical view endorsed a certain
conceptual connection: if you grant that history is irreversible because
physical time is irreversible, then you must also agree that either history
is no more than the chronicle (or actual passage) of physical time or that,
if it is not that, it is never more than extrinsically imposed on events
collected entirely in terms of physical time (whatever their nature) and
interpreted according to our contingent interests.

On the canonical view, then, history is not intrinsically apt for in-
terpretion, or it is merely heuristically interpretable. But this option goes
entirely against certain common intuitions. However, the narratizable
structures of history cannot be construed in realist terms except by

linking them to the real nature of human existence, by grasping the fact
that human existence *is* historicized. But to concede that is to concede
the force of Gadamer's insistence on the metaphysics of understanding.
Hence, the *radical* conception of history must employ strategies (2) and
(3), tallied just a moment ago.

There is a corollary. Grant: (1) that historical narratives may be true
or false, (2) that they may represent in a realist sense what actually
obtains in the human world, and (3) that they entail the inherent interpretability of human events. Grant all that: you must then deny any
necessary connection (of the sort the canon favors) between physical time
and *history* (as distinct from historical *time*). The two doctrines, the
canonical and radical views of history, are incompatible. *But the alterability of history and the historical past is not incompatible with the
irreversibility of physical time.* That is what is surprising. The two
notions can be reconciled if they are not taken to be equivalent or
identical—if, indeed, historical time and the historical past are not the
same as physical time and the physical past. The two conceptions of
history are mortally opposed to one another, but the distinction between
the historical past and the physical past is viable.

The contest rests on two considerations: first, on whether the necessary connection thought to hold between physical time and history is
genuinely compelling—which, of course, it is not (since its denial is not
self-contradictory); and second, on whether there is a possible (metaphysical) reading of the historical past compatible with the irreversibility
of physical time—which, of course, we have no reason to deny a priori
(but which we also have as yet no reason to support). What we sense is
the ineluctability of theorizing about the human condition directly.

Let us close this much of the argument with a single suggestion. Grant
that the historical past *entails* the physical past, but is not reducible to
it. Imagine that the historical past is conceptually more *complex* than the
physical past but indissolubly *incarnated* in it, logically *emergent* with
respect to it. That much, you must admit, is formally coherent. Now
then, if the phenomena of the human world (as opposed to mere physical
events) have (or "are") real histories, if such histories are Intentionally
structured, if they are interpretable for just that reason, if they are
capable (for the same reason) of supporting realist narratives, then it is
possible to hold that *what is* reversible or alterable *in* history is confined
to what is Intentional, significant, interpretable—without violating the
strong constraint: namely, (1) that *physical time is irreversible*; and (2)
that *events, once past, are, qua past, unalterable in any merely physical*

sense. (Notice also that it is entirely possible that *physical* events are themselves profoundly interpretable, though not for the same reason that human or cultural events are: they may be interpretable in the sense that their characterization is inseparable from the particular theories that legitimate this or that characterzation and that those theories are them- selves replaceable. (Think of the interpretability of the Olduvai Gorge.) This, of course, is just the sense in which Thomas Kuhn speaks of Priestley and Lavoisier as living in "different worlds."[49] And yet, on the familiar argument, physical events lack intentional properties. This is just what we had anticipated in speaking, earlier, of the double function of the notion of the Intentional.

There is a benign equivocation here. We were saying that a building (already built) may be torn down. A given *state of the world* may be reversed, but not physical time: *that* the building was built at *t* remains as timelessly true as any physical fact can be (if, indeed, that is the right idiom to favor about truth); the building's no longer standing does not affect any facts about its physical past—*a fortiori*, does not violate any physical laws. But, on the usual argument, the phenomena of a merely physical world lack Intentional (intentional or intensionally significant) structures altogether. (To speak of such structures in the physicalist's world is no more than a *façon de parler*.) That was the point of Hempel's treatment of history as a piece of rhetoric: its Intentional or interpretive focus shows only that it is irrelevant for science! Physicalism has no need for history, though it may well tolerate it.

So we've come to the decisive question. We've certainly not answered it. But we have gained two advantages at least: we have shown that the canonical theory cannot claim to rest on a necessary truth, and we have shown that the alterability of history and the historical past need not violate the principle that physical time is irreversible. All that is now required for a severely robust defense is that we distinguish satisfactorily between physical time and historical time and between the physical past and the historical past. *Any* theory that coherently yields in these regards yields in the direction of radical history. We have suggested what such a theory would require in the way of avoiding reductionism and dualism; and, anticipating that such a theory will prove viable, we have already collected a set of strenuous constraints—items (1)–(13), at the start of this chapter—which, once accommodated, would make the theory both reasonable and extremely challenging. But to test the possibility we must make a new beginning.

Let us take a brief moment, however, to spell out a few useful distinctions regarding the conundrum of time. First of all, clock time (or the chronicled reading of past, present, and future) does not afford any picture of real time at all, for, on any plausible view, it says nothing about the real extent of the *present* or about what is real or unreal about the past or the future with respect to the present or about *how* things are present in the present. It is only a convention (a good one) for measuring time uniformly and extensionally, but it says nothing about the nature of the *temporal persistence* of the very clocks by which time itself is measured. The distinctions "before" and "after" and "earlier than" and "later than" are merely anecdotal approximations to the systematic distinctions of clock time. As they appear in Aristotle, for instance, they do not even entail the notion that there is a single comprehensive order of real time to which they belong. They need be no more than episodic and story-relative. The tenses, then, are story-relative referential devices. They say nothing about the metaphysics of time.

Again, the "passage" of time in the real world cannot, coherently, be thought to "take time," to be located in a more inclusive time: the regress would be intolerable.[50] (It is a complaint Aristotle lodges against the *Timaeus*.) The only way to make coherent sense of all these approaches to time is to take time (1) to be real; (2) to be inseparable from the persistence of particular things; (3) to link the reality of past, present, and future to the persistence of all real things; and (4) to take real time to be formed as a single encompassing order by and only by the procress involved in the persistence of all aggregated things (that is, creation, change, destruction). If we commit ourselves to this alone, then nothing so far said need disallow the distinction (though not the separation) of physical and historical time and the physical and historical past. From this point of view, the study of time is inseparable from the study of the various ways in which things change and persist in the real world; for that cannot be told except in terms of what we discover the world to contain. For the same reason, the coherence of our theory of time is inseparable from that of our theory of reference.

SEVEN

Two Modes of Reality

I

We are gathering in the harvest now.

We have contrived a contest between two fundamentally different theories of history: the *canonical* and the *radical*, together with their larger doctrinal families. We found the canonical theory defective but coherent; and we found the radical theory coherent but incompletely formed. The defects of the first we took to be more damaging than the absence of detail in the second.

The canonical view goes clearly contrary to certain strong intuitions about ordinary history: contrary, for example, to (1) that histories take truth-values, may be true or false; (2) that historical narratives represent in a realist manner what actually obtains in the human world; and (3) that histories entail the interpretation of the intrinsic (Intentional) attributes of human events. (As we shall soon see, these are extremely quarrelsome notions.) The canonical view also goes contrary—or rather, the more fundamental conception of science and reality on which it rests goes contrary—to the strong strategic findings we were able to draw out, independently, regarding the profoundly historicized nature of reference and predication. Given these and related constraints, canonical history proves an impoverished notion, one that, although enormously influential, is unable to answer its fairest critics—unless, again and again, by the blunderbuss claims of physicalism and inductivism. On the foregoing argument, the radical theory is the more promising, but it has yet to answer its own questions. Fair enough.

We have, it is true, managed to show that it is possible, even plausible, to distinguish between the physical past and the historical past and between physical time and historical time, and to ensure in a formal way that the alterability of the historical past need not violate the irreversibility of physical time. That is a very large gain, but it is hardly enough. The radical theory would have been impossible but for the coherence of this last distinction. Still, we cannot help wondering whether a paradox comparable to the one we have provisionally met, this time unanswerable, lurks somewhere in the intended harvest. There can be no final assurance, of course, but we do see where the important challenges remain to be met if the theory is ever to prove compelling and robust.

The questions that remain are not mere artful tricks, any more than those that challenge the canonical theory. The canonical theory features the would-be rigor of its methodology as it marches to encompass the world under a single banner; the radical theory features its grasp of the human condition and, as a result, the problematic nature of every cognitive undertaking. One makes a virtue of its rational patience, confident of ultimate victory; the other makes a virtue of its scrupulous humanity, no matter what the consequences for the favored vision of rational order. We seek a middle way: one that favors conceptual rigor *in* the context of the human. To put the point a little unpleasantly: in comparing Grünbaum and Gadamer, we were comparing what, in the canonical picture, was methodologically irresponsible regarding the human world (the regimentation of psychoanalysis, for instance) and what, in the radical picture, was still unresponsive to the needs of reflexive inquiry (the disregard of truth-claims). We seek to escape these limitations.

The key to the resolution of the contest lies with what we may fathom in the doubly strange circumstance: (1) that humans, and only humans, understand themselves—both in understanding themselves as they understand others, and in understanding others as they understand themselves; and (2) that they are preformed by social forces that form their competence to understand themselves, and that, in exercising that ability, they alter themselves and others in the process, and alter the preformative conditions under which others, coming later, master a comparable but specifically different such competence. This is the original Hegelian theme, possibly anticipated in some measure in the short interval of German thought between Kant and Hegel, certainly obscured by the purple prose of the nineteenth century, and now again salient as the very nerve of our own late age. It concerns, you may say, the deep contest between the theory of the human self formed and functioning in a historicized world (according to Hegel and Marx, for instance) and the theory of the abstract rational self posited ahistorically as the competent site of all systematic inquiry (according to Descartes and Kant, for instance). It has surfaced in our own time in the important disagreement between Gadamer and Habermas, and it hovers, more elusively, in "analytic" quarrels between extensionalist and nonextensionalist visions of rational inquiry.

Items (1) and (2) together define the hermeneutic problem of historicism (not to be confused, you remember, with the classical historicism of Ranke). Gadamer is extraordinarily clear about the essential puzzle but disappointing in every regard that bears on the actual logic of inquiry under historicist conditions. He offers the boldest, most sensible picture of the hermeneutics of understanding and the leanest account of its metaphysics; but he has nothing to say about managing truth-claims under that condition. So, for instance, he observes that "interpretation is not an occasional additional act subsequent to understanding, but rather understanding is always an interpretation, and hence interpretation is the explicit form of understanding."[1]

Gadamer adds two very perceptive complications: first, that all understanding (*Verstehen*) obtains under the constantly changing history of the continuum of actual understanding, that is, of our being altered in our very "being" or "nature" as a result of the ongoing process of effective understanding; and second, that every act of understanding another (who is also capable of understanding) entails (depends upon) self-understanding ("application," *subtilitas applicandi*) and affects, in turn, all self-understanding (all further self-"application") by inherently altering the continued power of subsequent understanding. This is the precise meaning of what Gadamer terms "effective-historical consciousness" (*wirkungsgeschichtliches Bewusstsein*).[2] Clearly, it threatens paradox, perhaps unmanageably. (It also bears in a profound way on the problem of universals—hence, on predication, everywhere.) It needs to be said that Gadamer cannot claim to rely on any older sense of philological or interpretive objectivity; for, of course, his entire theory has the effect of undermining the pretensions of those older practices. If there is something to be genuinely salvaged there—methodologically—he never bothers to advise us how to reclaim the pertinent part of the older practice.

Gadamer is clearly uneasy about the radical implications of his own view, which derives significantly from Heidegger. He exposes the failure of "historical objectivism" (classical historicism) to come to terms with the historicity of its own critical method; and he warns us, quite rightly, that there cannot be a timeless "method" that would overtake the "effectivity" of history.[3] But he never presses beyond his own warning, never moves to examine the *logic* of interpretation. He has nothing to say about the role of truth and falsity regarding particular interpretive claims. And, fearful that his own view may lead to skepticism or relativism or sheer anarchy, he relents and appears to fall back to a most dubious position.

We understand nothing, Gadamer says, except from within the horizon of our tradition; and we affect and are affected by every new effort at such understanding. Also, *we* are nothing but the emergent artifacts (the "I and thou") of some effective community of understanding.[4] Nevertheless, through all this, Gadamer manages (as we have earlier remarked) to recover some magical invariance from within history itself:

> The historical movement of human life [he says] consists in the fact that it is never utterly bound to any one standpoint, and hence can never have a truly closed horizon. The horizon is, rather, something into which we move and that moves with us. Horizons change for a person who is moving. Thus the horizon of the past, out of which all human life lives and which exists in the form of tradition, is always in motion. It is not historical consciousness that first sets the surrounding horizon in motion. But in it this motion becomes aware of itself.

This poses an enormous conceptual danger for Gadamer—one, it seems, that is blessed with an inexplicably favorable resolution:

> When our historical consciousness places itself within historical horizons, this does not entail passing into alien worlds unconnected in any way with our own, but together they constitute the one great horizon that moves from within and, beyond the frontiers of the present, embraces the historical depths of self-consciousness. It is, in fact, a single horizon that embraces everything contained in historical consciousness.[5]

The "single horizon" mentioned is what Gadamer means by the "classical," which, he says, is "a consciousness of something enduring, of significance that cannot be lost and is independent of all the circumstances of time"—a concept that possesses a distinctly "normative sense."[6] It is also the clue to Gadamer's resolution of the hermeneutic circle:[7] to understand oneself or another, or a meaningful text, is (some-

how) to understand humanity as a whole. But the meaning of the claim
is far from clear. What, after all, is it to understand humanity as a whole?
(It is easy enough, you see, to universalize a parochial vision. That, for
instance, is just what Marx, in criticizing the Gotha program, had seen
in Lasalle's socialism.)

The point at stake is an extraordinarily subtle and strategic one: the
continuity of understanding the "discontinuities" of different historical
ages (construed so differently, for instance, by Hegel, Gadamer, Habermas, and Foucault) is not equivalent to (does not entail) the *universality* of the norms or concepts or forms of rationality by which that
understanding obtains. No, *that* continuity is no more than an artifact
of historical life reviewing, from its own horizoned vantage, the discontinuities it there discerns. To assume the validity of the universalist
thesis on the strength of the formal inclusiveness of discourse (speaking
ambigiously of the "whole of mankind") is to "Kantianize" discourse
illicitly and prematurely. It's a natural enough mistake: one that is surely
implicated in Hegel, Marx, Gadamer, Habermas, and possibly Foucault,
as well as in standard views of history affected by these thinkers.[8] But
it is a mistake nonetheless—a complete non sequitur.

There are three standard options for saving the "classical." The first
argues that Gadamer simply means to recover certain familiar specific
normative invariances ("universals") from within the flux of tradition:
recovering these, Gadamer would be no better than a traditionalist, the
(Hegelian-like) counterpart of the weak (Kantian-like) progressivist we
found Habermas to be—and he would surely fail as well. The second
holds that Gadamer means to claim only that, whatever the content or
supposed historical relevance of particular normative claims, such claims
can be legitimated only insofar as they are interpreted in accord with the
(mere) formal universality of rational concerns assigned to humanity as
a whole: in that case, Gadamer would have abandoned historicism
altogether and fallen back to something indistinguishable from a strong
Kantian formalism. The third maintains that whatever determinate
norms conform with the second can be legitimated by a historically alert
rationality; or that whatever can be legitimated for particular historical
conditions (but not perhaps for all) can also be legitimated in the name
of a historically progressive vision of universal humanity: in that case,
Gadamer would either side (again) with Habermas (by the first disjunct)
or, more interestingly, with Hegel or Marx (by way of the second). There
is some evidence that he has sympathies for what is common to the first
option and the first disjunct of the third.[9] There is also evidence that he

favors the Hegelian option (hardly the Marxist) wherever it can be fortified by the other.[10]

But he has no liking for a historicism that repudiates altogether the pretension that there *are* stable norms ranging across all histories (the "classical") that can be recovered *from* every time—if not also, operatively, *for* every time. So there is, in reading Gadamer, a nagging sense that his vision is a sort of benign blackmail. He dangles the empty vision of a universal (or "common") humanity before our eyes, all the while he reminds us, by an unspoken word, of the barbarism of the recent past.

Every historicist (in the modern sense) who recovers universal norms or categories of understanding (exceptionless, necessary, constitutive, regulative, essential, nomological, transhistorical, ideal, or similarly encumbered)—norms said to be suitable for the whole of historical humanity—has confused or conflated the notion of the constant, logical, atemporal (role of the) self functioning as the epistemic subject of all discourse and the notion of the historically formed human self horizoned by its enabling praxis in its effort to understand the world in the context of actual life. Such a commitment (the conflating) may reasonably be termed "Kantian," in a pejorative sense that links Kant and Descartes (and, in our own time, Habermas and Karl-Otto Apel, and Gadamer when he lapses into his defense of the "classical," and even Foucault when he is tempted to think of the "historical *a priori*" as "continuous" with the universal conditions of understanding);[11] but the rejection (or problematizing) of the compatibility of the historicist and universalist themes is just what distinguishes the radical concerns of the late twentieth century.

Furthermore, as we have noted, when he speaks of the "single horizon" that embraces "everything contained in historical consciousness," Gadamer is surely debasing an insight of Husserl's.[12] What is "one" or "single," here, is simply what, in the most vacuous sense, is (formally) included "in" any consciousness or discourse. The notion of a "single horizon" signifies only the paradox of alluding (negatively) to "what" we might pretend to "exclude" from consciousness or discourse. In this sense, "single horizon" lacks number, cannot be used criterially with regard to *any* determinate claims, and is entirely indifferent to particular questions of meaning, truth, value, or the like. So it cannot be used in the way Gadamer favors. However, the diverse "horizons" of different speakers are not affected in any substantive way by their "entering" into "one" discourse. Every discourse is global in this sense, precludes nothing; but, by the same token, it does not positively include anything worth disputing. It cannot pretend to include, distributively, what, holistically, it cannot coherently exclude. In that sense, the exclusive "single horizon" harbors no significant universality at all. If we conjecture that any functioning discourse is also horizonal (as Gadamer insists), then we cannot vouchsafe—except as a matter of intention—that it *is* genuinely universal (all-inclusive) just where it is substantively significant (normatively binding, for instance); and if our intention *is* universal in this sense, it cannot (yet) claim universal (universally valid) norms or principles or conditions of intelligibility or legitimation of any kind. "Single" in the first sense entails nothing regarding what is specifically interpreted or valued (or legitimated) in the second.

In this sense, the most promising option before us, the one most consistently in accord with the full historical flux, and the most distant from Gadamer's philosophical taste, is the one attributable to Marx—at least to the Marx of Marx's boldest moments. There, Marx (1) insists on the impossibility of separating theory and practice from the actual historical praxis of producing and reproducing life; (2) completely dismisses Aristotle's notion of the invariant normative potencies of the species; (3) still preserves the formal (but only formal) universality of a normative concern for the whole of humanity, the "species-man" (*das Gattungswesen*); and (4) manages withal to mount an empirical argument to show that *that* universality (at once substantive, historically emergent, and species-wide) becomes a viable nonutopian goal (for the first time) only in the present historical era in which the proletariat becomes capable of assuming political power.[13]

We are not here concerned, of course, with the fate of Marx's doctrine. It is clearly flawed on its empirical side; also, in terms of its pretense to have discovered a nomologically exceptionless science; also, in terms of its teleologism; also, in terms of the incompatibility of the import of the theme of praxis and these variously failed strains. But the fact remains that it is the most articulate specimen of the attempt to reconcile, consistently, the rejection of determinate normative invariances, the advocacy of a universalist morality and politics, and an adherence to an uncompromising historicism.

The coherence and daring of Marx's feat hardly depends on the fate of communism, and hardly depends on Marx's own political values. It is also historicist in a sense quite different from that of Hegel's option: because, on any reading of Hegel, the attempt to legitimate a particular emergent stage in the development of an all-inclusive (a "universal")

Geist would presuppose the legitimation of every preceding stage that was dialectically continuous with itself. There is no such Hegelian "universalism" in Marx's vision. Furthermore, by its immense historical detail, Marx's historicism severely challenges (even where it is contestable) Gadamer's historically thin concept, as well as Gadamer's entitlement to the baffling optimism of the "classical."

There is no inclusive "world history" in Marx. Furthermore, on the best reading, Hegel's universalism, precisely because it addresses the problem of a "world history," must be entirely retrospectively supplied—neither realist nor objectivist. If it proceeded prospectively, as in the lectures on history, then it would be an objective teleologism; but if it admitted only that narrative history has a telic structure, then, to escape Heidegger's harsh verdict (that its historicism was a sham), it could not go on to make any determinate claims of a realist or objective sort. It is also true, of course, that, in much of what Marx writes, a science of history is certainly presumed to be in place—a science complete with the laws of objective historical change. There, Marx is surely committed to some sort of teleologism.

Nevertheless, it *is* possible, as it is not in Hegel, to discern in Marx's best vision (regarding *das Gattungswesen*) a distinct form of universality that *is* determinate and that is neither essentialist nor committed to teleologism. It rests entirely on the radical historicism of the theory of praxis, on the bearing of praxis upon the formation of the horizonal resources of human concepts. In this sense, Marx is able to give determinate form to Hegel's best vision: *by* rejecting (Hegel's) world history altogether and by recovering the forward-looking judgments of the agents of history solely within the terms of *their* perceived, evolving, perspectived, "interested," collective, and socially constructed reality (the world of their praxis).

It is precisely because history is never a world history (for Marx: that is, a history of the *Weltgeist*) that the telic projection of particular histories by socially constructed human agents need never entail a real telos in history. (The option is not available to Hegel.) This yields a sense in which Marx more then adequately anticipates the main thrust of Foucault's genealogism. It is a sense in which the agents of history, reflecting on the social conditions they both perceive and effect, spontaneously construe their evolving history in terms of the telic possibilities of themselves and the whole of humanity. (It needs to be said again that this is a discernibly large theme in Marx, not the constant meaning of all of his most important statments.)

The point of pursuing the meaning of the "classical" (in Gadamer), by way of contrast, is to make as clear as possible Gadamer's neglect of the matter of truth-claims *under* historicist conditions; for, of course, *if* his view of the "classical" could have succeeded, then his philosophical negligence would have been benign enough. But Gadamer's judgment cannot prevail; or, rather, it cannot without invoking the very competence Gadamer fails to establish—the competence he actually opposes and cannot possibly provide—that would (if it succeeded) defeat his own vision by thus succeeding. So the paradoxicality of Gadamer's position looms more threateningly. Truth, in the context of history, is essentially consensual: not in the sense that consensus functions criterially, only in the sense that consensus is already socially implicated in the ongoing constitution, reconstitution, and recognition of the very structures of human existence. Marx's theory of praxis, therefore, affords a conceptual basis for melding a sense of objective history and the legitimation of universal norms that escapes at one and the same time every essentialism, every teleologism, every historical privilege that threatens. That we must also admit that Marx did not always see his best option in all of this is neither here nor there. He did not retreat to traditionalism, however.

II

There are actually two different but closely connected paradoxes that Gadamer's theory subtends. The first is central to his "metaphysics" of understanding (as well as to any historicism); the other he does not seriously discuss at all. The second is also a consequence of the larger conception of historicism Gadamer shares with others, though it does not depend in any narrow way on his particular vision.

We need both. They may be formulated as follows: (1) the interpretation of interpretable referents changes their "nature" without disqualifying, or rendering impossible, their continued identity as one and the same, or their being recognized as such through such changes; and (2) the ascription of truth-values to interpretations (bivalent values or some many-valued alternative)[14] preserves objectivity or realism, though there is no pertinent sense in which correct interpretations "correspond to" reality—no sense like that in which truth-claims about physical nature are informally said to "correspond to the facts" (despite intransparency and symbiosis).

We need both "paradoxes," and each is benign. Paradox (1) goes contrary to the strong tradition in Western philosophy, classically formulated in Aristotle's *Metaphysics*, now no longer bound to *de re* essentialism: namely, that, at least *de dicto*, the individuation and re-identification of particulars logically require their assigned *natures* (quiddities) to be held constant. Reviewing the puzzle of reference, we have already demonstrated that reidentification implicates and relies on a narratized memory of specific individuative and reidentificatory practices (*not* criterially fixed essences or haecceities); and that those practices are able to function coherently enough even when we replace "natures" by "histories." Predicatively, on that view, referents have only histories; referentially, they are "histories." Item (2) goes to the heart of explaining what sort of realism is available to the human sciences. It need not be taken to entail or preclude relativism. (This is also true of the bolder version of Marx's universalism, just reviewed.)

We must remind ourselves that we are now concerned to supply the missing details of the radical conception, in order to judge whether any insurmountable difficulties are likely to arise. Our bet is that there will be none; and, of course, if there are none, then, on the argument, the radical theory will have won hands down.

In any case, we need to bring our themes together in a compendious way, that is, items (1) and (2) collected above, the master theme of Intentionality, and the critical thesis we recovered from an earlier argument, namely, that altering the historical past need not entail violating the irreversibility of physical time. There you have the threads of the argument needed. If we can hold them all together coherently—in a theory congenial to those themes of history the canonical view cannot manage satisfactorily (in particular: that histories take truth-values, that historical narratives have a realist standing, that histories entail the interpretation of Intentionally complex events and artifacts)—we can easily move to complete the (radical) picture of historical understanding. There you have the object of the game.

The first of the two paradoxes introduced, item (1) above, already accords with our analysis of reference and predication. So it is coherent as it stands. It also signifies that whatever is interpretable is interpreted in virtue of having (or being) a history. If, then, we adopt something like Gadamer's notion of *wirkungsgeschichtliches Bewusstsein*, we may take the history of any interpretable referent to include its altered and alterable properties. But it is in virtue of a referent's possessing Intentional properties that it has a "history" at all—that it *is* interpretable; so, if a referent's history includes its past, and if its past is interpretable, then, on the argument, a referent's historical past will be alterable. But that is just what we had originally set out to demonstrate.

We may be reasonably sure, therefore, that the radical conception is coherent. But if so, we may venture another step. We may conjecture that histories of the sort just mentioned are open to indefinitely many interpretations and that every such interpretation may enter into indefinitely many histories.[15] For many this will be alarming news: no one can pursue them all, and to court too many would invite disaster. But the worry is only a practical matter: no incoherence threatens.

III

What then do we mean by the realism of the human world? Whatever we elect to mean, we cannot avoid a deeper paradox than the ones already collected. For, as you remember, we raised (much earlier on) the possibility that a judgment might be true, in a realist sense, without its being true, *in principle, in virtue of independent facts or states of affairs to which it could correspond.* You may think this story impossible to defend, but it is not. It is (now) very nearly ineluctable. The point is that the issue it raises can be decided only in accord with our *theories* of truth and reality. Any criterion (of truth or reality) we invoke will, on the argument, already be an artifact of such theories, especially if we admit (as we have) that reality is intransparent and symbiotically linked to the structures of historicized thought. (Once this is admitted, our option outflanks at a stroke the quarrel we have already mentioned, between Putnam and Dummett, about the regulative function of truth. That function cannot fail to be more "internalist" than Putnam would ever allow.)

That is also the implication of Kuhn's well-known remark, which was of course originally meant to apply primarily to the physical world: "The historian of science [Kuhn observes] may be tempted to exclaim that when paradigms change, the world itself changes with them."[16] Indeed, Kuhn is distinctly puzzled (even worried) about his own inclination to assert that "Lavoisier . . . saw oxygen where Priestley had seen dephlogisticated air and where others had seen nothing at all. . . . Lavoisier saw nature differently . . . after discovering oxygen [he] worked in a different world."[17]

Kuhn need not have worried. For, by historicizing the "world," he need not have precluded (in fact, he does not preclude) the recovery of the conception of a physical world independent of human inquiry, in virtue of which the truth-claims of a symbiotized science might still be (said to be) tested in "correspondence" terms: all he needed to concede was that that conception was itself an artifact of the same symbiosis, though hardly, for that reason, an arbitrary posit. On the contrary, the search for nomological invariances, the precision of prediction, the effectiveness of technological intervention confirm its plausibility.[18] The *realism* of the physical world is postulated for just such reasons—and readily cast, therefore, in correspondentist terms.

The independence of the physical world is a dependent but altogether compelling posit made from within the symbiotized world. The important point is that realism is always a theoretical and legitimative posit; otherwise, assuming intransparency, there could be no criterion of correspondence. The cultural world will not support a similar view, if the complexities of the Intentional cannot be eliminated. (We are betting that they cannot be eliminated.) But, its own appropriate realism will similarly be a theoretical and legitimative posit; and the condition on which the realist posit is taken to depend (consensus, as we have indicated a number of times) need not be treated in correspondentist or criterial terms at all.

Kuhn, however, must surely have realized that, adhering to the view he favored, he must have subverted by his own hand all the standard pretensions of the unity movement to which *he* wished to adhere (which, in fact, had sponsored the publication of *The Structure of Scientific Revolutions*). For the unity theorist (Hempel, for example) flatly denies that the real structure of the world depends in *any* way on the constituting power of human thought. What Kuhn does not explicitly admit, what finally alarms him, is the idea that, by adhering to his own historicism, such notions as those of nomological invariance, *de re* and *de dicto* necessity, the fixed pertinence of bivalence, the extensional structure of realist descriptions of the physical world, the ultimate impossibility (therefore) of conceptual incommensurabilities among correct descriptions and explanations of physical nature can no longer even be reliably claimed. That's what worries him about Lavoisier and Priestley, what "forced" him to be a progressivist of sorts.[19] For, he could not yield on symbiosis and intransparency.

He realized he could not jointly salvage the posited independence of physical nature *and* the legitimation of the unity of science program. Only a progressivism seemed capable of bridging the new paradoxes historicism spawned; and indeed it was the only possible way for him, given his philosophical ukase. But it was doomed to fail. The lesson of

Kuhn's reflections is simply this: the *posited* independence of the physical world depends on the genuine achievements of empirical science: historicism cannot discount that. But that alone neither supports nor is supported by the validity of the unity program: historicism has scuttled any such presumption.

The human world is significantly different from the physical—in possessing Intentional structures; it is conceptually richer and more complex in virtue of incorporating the other—and more. The physical world must be older, we say, than human life, and independent of human inquiry; otherwise, all our conjectures make no sense. But (we continue) the world of human culture is surely a construction *of human societies*; it cannot possibly predate *them*, or exist independently of *their* activities; and yet, on their side, human societies and their competences are also artifacts arising and persisting *in* the prior "space" of human history. There's a paradox there, embedded in our deepest intuitions: it's hardly the result of an occasional theory. What is it, then?

Try this: there can be no science, no *sense* of reality, if there are no human societies, no human agents real and competent enough to pronounce on what to regard as real. But if such aptitudes are formed only in the enculturing processes of particular societies, then the human world, the world of language and art and history, must also *be real—as real as* the physical world we claim to know, however different the "two" may be. Furthermore, the human world cannot be disjoined from the physical world: it must be *in* and *of* it, it must partake of it; for, otherwise, we should be obliged to explain its separate *materia* along the lines of the familiar caricature we call dualism. No one is prepared to take that course. Hence, the issue lies entirely with the (adverse) fortunes of physicalism. (We shall have to take all that for granted. It would be too much to pursue the full argument here.)[20]

There is no effective argument that would deny the existence of persons or (cognizing) selves, or eliminate altogether their distinctive aptitudes. Science and argument are themselves inseparable from the existence of persons. There is also no compelling argument that demonstrates the numerical identity of the cultural and the physical (or, more narrowly, the mental and the bodily), or that demonstrates in general the extensional equivalence of sentences about either of these two pairs of referents.[21]

There is only one conceptual option that could accommodate all these constraints: culturally distinctive particulars must be *complex* entities of some sort (harboring, possessing, the sui generis features of the human world but in a way completely embedded in the physical world). They must be: (1) logically, causally, and historically *emergent* with respect to the physical;[22] (2) distinct from the (merely) physical, in virtue of possessing Intentional (*intensionally articulated intentional*) properties; (3) *adequated* in their "natures" to such possession, that is, conceptually capable of possessing properties congruent with whatever properties are assigned them intrinsically (as their "natures"); and (4) actually *embedded indissolubly*, indivisibly—both such particulars and such properties—*in* counterpart physical particulars and physical properties.

Cultural particulars (we may say) are *embodied* in physical particulars (persons, in the members of *Homo sapiens*; Michelangelo's *Pietà*, in a certain block of marble; the uttered sentences of this disquisition, in sounds or marks or the like). By parity of reasoning, culturally significant (or "mental" or informational or semiotic) properties are *incarnate*, or incarnated, in physical or bodily properties (thinking, in neurophysiological processes; a period style, in the actual daubs of paint lying on a canvas; the meaning of a word, in sensory marks that fall within a certain range of variation). (Bear in mind, of course, that nothing so far said settles those questions about truth and method that Gadamer neglects, and that others have been so quick to answer—the romantic hermeneuts, for instance: Emilio Betti or E. D. Hirsch; or those late Kantian thinkers, Habermas and Apel.)

We can afford to risk the incompleteness of this metaphysical picture of human culture. (It corresponds, of course, to the catalogue of what Gadamer pursues in terms of the hermeneutics of history and understanding.) We needed a sketch of it at least, but we need not give it a completely polished form. We cannot stay to answer all the fair questions the sketch invites. It is enough to sense that it can make its way against the philosophical crowd. We are more interested in the ultimate paradox it harbors. We can identify that now as clearly as we wish. Thus, (1) the *human world*, the world of meanings, significant structures, deliberate habits of life, actions, practices, ideologies, institutions, traditions, artifacts, texts, artworks, and the like, is *real* insofar and only insofar as it is produced, constructed, made, enacted by—and for that reason discernible to—suitably apt *persons*, real enough *for that*; but (2) such persons and their competences are themselves first formed and recognized within a society reflexively apt and real enough *for that*. Hence, *neither* (the artifactual world nor persons) *can be real without the other.* Persons and the artifacts of their world are inextricably symbiotized (between themselves) in a deeper *consensual* way than the physical world appears to require of its own observers. The symbiosis of nature functions holistically only. It was Kant's and Husserl's error to suppose that it could be construed distributively and criterially—constitutively, in that sense. However, the symbiosis of culture functions only within the other, though mere consensus is no criterion of what it distributively contains. Still, *what is Intentionally real is consensually real.* All the puzzles of history depend on the fact that there cannot be any unique criterial consensus about that constituting consensus: it has its own history, you see; it is a history.

The paradox is benign enough. The reality of *persons* and (within the human world) the reality of *meanings, deeds, artifacts, products, histories* must be of the same sort. It is a realism of consensus, a realism of reflexive understanding, of the operative identity of cognizer and cognized, of the sharing of *Lebenswelten, Lebensformen, epistemes,* modes of production, the *Geist* of one or another age, traditions, ideologies. It is a *verstehende* consensus, a consensus of interpretation.

The human world must be embedded, we were saying, in the physical world. For the *realism* of the physical world precludes (on the usual view) the *reality* of intensional or intensionally qualified intentional structures; but the realism of the human world *is a realism of just such structures.* Also, the realism (not the reality) of the physical world is a posit of the human world! Once the reality of persons is admitted, once dualism is judged inadmissible, once reductive physicalism and eliminationism fail, only a theory that countenances the complex emergence of an Intentionally structured reality *within* the physical world could possibly be viable and adequate enough for our conceptual needs.

We cannot fail to see how utterly opposed to this are the claims of the unity program and the claims of those looser philosophical eddies that in the last half-century have dominated Anglo-American analysis. One example should suffice. Try this one for instance, by Daniel Dennett:

> Intentional objects are not any kind of objects at all. This characteristic is the dependence of Intentional objects on particular descriptions. [On the Intentionalist view,] to change the description is to change the object. What sort of thing is a different thing under different descriptions? Not any object. Can we not do without the objects altogether and talk just of descriptions. [For, it would be enough to say that] Intentional sentences are *intensional* (nonextensional) sentences.[23]

Dennett goes on to link this completely unsupported proposal with another (that is equally undefended) baldly intended to eliminate all talk of persons altogether.[24] But the linkage is gratuitous. The trouble is simply this: *no* champion of the reality of intentional or intensionally complex structures ever held that a change in the description of physical or natural objects entails a change in *such* "objects." The only question they ever (and properly) raised in that regard concerns the logical bearing of such complexities on the actual management of truth-claims about such (physical) objects. (The possibility of altering, as by interpretation, *Intentionally* qualified entities is another matter that Dennett never discusses.) Furthermore, the elimination of "Intentional objects" (including selves) leaves us with the utterly unexplained puzzle of *what, regarding the human, remains to be described and explained—and what description and explanation themselves amount to.* No eliminationist has ever answered the query.

All this is already a grand advance gained at a very small price. For it promises a less parochial sense (than Gadamer supplies) of the phenomenon Gadamer himself identifies as *wirkungsgeschichtliches Bewusstsein*: we need no longer be bound to Gadamer's conceptually unwieldy affiliation with hermeneutics and *Lebensphilosophie* and Heidegger's idiosyncrasies. We have found a formula generous enough to span whatever we may care to draw from both Anglo-American and continental European philosophies. It was only the refusal of "analytic" and "hermeneutic" theorists to talk together, to examine one another's notions, that made it so difficult to find alternative ways of rendering the other's discoveries in the resources of one's own idiom: it merely seemed as if Gadamer's insight required all of Gadamer's language and unanswerable questions. But that's not true. For another thing, we have now identified a distinctive symbiosis of the human world, one that is more specialized (and more invisible) than what we had already marked as the (Kantian-like) symbiosis of the natural world. For a third, we can explain the sense in which (we had said, earlier, that) statements may be true *about* the human world without there being any *independent* such world to which (*qua* true) they *correspond* (criterially). And, finally, we can now answer all the methodological questions Gadamer had simply abandoned.

IV

The issue is realism of course. There must be two distinct but compatible notions of realism at work here. Perhaps the following device can be made to tag their difference: the things of the human world, let us say, are *real!*, whereas physical things are *reall*. The conventional realism assigned the physical world holds that what is *reall* is independent of whatever is *real!*, however much its being posited (or "made" intelligible, or produced by a technology) depends on the powers of the other; whereas the realism of the *real!* confines within the space of the *reall* all that *that* includes, restricts its scope to whatever is shared *there* between cognizer and cognized—in effect, *Intentional structures*.

In the human world, cognizer and cognized are paradigmatically the same—persons, ourselves—reflexively interpreted and understood in the manner in which the members of a society communicate and share their practices. The human world is the consensual "space" of encultured persons and what they do and make: the space of history.[25] It is a congeries of collective habits of life that every generation of every society internalizes (in becoming the apt new members of that society) and, in spontaneously exercising those same habits, ineluctably alters (thereby becoming—the altered habits, that is—the enculturing network of subsequent generations of the same society).

This is the generic sense of what Wittgenstein means by a *Lebensform*, although Wittgenstein never speaks of forms of life except synchronically.[26] In the *Investigations*, for instance, Wittgenstein is surely speaking of the processes of history. It's only that he never confronts its actual puzzles: he has no interest in them. In this regard, his is a vastly different voice from all those other voices that treat as fundamental the temporal order of collective human life: the voices of Hegel, Marx, Nietzsche, Dilthey, Heidegger, Merleau-Ponty, Gadamer, Foucault, Giddens, Bourdieu—even Husserl (speaking of the *Lebenswelt*).

We need a moment more to fix our theme. We are trying, after all, to understand how historied things *exist*. To say that the physical world is *reall* and the human world, *real!* is merely to sort the *predicables* of those two contexts. Their referents fall within—*exist in*—the same real world. We distinguish between the *existence* of referents of either sort and the modes of *reality* proper to each. We need not abandon the univocal sense of "exists" in endorsing an equivocal sense of "real." But the caveat helps to explain the point of insisting that the human world cannot be detached from the physical world: it partakes of it, it exists in the same way the other does. Yet it remains, as we have said, incomparably richer.

The implied asymmetry is also important. *The reality as well as the realist structure of the cultural world presupposes the reality of the physical world*: it is embodied in it. However, *it is the realism rather than the reality of the physical world that presupposes the human*: realism is insuperably symbiotized, we have been claiming. The result is that, although we conjecture (reasonably, of course) that the physical world is older than the advent of human culture, the conjecture itself occurs only within the space of the human: knowledge is a cultural artifact; also, the determinate structures we impute to the physical world (what we take realism to signify) are, on the foregoing argument, logically inseparable from the emergent powers of the human world. In short, our theories of the physical world are endogenously horizoned by the cognitive history of human science. There is no insuperable paradox here.

What is *real*, actual particulars—that is, what is *real!* and/or *real!*—*exists*. On a realism restricted to the first option, the reality of the *real!* requires (it is said) no predicates drawn from the second option; but a realism of the second entails that the predicates of the *real!* apply only to some subset of whatever the predicates of the *real!* apply to; the predicates of the second qualify what is embodied in what the predicates of the first qualify. Only the referents of the second may be qualified by ("adequated to") the predicables of both options;[27] also, predicables of the second sort are indissolubly incarnate in predicables of the first sort. There's an irony, therefore, built into the very soul of the unity program and its allies. For how, reflecting on its own work, its own theorizing, could it possibly offer such restrictive physicalisms as those of Hempel and Davidson and Grünbaum and Dennett and Churchland? *What* is distributed in the *real!* world requires no predicates drawn from the *real!* world, *except of course for whatever qualifies the cognizing powers by which the first is discerned*; for those same powers, granted the global symbiosis we have already supported, are ingredients in the constituting structure of whatever is specified as *real* (*a fortiori*, of whatever is specified as *real!*). There you have the insuperable *pons* of every physicalism. In short, on the argument just supplied, *realism* makes no sense if we eliminate or impoverish the reality of the human world. Hence, similarly, it would (then) make no sense to claim that this or that was a real property of this or that real particular. That comes as a surprise to the partisans of the most recent physicalist readings of the cognitive sciences; for they have never demonstrated the coherence of eliminativism (Churchland) or the viability of a naturalizing of cognition (Quine, Dennett, Goldman).[28]

We have now recovered Gadamer's two principal themes about the "metaphysics" of culture—"effective-historical consciousness" (*wirkungsgeschichtliches Bewusstsein*) and the "fusion of horizons" (*Horizontverschmelzung*)—without catering at all to Gadamer's shadowy hermeneutics. The first theme confirms that truth-claims about the In-

tentional structures of the human world cannot be said to match an
independent world (in the sense usually reserved for physical nature).
Our claims cannot "correspond" to such a world; but a *real!* world exists
nevertheless and truth-claims about it do enjoy a characteristic objectivity. (In a way, this is Vico's theme.) The second theme should have
fixed the logic of historical claims within the space of the first. Gadamer
never makes good on that encumbered debt. He flinches, hides among
the pages of his metaphysics. But without the second labor, the labor of
the first would be too slack.

The subtlety of what remains to be made clear may still elude us. You
may catch a glimpse of it in the following alien remark of Michael
Dummett's. Why mention it then? Because it exposes so brilliantly by its
own deliberate silence what it would hide, namely, the ubiquitous indeterminacies of history that affect so adversely whatever we pretend still
count as *de re* and *de dicto* necessities. The most important of these is
this: that bivalence and all alternative logics may forever fail to guarantee
the objectivism of science and reason. Dummett's vision, for instance,
insinuates (everywhere) the unsupported presumption that there *is* an
independent, prior, relatively homogeneous order of reality that inquiry
(rightly instructed intuitionistically) can effectively fathom. There you
have a version of the same master stroke the unity program and the whole
of analytic philosophy variously favor: the posit of *the conceptual priority and assigned invariance of logic and semantics over the whole of
reality*, the certainty that nothing in the world could upset the adequacy
of our idealized organon of thought:

> A meaning-theory which substitutes [says Dummett], for the two-valued
> semantics, a finitely many-valued one represents *a very trivial variation* on
> this [two-valued semantics]; we have merely been provided with a slightly
> more complicated mechanism for determining the truth or otherwise of a
> complex sentence in accordance with its composition from [its] subsen-
> tences. In such a semantic theory, truth, as we have been using this notion,
> corresponds to having a designated value. If there are distinct designated
> values, these therefore represent different ways of being true, while the var-
> ious undesignated values represent different ways of failing to be true; the
> distinction between the various values are needed solely to explain how the
> truth of a complex sentence is determined *in accordance with its composi-
> tion*. The essential conception of the way in which meaning is given *remains
> the same: a grasp of the meaning of a sentence still involves an awareness
> that the sentence objectively possesses some determinate one of the finitely
> many statement-values*, and it remains the case that our knowledge of what
> must hold for it to have any particular one of these is, in general, *given
> independently of the means which we may have for recognizing which of the*

different values it has. Hence the distinction between a meaning-theory based on the two-valued semantics and an *n*-valued one, for finite $n > 2$, is comparatively insignificant.[29]

One sees at once the sly insinuation of Dummett's unexplained priorities: nothing is real that fails to conform to this or that semantic (*a fortiori,* logical) constraint. Dummett insists, it's true, that "a theory of meaning does have metaphysical consequences," but his own plan is to require metaphysics to conform to the *prior* terms of his meaning-theory; he is unwilling to concede any cognitive parity between metaphysics and "meaning-theory." But metaphysics and "meaning-theory" are already indissolubly symbiotized: the verdict follows from the *two* sorts of symbiosis we've already introduced.[30] (Dummett never addresses the question directly.)

A similar strategy (by way of an altogether different tactic) appears in Quine's treatment of indeterminacies among diverging (even incompatible) "metaphysical" parsings of shared "stimulus meanings." There is no fact of the matter here, says Quine; but *that* (it seems) never leads to truth-value gaps or doubts about excluded middle![31] Still, though Quine is obviously skeptical about ever fixing a unique metaphysics for our world (the lesson of his "analytical hypotheses"—a compressed concession to historicity), he is every bit as certain as Dummett that his own extensional semantics *antecedently* determines the form of all eligible metaphysics *and* the adequacy of a bivalent logic.[32] But if we merely remind ourselves of Peirce's incisive speculation about the real occurrence of the vague and the general in nature, then Dummett's and Quine's presumption becomes entirely transparent: there can be no knockdown reason, empirical or a priori, for supposing that *any* form of correspondentism or extensionalism or physicalism invariably fits each and every sector of reality.[33] To abandon metaphysical realism is to abandon all these presumptions. But very few see the connection: certainly not Quine, nor Davidson, nor Putnam, nor Dummett. (It needs to be said as well that, in Peirce's case, real vagueness and indeterminacy are only part of what is meant by "thirdness"; what is generic to thirdness is being developed here, in a fresh way, in terms of Intentionality.)

Neither Dummett nor Quine addresses the deeper metaphysical issue. They have no more interest in it than Hempel or Davidson or Dennett. But they are quick enough to insist on a uniform objectivism for the whole world. At the very least, they neglect Kuhn's and Peirce's and Gadamer's challenges—though the point at stake is more than gossip, it concerns the historicity of thought itself. It goes to show that there cannot be a general or a priori logic for all truth-claims; there cannot be a general logic of predicates; there cannot be a principled disjunction between an uninterpreted logical calculus and an interpreted calculus; there cannot be any strictly necessary invariances governing any of these distinctions. To admit all this is to deny the priority of semantics over metaphysics, to deny every form of cognitive privilege and every *de re* and *de dicto* necessity. (Needless to say, the objectives just tendered are not themselves independently necessary: they are no more than the expression of a dialectical bet.)

Peirce may be the deepest discussant of the matter. He does not bifurcate the physical and human worlds, because he sees nature as entirely semiotized already. He treats the world as harboring real inde-terminacies that can be *made* increasingly (never completely) determinate through historical inquiry and man's interpretive intervention: "The entire universe [he says]—not merely the universe of existents . . . —all that universe is perfused with signs if it is not composed entirely of signs." "[T]he meaning of a thought," he adds, that is, the meaning of every (such) sign—man himself being a sign, as is indeed the universe—"is altogether something virtual,"[34] something never completed in real-world time. As it happens, Peirce himself has no interest in pursuing the special complexities of human history. They are simply lost in his cosmic optimism and global semiosis.

You may feel the question of history slipping through our fingers, but it's not true. We are tracking it in the strongest possible way. You have only to remember that we demonstrated, earlier, the impossibility of casting the analysis of reference and predication in objectivist terms. That's what Dummett and Quine intend to offset by prioritizing their own semantic theories over metaphysics; and that is what they cannot do convincingly. If we now collect all the specimens from the unity of science and the whole of analytic philosophy, if we remember what we found true of all of them, we may safely say: *there is no known argument that disqualifies, or shows the incoherence or untenability or even im-plausibility of, the realism of the real!*

Of course, that leaves us still with Gadamer's failing.

V

On the historicist's view, history and interpretation are twin ventures: interpretation can claim no fixity in the "natures" of its referents—they are "histories" (*real!* "texts," let us say); and histories (that is, texts constructed to represent *real!* "texts") are formed by threading together the persisting unity of a referent's Intentional structures—we interpret such structures narratively. The point of invoking the notion of the *real!* is simply that narrated histories can still be shown to support truth-values; the "objectivity" they sustain, however, is suited to their particular world, not to the world of mere physical things. Theirs is a consensual objectivity at least and at most, but it is not a mere consensus. (No a priori semantics of Dummett's or Quine's sort can discredit that possibility.) In fact, the *real!* supports a genuine perceptual practice within the space of the forms of life of this or that society; it's only that the perceiving of what is thus perceived—Intentional structures incarnated in physical things—must be rightly informed Intentionally if it is ever to claim objective standing. That is what Grünbaum misses in his "unity" reading of psychoanalysis. The same preparation is needed for the perception of artworks and the perception of human behavior. (In this sense, let it be noted, speaking of "texts" is *not* an idealism but a recovery of the symbiosis of the cultural world.)

The lesson is already limned in Gadamer's borrowings from Heidegger:

> The anticipation of meaning [the "prejudice," the preformation of our aptitude for interpreting what is interpretable] that governs our understanding of a text [any interpretable referent] is not an act of subjectivity, but proceeds from the communality that binds us to [our own] tradition. . . . Tradition is not simply a precondition into which we come, but we produce it ourselves, inasmuch as we understand, participate in the evolution of tradition and hence further determine it ourselves.[35]

Gadamer fills out the historicist significance of Wittgenstein's *Lebensformen*. In effect: he offers us the notion of *Horizontverschmelzung*. But there *are* no actual horizons, there *is* no unique "horizon of the present": "There is no more an isolated horizon of the present than there are historical horizons. Understanding, rather, is always the fusion of these horizons which we *imagine to exist* by themselves."[36]

We favor Gadamer's theme here, if not his idiom, because "every encounter with tradition," every would-be interpretation of a "text," entails a sense of an "encounter with the past."[37] The historical past *is an interpretive construction projected from the present*. To live as a human being is to be aware, in the middle of life, that we ourselves are the encultured creatures of our own preexisting tradition: knowing that, we reconstruct our past again and again (as we must, under change) and then interpret, according to our lights, what we have thereby reconstituted (a particular interpretable text or history: ourselves, for instance). There cannot be a straightforward "correspondence," therefore, between *real!* texts and the texts that represent them—both said, equivocally, to be "histories" in the familiar idiom. For, the interpretable texts we reidentify through a given interval are themselves serially reconstituted by consensually approved interpretations (and reinterpretations) of the narratized structures they are imputed (or "perceived" to have). Their narrative structure—their past, for instance—is, as we have said again and again, always subject to further change by way of further interpretation. Nothing like this obtains in the physical world, although, even there, Kuhn's warning is too often neglected. (There is an instructive analogy here, of course, that supposes that the physical sciences form a peculiarly powerful abstraction *from* the inclusive space of the human sciences.)

Historians and interpreters play a double role, then: (1) they first identify—they must first fix, referentially—the interpretable texts belonging to their shared tradition: hence, also, the then-imputed properties of those texts (their Intentional structures, their intrinsic "natures"); and then (2) they interpret those now-stable "story-relative" texts, they "apply" their interpretations reflexively (and reciprocally) to themselves, to their own mode of self-understanding, and to other texts; hence, they continually reconstitute the "natures" of the interpretable texts they interpret.

All this would fail if reference presupposed the fixed, extensionally reliable natures of all individuatable things. But it does not. Indeed, on the argument, *it cannot*; and, because it cannot, reference and predication must be historicized undertakings. These distinctions may be made compatible with Peirce's and Gadamer's particular doctrines; but neither Peirce nor Gadamer (progressivist and traditionalist, respectively) ever pursues the possibilities we are now uncovering.

We may pause here to redeem one promissory note signed earlier: *of course the historical past can be altered* (consistently with the irreversibility of physical time), for *that past is a "prejudiced," horizonal, Intentional, diachronized construction (of incarnated meanings) projected from the historical present.* There would be no history at all, in this sense, if reference and predication were not already historicized, or if the world did not include phenomena that were intrinsically Intentional in structure. The first obtains even in the physical world. But if it does, then every science addressed to physical nature implicates the existence of cognizing subjects who are themselves Intentionally structured; and if that is conceded, then there is no compelling reason to refuse to allow, as real, all the dense phenomena of the cultural world. Q.E.D. Otherwise, history would reduce to no more than that expendable chronicle that Hempel sets aside, and cognizing selves would be reduced or ultimately eliminated in the physicalist's way.

We claim that narrated histories take truth-values in spite of the oddity of the *real!*. More than that, we claim that *that* is a direct consequence of the caveat we have just tendered: *history is an Intentional flux, discursively arrested within a tradition, represented or reported in accord with a society's consensually narratized memory of its own practice of reference, predication, individuation, reidentification, and the like.* The formula is not only coherent, it is unavoidable. It not only specifies the metaphysics of human existence, it defines the conditions of historical objectivity. There is an elegantly simple corollary of all this that settles the most strategic part of the dispute once and for all. It is this: even the referents of the *physical world* depend for *their* identity and reidentification on the human aptitude for effectively determining—"objectively"—*the narrative history of its own discourse about that world.* (This is what we were unmasking in Dummett and Quine.)

Grant this much, and you will have gained the high ground leading to our conclusion. For, now, all truth-claims will presuppose the narrative structure of *that part of the real world* (the narratized human world) through which alone *their* proper truth-values are objectively assigned. All realisms, therefore, encompass the *real!*. Furthermore, there is no *real!* (no human world) unless the things of that world *do actually possess* the narratizable structures that histories "objectively" impute to them. That's all. The contest is already lost, therefore, as far as the unity-minded or reductionist theorist is concerned: on his view, nothing really has a history; historical narrative is no more than a *façon de parler* governed by our transient and extrinsic interests. Even so, he has never eliminated those "extrinsic interests."

Still, to say that things have histories is not to say that histories are in principle uniquely fixed. That would save the *real!* but it would also favor an objectivism like Schleiermacher's or Vico's or Collingwood's again. Real history is not available to the unity theorist at all. But *we* must still choose between an objectivist and a fully historicist account of history.

VI

There is a deep uneasiness in contemporary efforts to reconcile the bifurcated and unity visions of the human sciences. It appears most pronouncedly in Paul Ricoeur's theory of history, but also in Hayden White's, which is influenced by Ricoeur's. It affects the very idea of narrative structure. Neither Ricoeur nor White is straightforwardly prepared to affirm that the *real!* referents of the human world—notably, persons and their actions—*have* narratizable attributes, *have* histories, have suitably complex properties apt for narrative reporting or interpretation. They do not deny that narrative histories are paradigmatically suited to our understanding of human life. On the contrary, they insist on bifurcating nature and culture in just this respect. But they are impressed with the apparent fact that the past is "gone," no longer *real!*, never actual. As a result, they have persuaded themselves that the narrative *recovery* of the past (*a fortiori*, the recovery of the whole of narratized life) must be essentially figurative and fictional. They risk the reality of the *real!*, therefore: they admit the reality of persons, of course, but they are unclear about the full import of that; they worry about bringing their own theory of history into accord with the "superior" constraints of the physical sciences, but they are unwilling to give up whatever a viable history requires. So they fall back to the tricky resources of metaphor and fiction.

History, they say, is both metaphorical *and* an apt figuration (not quite realistically mimetic) of the Intentionally complex meaning of human life. Both Ricoeur and White combine in one account a view of history anchored in the most uncompromising physicalist conception of time (one, say, that Hempel would be entirely willing to accept) and whatever of the intensionally rich structure of the cultural world may be needed to represent the actual reflexive and purposive life of human subjects (what, for instance, the hermeneuts would be prepared to include). They believe, therefore, that they have no choice but to treat history as uniting a *mimesis* and *diegesis* in such a way that: (1) the *diegesis* is figurative with respect to *time* but realist (enough) with respect to the Intentional structure of the essential life of its subjects, and (2) the *mimesis* is realist with respect to essential human reflections on temporal existence (already refigured by the choice of one literary trope or another) but not quite realist enough with respect to the resultant *story*.

This yields a wonderfully tortured conceptual vision that masquerades as one form of wisdom or another (theological and poetic, primarily), without ever sensing a need to abandon any of the essential ingredients of historical understanding. But the thesis is an extravagance. We can replace it quite easily now, if only we distinguish between physical and historical time and past, if we treat the historical as incarnate in the physical, and if we strengthen the realist standing of both sorts of time. Ricoeur and White have made too much of the real "absence" of the past: they cannot meet the conceptual needs of the physical sciences, that is, *the reality of the physical past*;[38] and they have made too little of the difference between the *real!* world of human culture and the *reall* world of physical nature. They thereby subvert the objective standing of history itself.

Both are caught up too much with the mimetic tradition of poetry (with Aristotle's *Poetics*, in particular). In Ricoeur's case, the underlying worry (about the realism of reflexive history) is strengthened by his theological concerns (via St. Augustine's *Confessions*, Book XI)—by the thought, that is, that mere humans cannot ever rightly construct the true (divinely appointed) narrative that fits each mortal self.[39] Man presumes to invent a totalized and smoothly continuous history for himself out of the necessarily discontinuous and fragmented episodes of his remembered life. In White's case, it is, rather, the supposed continuation of Aristotle's insistence on the mimetic that counts: the adequacy, in realist terms, of an ideally artifactual (fictional) construction of a represented life (via Northrop Frye's *Anatomy of Criticism* and its Vichian sources).[40]

Both visions are extravagances, and neither really works. Both presume on the validity of Aristotle's distinction between history and poetry.[41] Both insist on the quiddity and haecceity of human existence. It is in fact the supposed reliability of the human essence that assures us that a *fictional* treatment of the *diegesis* of a particular life may be counted on to conform with a *realist* recovery of historical *meaning*; for historical meanings must be structured in accord with those literary tropes (tragedy, for instance) that successfully capture—because they do so poetically (that is, better than mere particular chronicle)—what, *generically*, is mimetically true of human existence. Histories represent particular natures; but narrative structure is not part of the real (*real!*) world: as such, it cannot be directly or objectively represented. In Ricoeur's argument, *narrative histories are part of the rhetoric of representational acts only*. Temporal structure is restricted to what is conformable with physical time; the historical past, bound by the irreversibility of physical time, is simply what was but is no longer actual in the space of human events. As a consequence, narrative is treated as a construction of some sort—an imposition of meaning—upon human events viewed solely in terms of physical chronicle. And yet, of course, it is only human existence that *is* meaningful and the source of meaning! In short, Ricoeur and White fail to consider that the *real!* nature of humans is already languaged, encultured—hence, that language and cultural meaning are themselves incarnate. But if that is so, then so also are the narrative structures of human life.

It's not that the events of the "present" are not meaningful for White and Ricoeur: they merely neglect to provide a theory of human events that rightly ranges over the whole of human time. Consequently, they fail to air the implications of actually ascribing, to *present referents* (whether Intentionally structured or not), whatever attributes they have or had. They thereby lose the realism of the historical (and the physical) past.

The issue is straightforward. Once concede that narrative structures are not real—that is, not (even) *real!*: every principled distinction between history and fiction founders. That alone would not be troublesome, say, for Aristotle (or for Aristotle on Ricoeur's interpretation); for, for Aristotle, poetry, even more than history, represents the verisimilitudinous with regard to the human *quiddity* (the "possible," what "might have been"). On just that sort of reading, Ricoeur asks: "Free from the external constraint of documentary proof, is not fiction internally bound by its obligation to its quasi-past, which is another name for the constraint of verisimilitude?"[42]

Ricoeur means us to understand, here, not that history is merely fiction (or as free as fiction) but rather that it cannot complete its task except through an "interweaving" of the resources of fiction and reality. Ricoeur holds that that *is* a "realist" undertaking. But what he means is that it does not violate or depart from the thread of physical time:

> History [he affirms] reinscribes the time of narrative within the time of the universe. This is a "realist" thesis in the sense that history locates its chronology on the single scale of time common to what is called the "history" of the earth, the "history" of living species, the "history" of the solar system and the galaxies. This reinscription of the time of narrative within the time of the

universe in accordance with a single time scale marks the specificity of the referential mode characteristic of historiography.[43]

Unfortunately, this obscures the point that *the narrative time of history—not* the physical time history must also inhabit (must be incarnate in)—*is (on the theory Ricoeur offers) not real (or real!) but merely fictional* ("mimetic," as Ricoeur has it, rather than "imitative").[44] Ricoeur misses the point that a *realism* of history requires a realism *of* historical time, *of* the historical past, *of* historical narrative. There is no other way to distinguish fiction from history. Ricoeur is so busy reconciling fiction and history in terms of shared meanings that he scants the realism of time (and past) he himself requires.

White distances himself from Ricoeur in this regard—initially but not successfully.[45] He isolates what a full realism regarding history would require. He does not himself endorse that requirement, because (like Ricoeur) he too falls back to an Aristotelian view of man: to an acceptance of the *realist import of fiction* vis-à-vis man's quiddity—which of course *is* just Ricoeur's essential maneuver.[46]

On White's view, it's true that Ricoeur disputes Aristotle's distinction between *mimesis* and *diegesis*; but Ricoeur disputes it (as White shows) in order to build *into* historical *diegesis* the mimetic (and fictional) power of narrative.[47] And that now means that the would-be realism of history *requires* the fictional or allegorical feature of narrative (its supposed mimetic function). It is "realist" in the sense of Aristotelian (generic) "possibility," *not* in the sense of (particularized) historical time. It cannot be that, on White's account. That's why White insists that "the 'truth' of narrative form can display itself only indirectly, that is to say, by means of *allegoresis*":

> This transition [that is, the "transition from the level of fact or event in the discourse to that of narrative . . . the logic of figuration itself"] is effected by a displacement of the facts onto the ground of literary fictions or, what amounts to the same thing, the projection onto the facts of the plot structure of one or another of the genres of literary figuration.[48]

But what *is* historical "truth"? you ask. Here is White's answer:

> Precisely insofar as the historical narrative *endows* sets of real events with the kinds of meaning found otherwise only in myth and literature, . . . we should regard it as allegorical, that is, as saying one thing and meaning another. . . . This is not to say that a historical discourse is not properly assessed in terms of the truth value of its factual (singular existential) statements taken

individually, and the logical conjunction of the whole set of such statements taken distributively. . . . But such assessment touches *only* that aspect of the historical discourse conventionally called its chronicle. It does not provide us with any way of assessing the content of the narrative itself.[49]

Truth (in the "strict" sense) is confined, anchored, to what obtains in the space of physical time. White and Ricoeur never say just *what* falls within that space: if they had admitted *real!* structures as well as *real!* time, then historical narrative would implicitly have been admitted to be real; but in denying that status to narratized properties, White and Ricoeur are logically bound to deny it as well to *human events in the present*—which they cannot really acknowledge consistently, but which they have no way of describing in fully realist terms. White is bent on excluding the "content" of historical narrative from the range of truth in the "strict" sense. (He says he will recover its [generic] realism "indirectly"—through fiction.) In that sense, White has abandoned the reality of the human world—which of course is hardly what he intends. There's a great muddle here. There cannot be a convincing disjunction between the narrative form of human life and its interpretable import. "Both" are Intentional and for the same reason. They are in fact indissoluble aspects of one and the same human career.

Irwin Lieb, we may belatedly note, offers a most subtle improvement of the thesis in question, but an improvement that still fails for related reasons. He speaks of the "imposture" of history:

> The imposture in supposing that history says what was as it was when it was present is that historians know, in telling or constructing the narrative, how it all comes out, but when things were as they were at a present, no one knew how they would come out. A historian's knowledge of outcomes affects either the telling of the story or the story itself. . . . A historical narrative should not be construed as a plausible or even an interesting rendering of things as they in fact occurred. It is an imagined world in which imagined individuals are imagined to act in ways that real individuals could never have acted.[50]

Lieb means of course, among other things, that agents in historical time could not (normally do not) know the literal outcome of their complex histories as they live and act *in the present*. Nevertheless, they *do* rehearse all sorts of possible narrative outcomes *as they act*. It's the very mark of rationality. There *are* narrative characterizations, potential telic outcomes, that they reflexively entertain *in the present*. This shows the reasonableness of construing narrative structures as *real!* That the closure of history is a function of its interpretation "after the fact" is both compatible with that (in fact, it is informed by such reflections) *and* interpretively open to being judged (for that reason) plausible or implausible, on the general caveat that human agents cannot be expected to grasp such structures in the middle of life. The narrative structure of history is judged in accord with the narrative model of rationality. That there is no single such model, that such a model is itself an artifact of diverging histories, is just what marks the ultimately antihistoricist themes in Vico and Collingwood and Peirce and Ricoeur and White and Habermas. It goes to show that the historical past *is* an interpreted construction of the meaning of events "completed" in the physical past. Also, of course, the openness of the present is informed, for humans, by their memory of endless other histories that they have entertained about past presents.

Only grant the analysis, only oppose White's and Ricoeur's (and Lieb's) arguments: you will find yourself inexorably drawn to a more radical historicism.

Epilogue: Historicism

I

Thinking has a history! There's the thread of the new historicism.

It's not a new theme, of course, but its meaning dawns on us in a new way. We must give it a final moment to settle in. Ordinary habits of reflection now spontaneously incline toward acknowledging the unfathomed contingent forces that form the way we think. It tempers what we think (and say and do); it seasons it. It cannot affect matters criterially, however. We are at once blind and sighted in a cognitive sense, endogenously limited by our own aptitude; and that aptitude varies and is altered historically in incompletely penetrable ways. We cannot discern our own cognitive limitations—*by* our cognizing labors. The theme is Wittgenstein's; also, Hegel's, Marx's, Nietzsche's, Heidegger's, Gadamer's, Foucault's. It is what is fatally neglected in Kant and Husserl and the objectivism of the unity of science.

Historicism civilizes what we say—piecemeal. It does not issue in any particular claim alongside others, except in terms of our second-order (legitimative) understanding of what we mean by what we say. We make reference as before, but we now understand the act in terms of its profound contextedness; we offer grounds for reidentifying this or that, but we now understand the insuperable informality of doing so. We historicize our lives by historicizing our understanding of our lives. And that makes a difference. But we cannot *expose* our limited horizon: we infer its presence from the horizoned critique of our past and the competence of other cultures; that is, we infer that it must be so. Fortunately, historicism produces no self-referential paradoxes, though it may seem as if it must.

This is not likely to be believed. Hilary Putnam, for one, risks his entire philosophical capital on there being an insuperable and vicious paradox lurking in historicism. It's the engine of his internal realism. So, for instance, he honors Hegel's innovation in a double way. Hegel, he says, "taught us to see all our ideas, including above all our ideas of rationality, our images of knowledge, as historically conditioned. . . . On the other hand [he adds], Hegel postulated an *objective* notion of rationality which we (or Absolute Mind) were coming to possess with the fulfillment of the progressive social and intellectual reforms which were already taking place."[1] He draws his lesson at once: "Thinkers who accept the first Hegelian idea, that our conceptions of rationality are all historically conditioned, while rejecting the idea of an end (or even an ideal limit) to the process tend to become historical or cultural relativists." And relativism, he assures us—"total" relativism, as he dubs it—is "self-refuting," "incoherent," "self-contradictory."[2] He does not linger long enough to identify relativisms that are coherent *and* afford an account of truth pertinent to the enterprise of science.[3] But let that pass.

What Putnam fails to consider is this: (1) that historicism does not—has not been, cannot be, shown to—entail the self-refuting forms of certain relativisms; and (2) that, within the terms of historicism, the "objective" notion of rationality and knowledge cannot be counted on to escape its own constraints, either by (externally) importing a criterion or by (internally) positing a progressivist rule that could ever, or at some ideal limit, confirm that we were indeed discerning the actual properties of the independent world. Putnam fails—utterly—to explain the sense in which we are rationally obliged to admit *that* there is a determinate "end" or "ideal limit" to inquiry *and that* anyone could rightly judge that we were making progress toward it without yet reaching it. He fails to show that *his* second condition ("idea of an end") does not violate his first ("that all our conceptions of rationality are historically conditioned"), or that Hegel has shown either the necessity of the compatibility of the two or the necessity of accepting the second (having accepted the first) or the operative possibility of ensuring the success of the second under the condition of the first. *No one has shown that.* There's a lacuna, therefore, that Putnam misses: it's possible to accept his second condition as an open option, should anyone care to try to show us how to make it work, while at the same time we admit (however sadly) that it seems impossible to satisfy.

The source of Putnam's error is important. It's this: Putnam believes that "positivism and historicism are both attempts to reduce epistemic notions to non-epistemic ones: syntactic ones, in the case of positivism, anthropological ones (e.g., 'structuralist' ideas) in the case of historicism or relativism." He (rightly) takes this to be an impossible task—that is, the reduction. "No one," he says, "would maintain nowadays that epistemic predicates are semantically or conceptually reducible to non-epistemic predicates."[4] (He's wrong in this, of course. It's hardly the same point. One has only to remember Quine's remarkably influential effort to "naturalize" epistemology.)[5] But the fact is that neither historicism nor relativism is logically bound to favor the reduction Putnam baits us with; all that is needed is that we *historicize both knowledge and reason—not truth*. That is just the point of the contribution Putnam finds in Hegel. Its true lesson, therefore, is deeper that Putnam's: namely, we must recover every conceptual question that science and inquiry generate, but we must do so under the condition that thinking has a history.

You may take this as a prophecy or a prescription for the next century. There are already fledgling efforts to begin the task. Hegel has identified its difficulty—and the glory of succeeding. We have ourselves already marked the conceptual weakness of Hegel's would-be recovery; and we have noted that Marx fails to escape the "Hegelian" weakness, though his theory of praxis affords an excellent clue for eluding the trap.[6] The various progressivist and traditionalist doctrines we have canvassed also confirm the difficulty.

Over this entire effort there now looms the threat of incoherence. We can see that it is no more than a paper threat: no sense has ever been given that would make it ineluctable. It is certainly fair to say, as we have already remarked, that Ranke's (classical) historicism does indeed generate self-referential paradoxes. But historicism in the contemporary sense (the sense of Hegel's "first" contribution) does not require any strict disjunctive isolation of the *Geist* of different ages; on the contrary, it resists it, as it does in Gadamer. Ranke's objectivism, by contrast, requires something like a divine occasionalism at every point at which the historian penetrates the archival traces of another age. It could only be by a large confusion, therefore, that Ranke's sort of difficulty would be attributed to ventures like Peter Winch's, say—ventures that had hoped to analyze the anthropologist's cross-cultural understanding of an alien society from the conceptual resources of its own. Winch addressed the matter as a Wittgensteinian, not as a Hegelian or a post-Hegelian of Ranke's stripe, certainly not as a Protagorean. Still, he was wrongly charged with having failed to consider the self-referential puzzles of cultural relativity.[7]

II

Now, the important point is that there *are* puzzles of historical understanding, both of the cross-cultural and the diachronic sort within "a" culture. But such puzzles are not—need not be—the puzzles of self-referential paradox. They concern, rather, *the meaning of objectivity under historicist conditions*. That's all! Once you grasp that, you grasp as well the needless extravagance of Foucault's forever dancing away from the question of the nature of truth in the context of history. Foucault sensed a paradox he could never satisfactorily formulate or resolve. He risked realigning his work with the canonical tradition—but not quite. Perhaps it was more in the interest of the peculiar pathos of his work to have left the puzzle unresolved. It is in fact quite easily resolved. Also, as it happens, Foucault could easily have answered. All that would have been needed is already suggested by his genealogism.

Foucault puts the matter thus, among the papers of his best period:

> My problem is . . . this: what rules of right are implemented by the relations of power in the production of truth? Or alternatively, what type of power is susceptible of producing discourses of truth that in a society such as ours are endowed with such potent effects?[8]

The paradox he has in mind is clear enough: in some sense, truth is at once a product of the historical processes of a society *and* the genealogical discovery of how the historicized normalization of truth obtains in this or that society. Are these functions reconcilable?

It will help to have before us the well-known (but entirely misleading) criticism of Foucault's project that Habermas presents; for Habermas's mistake, while canny enough, obscures a genuine possibility Foucault seems not to have noticed (or Habermas, apparently). It also obscures Habermas's failure to perceive the inadequacy of his own intended improvement. In trying to succeed—and in failing—Habermas has touched the philosophical nerve of the late days of our century. Nearly everyone is concerned to try to reconcile the universal, transhistorical scope of reason and the historicism that governs its emergence. The project is impossible, but it has not been generally admitted.[9] It continues to be the endlessly iterated puzzle of our age. Somewhere it will subside. When it does, the new century will have come to terms with the new historicism.

In one of his lectures on Foucault, collected in *The Philosophical Discourse of Modernity*, Habermas has the following to say:

> Foucault's genealogy of the human sciences enters on the scene in an irritating double role. On the one hand, it plays the *empirical role* of an analysis of technologies of power that are meant to explain the functional social context of the science of man. Here power relationships are of interest as conditions for the rise of scientific knowledge and as its social effects. On the other hand, the same genealogy plays the *transcendental role* of an analysis of technologies of power that are meant to explain how scientific discourse about man is possible at all. Here the interest is in power relationships as constitutive conditions for scientific knowledge.[10]

But though it is true that Foucault construed his question as akin to the Kantian-like question, How is a science of man possible?, it is emphatically not true that he actually recommends or employs a "transcendental" method in accounting for genealogy—that is, a *Kantian* method. Certainly, Habermas should have granted the point, since he himself (with noticeably less success) has always been engaged in distancing his "pragmatist" or "legitimative" second-order concerns from any full-blown Kantian reading.[11] But more than that, Foucault explains, in a paper of the same period:

> I wanted to see how these problems of constitution *producing* "objects" could be resolved within a historical framework, instead of referring them back to a constituent object (madness, criminality, whatever), but this historical contextualization needed to be something more than the simple relativization of the phenomenological subject. I don't believe the problem can be solved by historicizing the subject as posited by the phenomenologists, fabricating a subject that evolves through the course of history. One has to dispense with the constituent subject, to get rid of the subject itself, that's to say, to arrive at an analysis which can account for the constitution of the subject within a historical framework. And this is what I would call analogy, that is, a form of history which can account for the constitution of knowledge, discourse, domains of objects etc., without having to make reference to a subject which is either transcendental in relation to the field of events or runs in empty sameness throughout the course of history.[12]

There is no way to reconcile Habermas's charge with Foucault's intention. The irony is, it's Habermas rather than Foucault who plays the transcendental card (as a progressivist, to be sure, much like Putnam in the Peircean spirit), but as a Kantian nevertheless (sometimes even a full-blooded Kantian, in the manner Karl-Otto Apel favors).[13]

In fact, Habermas pursues his critique of Foucault in a way nearly indistinguishable from Putnam's Peirceanized "transcendentalism": Foucault's "putative objectivity of knowledge is itself put in question [he says] (1) by the involuntary *presentism* of a historiography that remains hermeneutically stuck in its starting situation; (2) by the avoidable *relativism* of an analysis related to the present that can understand itself only as a context-dependent practical enterprise; (3) by the arbitrary *partisanship* of a criticism that cannot account for its normative foundations. Foucault [he kindly observes] is incorruptible enough to admit these incoherences—but he does not draw any consequences from them."[14]

Habermas nowhere shows that his charges against Foucault, (1)–(3), are not entirely benign. Those charges need to be made more accurate in any case: they do not seem to entail any "incoherences" at all. Furthermore, it is certainly not clear that Habermas himself can escape whatever charges he lays on Foucault.

The escape he obviously plans is the same one Putnam favors (in his criticism of Dummett's antirealism). The strategy betrays itself in his critique of Heidegger in the same lecture series. Heidegger, he says, "fails to see that the horizon of the understanding of meaning brought to bear on beings [*Seiende*] is not prior to, but rather subordinate to, the question of truth."[15] Here, the point at stake is not to reverse Habermas's critique of Heidegger but to draw attention to the fact that he is unwilling to admit the full import of *the historicizing of the question of truth* and the equally troublesome fact that he attempts to escape its contextedness by progressivist means alone—which, as we have seen, are inadequate to the task.[16] (We are speaking here, remember, of the assignment of truth-values, *not* of the meaning of "truth.") Either that, or Habermas must be an old-fashioned Kantian after all, in spite of his protestations. It is a question Habermas has never faced or resolved, the same one Gadamer so compellingly exposed in the well-known exchange between the two regarding the fortunes of hermeneutics (which we have also briefly considered).

It is a question that cannot be answered in any way favorable to decontextualizing truth, without reclaiming some form of cognitive privilege. Once again: we are *not* speaking of the meaning of "truth" but of the operative conditions on which the actual ascription of truth-values depends (the epistemic, not the alethic, issue). Such a maneuver could not but be incompatible with the doctrines of symbiosis and intransparency. Habermas himself acknowledges his Marxist and Frankfurt-Critical sources. (How could he not?) But he has never explained just *how* he distinguishes between his own account of history and the historicism that is about to engulf him.

Another consideration is this. On purely textual grounds, Habermas is wrong to characterize Foucault's *genealogy* as playing "the empirical role of an analysis of technologies of power." For, the point of Foucauldian genealogy is to expose the "origins" of such technologies under the condition that their posit is itself an artifact of some such technology. There is no fixed origin and no secure exit from history (in Foucault's view) in virtue of which Habermas's charge of "presentism" could gain a footing. So Habermas is wrong on both interpretive counts: Foucault does not claim a straightforward "empirical" objectivity for genealogy, and he does not claim any transcendental "explanation" of the human sciences. On the contrary, he is quite prepared to insist, in a "Nietzschean" spirit: "Genealogy does not oppose itself to history as the lofty and profound gaze of the philosopher might compare to the molelike perspective of the scholar; on the contrary, it rejects the metahistorical deployment of ideal significants and indefinite teleologies. It opposes itself to the search for 'origins.'"[17] Nothing could be plainer. The entire essay in which this appears opposes any pretense of "constants," "origins," "rules" of inquiry, "absolutes," "continuities," or the like.

It is in the "archaeological" writings that Foucault ventures to speak of conceptual necessity and the transcendental; but he hardly means to support the full Kantian thesis. On the contrary, he treats these themes as having emerged historically as a distinctive view of man: "Man, in the analytic of finitude [he says], is a strange empirico-transcendental doublet, since he is a being such that knowledge will be attained in him of what renders all knowledge possible." He adds, lest anyone misunderstand (Habermas, perhaps, by a touch of precognition): "The threshold of our modernity is situated not by the attempt to apply objective methods to the study of man [as intended by Condillac and Kant], but rather by the constitution of an empirico-transcendental doublet which was called *man*."[18] "Man," then, is the emergent entity of eighteenth-century discursive regimes:

> Before the end of the eighteenth century, *man* did not exist—any more than the potency of life, the fecundity of labor, of the historical density of language. He is a quite recent creature, which the demiurge of knowledge fabricated with its own hands less than two hundred years ago; but he has grown so

quickly that it has been only too easy to imagine that he had been waiting for thousands of years in the darkness for that moment of illumination in which he would finally be known.[19]

It is clear at once that any necessities of thought or language appear to be such *to* the cognitional "constitution" of that "empirico-transcendental doublet." One begins to appreciate, therefore, Habermas's blunder—that is, his remark about the "irritating double role" of *Foucault's* genealogy. It's not the genealogy that's at stake; it's the dual role of *"man"*—*in* the invented sense Foucault reports. In fact, when he turns to the human sciences, Foucault explicitly adds:

> Man's mode of being as constituted in modern thought enables him to play two roles: he is at the same time at the foundation of all positivities and present, in a way that cannot even be termed privileged, in the element of empirical things. This fact—it is not a matter here of man's essence in general, but simply of the historical *a priori*, which, since the nineteenth century, has served as an almost self-evident ground for our thought—this fact is no doubt decisive in the matter of the status to be accorded to the "human sciences," to the body of knowledge (though even that word is perhaps a little too strong: let us say, to be more neutral still, to the body of discourse) that takes as its object man as an empirical entity.[20]

Foucault is obviously not promoting transhistorical necessities regarding the objective conditions of the human sciences: he takes himself to be accounting only for the historical emergence of that notion. Within its space—but not beyond, as far as can be seen—the distinction between the necessary and the contingent, and between the essential and the accidental, are simply internal to the discursive regime in which they happen to emerge.

III

The misfiring of Habermas's reading of Foucault is the dark side of his own advocacy of a return to Kantianism via a Peircean-like maneuver. In fact, the tables may be profitably turned on Habermas. Foucault mentions Habermas as one committed to answering the question, What is Enlightenment?—that is, the question Kant answered in 1784, responding to an open invitation from the *Berlinische Monatschrift*. Foucault identifies the question as one "that modern philosophy has not been capable of answering, but that it has never managed to get rid of, either."[21] Given what we have already said, would it be too much to see in this a sly repudiation of Habermas's entire enterprise? Recall that the

Enlightenment is an "event" to be interpreted and used—one that, by their reception of Kant's philosophy and similar labors, nineteenth- and twentieth-century thinkers (Habermas, for one) have been too quick to explain in terms of some would-be essential or universal or necessary condition of human rationality. In *that* sense, the question cannot be answered and has not yet been resolved. The historically emergent "empirico-transcendental doublet" becomes, *in Habermas* (and others), a straightforward topic for "objective" inquiry. That is what Foucault warns us about.

In the way of evidence, we may notice that Foucault mentions Baudelaire's conception of modernity. This is the same material Habermas mentions at the beginning of his own lectures on modernity, which eventually lead to his charge of "presentism" against Foucault. (*That*, as it happens, is a part of Baudelaire's explicit thesis: "Modernity is the transient, the fleeting, the contingent; it is one-half of art; the other being the eternal and immovable.")[22] But Foucault's objective is *not* to support Baudelaire in "the will to 'heroize' the present,"[23] but to interpret *Kant's* answer to the question about Enlightenment so as to permit *him* (Kant) *to introduce an original way of treating the present philosophically.* In this, Foucault turns the tables on Habermas without so much as a frontal assault. We are not concerned with the mere confrontation between Foucault and Habermas, of course (which, as it happens, was planned to take place in the flesh, so to say, but which never occurred).[24] It's rather that the implied contest illuminates *Foucault's* notion of history. With that in hand, we can outflank the limitations of both Foucault and Habermas. Have patience.

Foucault reads Kant's essay as "a reflection by Kant on the contemporary status of his own enterprise. . . . It is in the reflection on 'today' as difference in history and as motive for a particular philosophical task that the novelty of this text appears to me to be." He thinks Kant is the first philosopher to have viewed his own work thus "from the inside."[25] So it is true enough that Foucault emphasizes a certain responsiveness to the present. But his purpose is to draw attention to the fact that *Kant* is engaged (in *his* essay) in a kind of "historical ontology" (of man and human reason). Kant, we are led to understand, "is not seeking to make possible a metaphysics that has finally become a science; [he] is seeking to give new impetus, as far and wide as possible, to the undefined work of freedom."[26]

If we accept the comment at face value, then Foucault is *not* attempting to reconcile *his* genealogies *with* the acknowledged prior canon of

Kant's transcendentalism. He is instead reinterpreting the normalized use *of* transcendental arguments in terms of *their* having been first introduced, *by Kant, at* a historical moment, *as* a historically focused offer of a new conception for the role of reasoning (*räsonieren*)—the term belongs to the *Critiques*—"in the use of which reason has no other end but itself: *räsonieren* [says Foucault] is to reason for reasoning's sake."[27]

In effect, Foucault's essay serves to deliver an early salvo in the larger campaign we were prophesying a moment earlier would take hold in the twenty-first century: that is, the campaign to reclaim the whole of science and philosophy in accord with *Hegel's* "lesson." Foucault is bent, then, on domesticating, well after the fact of the nineteenth- and twentieth-century reception of *Kant*, the *genealogical* import of *Kant's* innovation: the very *presumption* of a universal science of reason (or of man), is made, genealogically, to be the principal witness and instantiation of the "historical *a priori*." Extraordinary! To think that Habermas misses the entire tale!

Foucault could not be more explicit:

> Criticism is no longer going to be practiced in the search for formal structures with universal value, but rather as a historical investigation into the events that have led us to constitute ourselves and to recognize ourselves as subjects of what we are doing, thinking, saying. In that sense, this criticism is not transcendental, and its goal is not that of making a metaphysics possible: it is genealogical in its design and archaeological in its method.[28]

Foucault, however, has never satisfactorily addressed the paradox of truth on which his own work rests. It needs to be resolved if the "Hegelian" project is ever to be seriously advanced.

There you have the point of challenging Habermas's criticism of Heidegger—which is ultimately the same criticism Habermas levels at Foucault and the Frankfurt Critical theorists: namely, that "the horizon of the understanding of meaning . . . is not prior to, but rather subordinate to, the question of truth." We have already examined this failed contention among the leading Anglo-American analytic philosophers—notably, among Davidson, Dummett, and (just a moment ago) Putnam. It's not that "the horizon of the understanding of meaning" is "prior" or "subordinate" to truth; it's rather that *meaning and truth (and reference and identity as well) are conceptually inseparable—on a par with one another—and, taken together, are (now) being irresistibly historicized.* There's the lesson stretching from Hegel to Foucault.

IV

The resolution of the paradox follows easily enough. The terms of historicism never function criterially. They function only to define the "limit-attitude" (Foucault's coinage) of a new philosophical outlook. "I shall [Foucault says] characterize the philosophical ethos appropriate to the critical ontology of ourselves [what we are calling historicism] as a historico-practical test of the limits that we may go beyond, and thus as work carried out by ourselves upon ourselves as free beings."[29] Historicism, therefore, is concerned with the question of conceptual coherence *at* the moment at which we act to replace one executive vision of reason and reality with another. The remark falls trippingly from the tongue; but to identify historicism thus is to grasp at once that the *constraints of coherence* (the logical underpinnings, if you please, of what has been functioning as the esssential part of the transcendental a priori in post-Kantian thought) are now radically reinterpreted as the contingently generated constraints of what Foucault calls the "historical *a priori*." This is the point of Foucault's "genealogy" of changing *epistemes*—including, now, his own "archaeologies."

Foucault does not thereby dismiss the *de re* or *de dicto* necessities of this or that *episteme*: *they* are rightly recognized *there* as the necessities they function *as*. But they are also not enshrined as universal, changeless structures of any kind (regarding world or reason): we are always invited to "test" for "the limits that we may go beyond." That's to say: *the invariances of any proposed transcendental limits of reason may be tested by exploring whether we can alter such a model of coherence convincingly, in a way that rests on historical change.* Neither Kant nor Husserl fully grasped the possibility. They never quite acknowledged that thinking has a history. Yet, on Foucault's analysis, Kant's answer to the question about Enlightenment betrays his (Kant's) *genealogical* discovery of the power of his own *Critiques*. That's what Habermas misses—in Foucault, in himself, in Kant, and in Hegel. *That's* the point of his contest with Gadamer: and, of course, Gadamer was dead right.

The resolution of the paradox may now be seen to rest on two distinctions, both of which have already been invoked. One is this: the syntactic and semantic dimensions of discourse are inseparable from one another *and* from our beliefs and understanding of the world. That alone reverses Habermas's critique of Heidegger, though it hardly vindicates Heidegger. The point was (you may remember) the focus of our critique of Dummett's prioritizing the analysis of meaning over meta-

physical speculation. There is no hierarchy of the sort Habermas pro-
poses.[30] The other distinction is this: historicism never functions criterially, which means that coherence—the rules of reason and the laws of
the world—is itself historically constructed, an artifact of the dawning
possibilities our horizoned experience happens to disclose. Hence, the
two distinctions cannot be disjoined. They deepen the internalism Putnam espouses, but in such a way that they reveal "the limits that we
may go beyond," that (as we saw) Putnam is himself unable to traverse.
Putnam cannot, at one and the same time, embrace internalism (symbiosis and intransparency) and preclude historicism (the historicity of
thought—*or*, the historicity of the supposed "regulative" function of
truth); and he cannot, admitting historicism, appeal to a rule of coherence that he then exempts from the contingencies of history. Hence,
admitting these contingencies, he cannot reclaim progressivism. (Neither can Habermas.)

Historicized critique is not arbitrary, but it cannot exceed its own
consensual resources. For example, all the would-be invariances of canonical philosophy may be reclaimed (if they can be reclaimed at all) *as*
constant *within* an evolving history: they are then and there no more than
the forms of the "historical *a priori*." But the claim is no weaker than
what the empiricists have always insisted on (Quine, for instance), and
it is entirely sufficient for our general needs. On the strength of Foucault's
example, then, we may suppose that this is the common lesson intended
in Hegel and Marx and Nietzsche and Gadamer—and perhaps, dawningly, in Kant himself. It is also, very probably, the philosophical horizon
of the twenty-first century.

In a word: truth-claims are historicized but "truth" cannot be. The
one is epistemic; the other, alethic. Furthermore, the distinction is neutral
to bivalence and relativism. Also, the historical legitimation of future
epistemes repeats the same benign distinction between the meaning of
"truth" and the responsible ascription of truth-values.

Beyond this conceptual plateau, there beckons a more unruly landscape. Fixity is gone. Thinking is a history. And the structure of reality
is inseparable from the structure of our historicized understanding. But
if you bring these notions together, if our own existence is marked by the
saliencies of thinking, and if the human world is altered by interpretation, then there is no limit to the diverging histories to which we may
belong—except by dint of our consensual memory and consensual tolerance. The referents of our Intentional world no longer have fixed
boundaries, and the fixed boundaries we assign the things of the physical

world are now hostage to our history. Having ended one trek, therefore, we might consider undertaking another.

Viewed in these terms, the history of Western philosophy exhibits a splendid simplicity. Aristotle, Kant, and Hegel now mark the principal phases of our reflection. In each there is a form of pre-established harmony between human cognition and cognized reality; and in each there is an attempt to escape from the contingencies of the context of human inquiry. In Aristotle, intuitive reason (or *nous*) reliably grasps the changeless structure of reality; in Kant, the intelligible structure of reality is necessarily imposed on the experienced world by the invariant species-wide structures of our perception and understanding. And in Hegel, the *Weltgeist's* self-understanding evolves historically but is entirely actualized at every phase of its career. In this sense, Hegel utterly breaches the charmed arrangement by historicizing human thought: there cannot any longer be closure in human thought, and there cannot be any human certainty about the *Weltgeist's* "thought." Late twentieth-century philosophy may be said to be engaged in fathoming what intelligible order is still possible under the condition that Aristotle's and Kant's presumptions are now historicized, and Hegel's presumption is now no more than a heuristic fiction we ourselves project. That, I suggest, is what the doctrine of the flux now signifies as we approach the beginning of the new millennium.

Notes

PROLOGUE

1. For an instructive and entertaining overview of the themes of time, change, and history, see J. T. Fraser, *Of Time, Passion, and Knowledge: Reflections on the Strategy of Existence*, 2d ed. (Princeton: Princeton University Press, 1990). The book functions best as an index of topics to be examined in greater depth, but it conveys a good sense of the alien quality of Greek speculation.

2. For a sense of the varieties of histories in the ancient world and ancient conceptions of history, see Charles William Fornara, *The Nature of History in Ancient Greece and Rome* (Berkeley, Los Angeles, London: University of California Press, 1983), particularly chs. 1, 3.

3. Thucydides, *The Peloponnesian War*, trans. Benjamin Jowett, in *The Greek Historians*, ed. Francis R. B. Godolphin, vol. 1 (New York: Random House, 1942), bk. II, chs. 34–46.

4. Thucydides, *The Peloponnesian War*, bk. V, chs. 84–114.

5. Thucydides, *The Peloponnesian War*, bk. VI, chs. 8–23.

6. Thucydides, *The Peloponnesian War*, bk. VI, ch. 24.

7. Aristotle, *Poetics*, trans. Ingram Bywater, in *The Basic Works of Aristotle*, ed. Richard McKeon (New York: Random House, 1941), ch. 9, 145a–b.

8. In the recent American literature concerned with moral and practical life, the Aristotelian theme has taken two distinct forms—both suspect: in one, certain novelists (Henry James and Joseph Conrad, for instance) are thought to have constructed "Aristotelian" accounts of human nature; in the other, Aristotle's ethical theory is thought to apply in some principled way to the altered history of the contemporary world. It should be noted, by the way, that the first is an undertaking altogether different from that pursued by F. R. Leavis in *The Great Tradition* (New York: New York University Press, 1967); for Leavis was frankly

interested in supporting a certain high native English moral tradition embedded in the actual *Sitten* of nineteenth- and twentieth-century life, without regard to any explicit moral philosophy of Aristotle's sort (to which, nevertheless—that is, Leavis's "great tradition"—James and Conrad contributed in important ways). The best-known late "Aristotelians" in this double respect are Martha C. Nussbaum, in *Love's Knowledge: Essays on Philosophy and Literaure* (New York: Oxford University Press, 1990); and Alasdair MacIntyre, *After Virtue*, 2d ed. (Notre Dame: University of Notre Dame Press, 1984).

9. Georg Wilhelm Friedrich Hegel, *Lectures on the Philosophy of World History (Introduction: Reason in History)*, trans. H. B. Nisbet (Cambridge: Cambridge University Press, 1985), 12. This is a translation of Johannes Hofmeister's edition of the *Introduction*.

10. Karl Popper enjoys savaging Hegel and Marx about such options. See Karl R. Popper, *The Poverty of Historicism*, 3d ed. (New York: Harper and Row, 1961); and *The Open Society and Its Enemies* (Princeton: Princeton University Press, 1950).

11. This last issue is the essential puzzle that has begun to dawn in contemporary Anglo-American philosophies of science following the reception of Thomas S. Kuhn, *The Structure of Scientific Revolutions*, 2d ed. enl. (Chicago: University of Chicago Press, 1970).

12. See Plato, *Republic*, bks. VIII and IX; also, Aristotle, *Problemata*, bk. XVII, ch. 3, 916a.

13. Aristotle, *Rhetoric*, 1356b.

14. For a (necessarily) brief overview of the Sophists, who clearly provoked Plato to resist their account of the reality of the changeable world, see G. B. Kerferd, *The Sophistic Movement* (Cambridge: Cambridge University Press, 1981).

15. Thucydides, *The Peloponnesian War*, bk. II, ch. 41.

16. Aristotle, *Nicomachean Ethics*, trans. W. D. Ross, in *The Basic Works of Aristotle*, ed. Richard McKeon (New York: Random House, 1941), bk. I, ch. 1, 1094a. See, also, *On Generation and Corruption*, trans. Harold H. Joachim, in *The Basic Works of Aristotle*, bk. II, ch. 11.

CHAPTER 1

1. Giambattista Vico, *The New Science of Giambattista Vico*, trans. from 3d ed. (1744) Thomas Goddard Bergin and Max Fisch (Ithaca: Cornell University Press, 1948), §331; see §§236–238.

2. *The New Science of Giambattista Vico*, §342.

3. *The New Science of Giambattista Vico*, §342.

4. *The New Science of Giambattista Vico*, §348.

5. *The New Science of Giambattista Vico*, §349.

6. *The New Science of Giambattista Vico*, §360; cf. §§147, 148, 346.

7. *The New Science of Giambattista Vico*, §342.

8. Chomsky may seem an unlikely member of this cohort. Still, two considerations favor his inclusion. One concerns his oddly insistent claim that there is no viable option to accounting for the linguistic aptitude in humans but the

assured functioning of an invariant linguistic "competence"—which he never actually demonstrates. The other concerns his increasing aversion to the deep contingencies of actual linguistic "performance"—so that his skillful adjustments to the "underlying" grammar are (always) already compliant with the unchallenged assumption of its invariant fixity. See Noam Chomsky, *Knowledge of Language: Its Nature, Origin, and Use* (New York: Praeger, 1986); *Rules and Representations* (New York: Columbia University Press, 1980); and Joseph Margolis, *Texts without Referents: Reconciling Science and Narrative* (Oxford: Basil Blackwell, 1989), chs. 5, 9.

9. An excellent summary of this view may be found in John Stachel, "Comments on 'Some Logical Problems Suggested by Empirical Theories' by Professor Dalla Chiara," in *Language, Logic, and Method*, ed. Robert S. Cohen and Marx W. Wartofsky (Dordrecht: D. Reidel, 1983).

10. This accords neatly with Foucault's notion of the "historical *a priori*." See Michel Foucault, *The Order of Things: An Archaeology of the Human Sciences*, in translation (New York: Vintage, 1973), ch. 10.

11. Wilhelm von Humboldt, *Linguistic Variability and Intellectual Development*, trans. George C. Buck and Frithjof A. Raven (Philadelphia: University of Pennsylvania Press, 1972), xix; see, also, p. 1. For an overview of Humboldt's work, see Hans Aarsleff, "Wilhelm von Humboldt and the Thought of the French *Idéologues*," in *From Locke to Saussure: Essays on the Study of Language and Intellectual History* (Minneapolis: University of Minnesota Press, 1982).

12. Humboldt, *Linguistic Variability and Intellectual Development*, 193.

13. Humboldt, *Linguistic Variability and Intellectual Development*, 1.

14. See Anthony Giddens, *New Rules of Sociological Method: A Positive Critique of Interpretive Sociology* (New York: Basic Books, 1976), ch. 3; and Pierre Bourdieu, *Outline of a Theory of Practice*, trans. Richard Nice (Cambridge: Cambridge University Press, 1977).

15. Humboldt, *Linguistic Variability and Intellectual Development*, 4.

16. Humboldt, *Linguistic Variability and Intellectual Development*, 195.

17. Humboldt, *Linguistic Variability and Intellectual Development*, 194.

18. Humboldt, *Linguistic Variability and Intellectual Development*, 193.

19. Humboldt, *Linguistic Variability and Intellectual Development*, xx, 6.

20. Humboldt, *Linguistic Variability and Intellectual Development*, 1.

21. Humboldt, *Linguistic Variability and Intellectual Development*, 192.

22. Wilhelm von Humboldt, "On the Historican's Task," (included) in Leopold von Ranke, *The Theory and Practice of History*, ed. Georg G. Iggers and Konrad von Moltke (New York: Irvington, 1983).

23. See Benedetto Croce, *History—Its Theory and Practice*, trans. Douglas Ainslee (New York: Harcourt, Brace, 1921).

24. R. G. Collingwood, *The Idea of History* (Oxford: Oxford University Press, 1956): for instance, "the historian need and cannot (without ceasing to be an historian) emulate the scientist in searching for the causes or laws of events" (214). For a sense of how Collingwood has been recovered in our own time, see Rex Martin, *Historical Explanation: Re-enactment and Practical Inference* (Ithaca: Cornell University Press, 1977).

25. Collingwood, *The Idea of History*, 258–260, 265–266.

26. The ambiguity in Humboldt's account is rather nicely matched, in the recent literature, in the altogether different undertaking E. D. Hirsch favors. (Hirsch is a romantic hermeneut.) For Hirsch believes that probabilizing literary "genres" in accord with which authors utter their poems or other literary pieces can be rightly taken to "approximate" the real fixed genres that govern them, even though the genres *cannot* be discerned but only inferred. See E. D. Hirsch, Jr., *Validity in Interpretation* (New Haven: Yale University Press, 1967), 173–180. See, also, Joseph Margolis, "Genres, Laws, Canons, Principles," in *Rules and Conventions*, ed. Mette Hjort (Baltimore: Johns Hopkins University Press, 1992). Habermas's counterpart attempt to recover the universal constraints of reason appears in his effort to validate, under the explicit influence of Karl-Otto Apel, the moral constraints that bind human behavior. See Jürgen Habermas, "Discourse Ethics: Notes on a Program of Philosophical Justification," in *Moral Consciousness and Communicative Action*, trans. Christian Lenhardt and Shierry Weber Nicholsen (Cambridge: MIT Press, 1990).

27. Collingwood, *The Idea of History*, 304–305. These materials belong to part V of the printed text, to what Knox titles "Epilegomena."

28. Collingwood, *The Idea of History*, 306.

29. Collingwood, *The Idea of History*, 307–308.

30. See R. G. Collingwood, *The Principles of Art* (Oxford: Clarendon, 1938), ch. 7.

31. See Fernand Braudel, *On History*, trans. Sarah Matthews (Chicago: University of Chicago Press, 1980); also, Paul Veyne, *Writing History: Essays on Epistemology*, trans. Mina Moore-Rinuducri (Middletown: Wesleyan University Press, 1984).

32. See Thomas Nagel, "What Is It Like To Be a Bat?" *Philosophical Review* XXXII (1974). The paper has been very widely discussed. But Nagel muddies the question in thinking that it calls into doubt our understanding of inner experience.

33. See Ludwig Wittgenstein, *Tractatus Logico-Philosophicus*, trans. (2d ed. corr.) D. F. Pears and B. F. McGuinness (London: Routledge and Kegan Paul, 1972), 5.632, 5.633, 5.6331.

34. See W. V. Quine, *Word and Object* (Cambridge: MIT Press, 1960), chs. 1–2; Hans-Georg Gadamer, *Truth and Method*, trans. from 2d ed. Garrett Barden and John Cumming (New York: Seabury Press, 1975), Second Part, II; and Michel Foucault, "Nietzsche, Genealogy, History," in *Language, Counter-memory, Practice: Selected Essays and Interviews*, ed. Donald F. Bouchard, trans. Donald F. Bouchard and Sherry Simon (Ithaca: Cornell University Press, 1977).

35. Collingwood, *The Idea of History*, 310.

36. See the exchange between John Watkins and Alan Donagan, following John Watkins, "Imperfect Rationality," in *Explanation in the Behavioural Sciences*, ed. Robert Borger and Frank Cioffi (Cambridge: Cambridge University Press, 1970).

37. Collingwood, *The Idea of History*, 216, 217.

38. Collingwood escapes the *aporia* of Ranke's historicism, and he avoids the Kantianism of Dilthey's view of the *Geisteswissenschaften*; but how he does that is not at all clear. That Collingwood is not a Kantian (or a Husserlian, by sympathy at least) may be gathered from the brief remarks he offers regarding the nature of mind in his first book, *Religion and Philosophy* (Oxford: Clarendon, 1916), 100: "Just as the mind is not a self-identical thing persisting whether or not it performs its functions, but rather is those functions; so the consciousness in which it consists is not an abstract power of thought which may be turned on to this object or that, as the current from a dynamo may be put to various uses. All consciousness is the consciousness of something definite, the thought of a thing or that thing; there is no thought in general but only particular thoughts about particular things." I have benefited here from a reading of W. J. van der Dussen, *History as a Science: The Philosophy of R. G. Collingwood* (The Hague: Martinus Nijhoff, 1981); the passage is cited by van der Dussen. My colleague Michael Krausz drew my attention to van der Dussen's book; I had not known of it before. Collingwood's argument is expressly antidualistic, anti-Cartesian—contrary to the account offered by Patrick Gardiner, in "The 'Objects' of Historical Knowledge," *Philosophy* XXVII (1952). See, also, W. H. Walsh, *An Introduction to Philosophy of History* (London: Hutchinson, 1951), 49–50.

39. These remarks are cited by van der Dussen, *History as a Science*, 271–281, from Collingwood's unpublished menuscripts. The longer citation is from a manuscript titled "Notes Toward a Metaphysics," dated 1933–1934.

40. Van der Dussen has done a fine bit of detective work in assembling the pertinent materials; see van der Dussen, *History as a Science*, 273–274.

41. Cited by van der Dussen, *History as a Science* (276), from "Ruskin's Philosophy," reprinted in *Essays in the Philosophy of Art by R. G. Collingwood*, ed. Alan Donagan (Bloomington: Indiana University Press, 1964).

42. Collingwood, *The Idea of History*, 205.

43. Collingwood, *The Idea of History*, 210–211.

44. Collingwood, *The Idea of History*, 212.

45. Collingwood, *The Idea of History*, 214–215; see 213.

46. Collingwood, *The Idea of History*, 215–216.

47. Collingwood, *The Idea of History*, 283; see 252–266.

48. See Collingwood, *The Idea of History*, 293.

49. See Hans-Georg Gadamer, *Truth and Method*, trans. from 2d ed. Garrett Barden and John Cumming (New York: Seabury Press, 1975), 467–469.

50. Collingwood, *The Idea of History*, 218.

51. Collingwood, *The Idea of History*, 219.

52. Collingwood, *The Idea of History*, 220.

53. See Joseph Margolis, *The Truth about Relativism* (Oxford: Basil Blackwell, 1991).

54. See Collingwood, *The Idea of History*, 223–225.

55. Collingwood, *The Idea of History*, 226, 227.

56. See Alan Donagan, "The Verification of Historical Theses," *Philosophical Quarterly* VI (1956); and van der Dussen, *History as a Science*, ch. 7.

57. Collingwood, *The Idea of History*, 234; see 231–233.

58. Collingwood, *The Idea of History*, 225, 226.

59. Collingwood, *The Idea of History*, 247.

60. See Collingwood, *The Idea of History*, 223.

61. R. G. Collingwood, *An Essay on Metaphysics* (Oxford: Clarendon, 1940), 48n.

62. See Collingwood, *An Essay on Metaphysics*, ch. 49.

63. Compare R. G. Collingwood, *The Idea of Nature* (Oxford: Clarendon, 1960).

64. See Yirmiahu Yovel, *Kant and the Philosophy of History* (Princeton: Princeton University Press, 1980), particularly Epilogue. Something of a Kantian analogue of "absolute presuppositions"—which, as we shall see later, accords with Jürgen Habermas's progressivism—appears in a recent paper by Ernst Tugendhat, "Reflection on Philosophical Method from an Analytic Point of View," in Axel Honneth et al., *Philosophical Interventions in the Unfinished Project of Enlightenment*, trans. William Rehg (Cambridge: MIT Press, 1992). Tugendhat's suggestion concerns identifying "concepts [which] look like Kantian *a priori* concepts, and are indispensable *for us* [which] means [that] such necessity is relative to us, to this language community." But, here, Tugendhat automatically assumes that this prepares us for "a progressive derelativization" of what "at present appears to us as indispensable." That is, "by being confronted with the understanding of other language communities, we can learn [he says] new possibilities for understanding, which we can then incorporate into an expanded 'We'" (123). The account is too brief to press in a strenuous way. But it noticeably ignores the question of the historicity of coming to understand "other language communities." That is, Tugendhat does not explain what is meant by the terms "expanded."

65. Collingwood, *The Idea of History*, 241–242.

66. Collingwood, *The Idea of History*, 242, 246.

67. See Collingwood, *The Idea of History*, 248.

68. See Collingwood, *The Idea of History*, 239.

69. Collingwood, *The Idea of History*, 245–246.

70. Collingwood, *The Idea of History*, 222.

71. Collingwood, *The Idea of History*, 248.

72. Collingwood, *The Idea of History*, 265.

73. See Michel Foucault, *The Order of Things*, in translation (New York: Random House, 1973), 341–345.

74. Collingwood, *The Idea of History*, 288.

75. Collingwood, *The Idea of History*, 290.

76. Collingwood, *The Idea of History*, 287.

CHAPTER 2

1. Van der Dussen's account of Collingwood's unpublished manuscripts appears to bear this out. It may be the only plausible conjecture about what Collingwood could have meant, though it is not itself plausibly developed. See W. J. van der Dussen, *History as a Science: The Philosophy of R. G. Collingwood* (The Hague: Martinus Nijhoff, 1981), ch. 4.

2. See Yirmiahu Yovel, *Kant and the Philosophy of History* (Princeton: Princeton University Press, 1980).

3. R. G. Collingwood, *The Idea of History* (Oxford: Oxford University Press, 1956), 239.

4. Collingwood, *The Idea of History*, 224–225.

5. See Thomas S. Kuhn, *The Structure of Scientific Revolutions*, 2d ed. enl. (Chicago: University of Chicago Press, 1970).

6. See Bas C. van Fraassen, *Laws and Symmetry* (Oxford: Clarendon, 1989).

7. The most undisguised example appears in Adolf Grünbaum, *The Foundations of Psychoanalysis: A Philosophical Critique* (Berkeley, Los Angeles, London: University of California Press, 1984).

8. Carl G. Hempel, "The Function of General Laws in History," in *Aspects of Scientific Explanation and Other Essays in the Philosophy of Science* (New York: Free Press, 1965), 231.

9. See Maurice Mandelbaum, *The Problem of Historical Knowledge* (New York: Liveright, 1938), chs. 7–8; also, "Historical Explanation: The Problem of 'Covering Laws'," *History and Theory* I (1961).

10. Hempel, "The Function of General Laws in History," 233, n. 1; italics added.

11. Hempel, "The Function of General Laws in History," 238.

12. For some specimen views, see van Fraassen, *Laws and Symmetry*; and Carol G. Gould, *Marx's Social Ontology* (Cambridge: MIT Press, 1978).

13. Davidson's argument is really better known than Hempel's because it explicitly applies Hempel's argument to the analysis of "reasons" and "explanations by reasons." But it clearly confuses the analysis of alternative conceptions of cause and alternative conceptions of causal explanation. See, in particular, Donald Davidson, "Actions, Reasons, and Causes" and "Mental Acts," in *Essays on Actions and Events* (Oxford: Claredon, 1980).

14. Hempel, "The Function of General Laws in History," 231–233. I have italicized the terms "every," "kind," "will," and "always"—except for the last use of "kind."

15. See Wesley C. Salmon, *Scientific Explanation and the Causal Structure of the World* (Princeton: Princeton University Press, 1984).

16. See, for instance, Nancy Cartwright, *How the Laws of Physics Lie* (Oxford: Clarendon, 1983), essay 6. This is not to endorse Cartwright's wholesale objection to theoretical laws.

17. Hempel, "The Function of General Laws in History," 233.

18. See Stephen Stich, *From Folk Psychology to Cognitive Science: The Case against Belief* (Cambridge: MIT Press, 1983); and Paul M. Churchland, *A Neurocomputational Perspective: The Nature of Mind and Structure of Science* (Cambridge: MIT Press, 1989).

19. See Davidson, "Mental Events."

20. Carl G. Hempel, "Studies in the Logic of Explanation," in *Aspects of Scientific Explanation*, 263; italics added.

21. Hempel, "Studies in the Logic of Explanation," 263.

22. For a brief overview of the objections to physicalism, see Joseph Margolis, *Texts without Referents: Reconciling Science and Narrative* (Oxford: Basil Blackwell, 1989), ch. 6; see, also, *Science without Unity: Reconciling the Human and the Natural Sciences* (Oxford: Basil Blackwell, 1987), ch. 10.

23. Hempel, "The Function of General Laws in History," 233.

24. Hempel, "The Function of General Laws in History," 236.

25. See Carl G. Hempel, "Aspects of Scientific Explanation," *Aspects of Scientific Explanation*.

26. Hempel, "The Function of General Laws in History," 243.

27. Hempel, "The Function of General Laws in History," 231.

28. See Stich, *From Folk Psychology to Cognitive Science*; and P. K. Feyerabend, "Materialism and the Mind-Body Problem," *Review of Metaphysics* XVII (1963).

29. Hempel, "The Function of General Laws in History," 239–241.

30. See Imre Lakatos, *Philosophical Papers*, vol. 1, ed. John Worrall and Gregory Currie (Cambridge: Cambridge University Press, 1978), *passim*.

31. Hempel, "The Function of General Laws in History," 243.

32. See Hilary Putnam, *Meaning and the Moral Sciences* (London: Routledge and Kegan Paul, 1978).

33. See Jürgen Habermas, *Knowledge and Human Interests*, trans. Jeremy J. Shapiro (Boston: Beacon Press, 1971).

34. I define relativism in just these terms. There is, however, no point in pressing the issue here, since Putnam does not favor it. But see, further, Joseph Margolis, *The Truth about Relativism* (Oxford: Basil Blackwell, 1991).

35. Hilary Putnam, "A Defense of Internal Realism," in *Realism with a Human Face*, ed. James Conalt (Cambridge: Harvard University Press, 1990), 41.

36. Putnam, "A Defense of Internal Realism," 41.

37. Hilary Putnam, "Realism and Reason," in *Meaning and the Moral Sciences*, 125.

38. Hilary Putnam, "William James's Ideas" (authored with Anna Putnam), in *Realism with a Human Face*, 225; italics added.

39. See Hilary Putnam, *The Many Faces of Realism* (La Salle: Open Court, 1987), 53, 83.

40. It may be helpful to suggest that one source of the tension about truth which may be found in Putnam (*a fortiori*, in Habermas) may be traced to the Frankfurt School's oscillation between an ahistorical and a historicized conception of reason. See, for instance, Richard Wolin, *The Terms of Cultural Criticism: The Frankfurt School, Existentialism, Poststructuralism* (New York: Columbia University Press, 1992), part I. In the American pragmatist tradition, it may (perhaps) be traced to the influence of Emerson. See Cornel West, *The American Evasion of Philosophy: The Genealogy of Pragmatism* (Madison: University of Wisconsin Press, 1989).

41. See, for instance, Putnam's discussion of his differences with Dummett in *Meaning and the Moral Sciences*.

42. Putnam, "The John Locke Lectures (1976)," in *Meaning and the Moral Sciences*, lecture 2: 20.

43. Putnam, "The John Locke Lectures," 21; italics added.
44. Putnam, "A Defense of Internal Realism," 40.
45. Putnam, "A Defense of Internal Realism," 41.
46. Putnam, *The Many Faces of Realism*, 26–27.
47. Putnam, *The Many Faces of Realism*, 28.
48. See Margolis, *The Truth about Relativism*. Putnam has never seriously considered the possibility of a coherent relativism. In his latest book (which I have only seen in manuscript), *Renewing Philosophy* (The Gifford Lectures, 1990), he returns (ch. 4) to trash once again the relativist who embraces self-referential paradoxes. In fact, he takes as his specimen Richard Rorty, who, in *Philosophy and the Mirror of Nature* (Princeton: Princeton University Press, 1979), construed truth as agreement with one's peers; but Rorty also "recanted," in *Consequences of Pragmatism* (Minneapolis: University of Minnesota Press, 1982), xxv—which Putnam reports. It is difficult to understand why Putnam merely repeats the same objection in each new discussion of relativism. For one thing, it is a gloss on Plato's ancient argument (in *Theaetetus*), which itself may be fairly read as misinterpreting Protagoras; and, for another, it hardly exhausts the resources of relativism.

CHAPTER 3

1. A compendium of the relevant texts in Peirce is provided in Philip P. Wiener (ed.), "Pragmaticism: A Philosophy of Science," *Values in a Universe of Chance: Selected Writings of Charles S. Peirce (1839–1914)* (Garden City: Doubleday, 1956).
2. See Martin Heidegger, *Being and Time*, trans. from 7th ed. John Macquarrie and Edward Robinson (New York: Harper and Row, 1962), 480–488 (428–437 in the German pagination).
3. See Søren Kierkegaard, *Repetition: A Venture in Experimenting Psychology* (bound with *Fear and Trembling*), ed. and trans. Howard V. Hong and Edna H. Hong (Princeton: Princeton University Press, 1983), for a very amusing and decidely oblique critique of Hegel. But see, also, *Concluding Unscientific Postscript*, trans. David F. Swenson and Walter Lourie (Princeton: Princeton University Press, 1944), 270–271.
4. Gillian Rose, *Hegel Contra Sociology* (London: Athlone Press, 1981), 92. See the rest of ch. 3.
5. Rose, *Hegel Contra Sociology*, 1–2, 33–36. See Andrew Arato, "The Neo-Idealist Defense of Subjectivity," *Telos* XXI (1974); cited by Rose.
6. I have had the benefit here of an unpublished paper by Tom Rockmore, "Hegel's Absolute Idealism as Relativism." (Rockmore's argument is congenial to the larger thesis being developed.) I only urge that care must be taken to distinguish the alethic definition of truth from the epistemic conditions of knowledge. The confusion of the two yields what has earlier been designated as the "relational" account of truth. It is, of course, the one that Putnam inveighs against. On Hegel's own statement, see *Hegel's Phenomenology of Spirit*, trans. A. V. Miller (Oxford: Oxford University Press, 1977), §§788–808 ("Absolute Knowing").

7. The decisive passages in Peirce may be found in Charles Sanders Peirce, *Collected Papers of Charles Sanders Peirce*, ed. Charles Hartshorne and Paul Weiss (Cambridge: Harvard University Press, 1960), 5.448, 5.505.

8. See Joseph Margolis, *The New Puzzle of Interpretation*, forthcoming, ch. 3.

9. Peirce, *Collected Papers*, 7.321. (Vols. 7 and 8 were added to the expanded edition of the *Collected Papers*, with the additional editorial responsibility of Arthur W. Burks, in 1966.)

10. Peirce, *Collected Papers*, 5.311.

11. Peirce, *Collected Papers*, 3.11, 8.315.

12. Georg Wilhelm Friedrich Hegel, *Lectures on the Philosophy of World History (Introduction: Reason in History)*, trans. H. B. Nisbet (Cambridge: Cambridge University Press, 1975), 26. It is worth citing, also, Hegel's intended recovery of philosophical history, which certainly obliges us to concede that he could not have been merely an ironist:

> But the sole thought which philosophy brings with it is the simple idea of reason—the idea that reason governs the world, and that world history is therefore a rational process. From the point of view of history as such, this conviction and insight is a presupposition; for it is proved in philosophy by speculative cognition that reason—and we can adopt this expression for the moment without a detailed discussion of its relationship to God—is substance and *infinite power*; it is itself the substance of all natural and spiritual life, and the infinite form which activates this material content. . . . On the one hand, it is its own sole precondition, and its end is the absolute and ultimate end of everything; and on the other, it is itself the agent which implements and realizes this end, translating it from potentiality into actuality both in the material universe and in the spiritual world—that is, in world history. That this Idea is true, eternal, and omnipotent, that it reveals itself in the world, and that nothing is revealed except the Idea in all its honor and majesty—this, as I have said, is what philosophy has proved, and we can therefore posit it as demonstrated for any present purpose. (27–28)

13. For opinions on this issue, see Tom Rockmore, *Hegel's Circular Epistemology* (Bloomington: Indiana University Press, 1986), ch. 5; Charles Taylor, *Hegel* (Cambridge: Cambridge University Press, 1975), ch. 15; and J. N. Findlay, *Hegel: A Re-examination* (London: George Allen and Unwin, 1958), ch. 8.

14. Findlay, *Hegel: A Re-examination*, 250–251. (The pagination is to the Oxford University Press Galaxy edition, New York, 1976). The references to Hegel are to *Hegel's Science of Logic*, trans. A. V. Miller (Atlantic Highlands: Humanities Press International, 1989), vol. 2, sec. 2, ch. 3.

15. W. V. Quine, *Word and Object* (Cambridge: MIT Press, 1960), 23. See, also, Richard Rorty, "Pragmatism, Davidson and Truth," in *Truth and Interpretation: Perspectives on the Philosophy of Donald Davidson*, ed. Ernest LePore (Oxford: Basil Blackwell, 1986).

16. Quine, *Word and Object*, 23.

17. Hilary Putnam, "The John Locke Lectures," in *Meaning and the Moral Sciences* (London: Routlodge and Kegan Paul, 1978), lecture 1.

18. See Quine, *Word and Object*, 12–13, 27. It is true, nevertheless, that Quine waffles (as he must) on the treatment of "stimulus conditions": sometimes

they are themselves within the scope of the holism, sometimes not. But that is a matter of little importance to our present issue.

19. See Joseph Margolis, "The Passing of Peirce's Realism," in *Transactions of the Charles S. Peirce Society*, forthcoming.

20. See Hilary Putnam, *The Many Faces of Realism* (La Salle: Open Court, 1987), lecture 2.

21. See Joseph Margolis, "*Praxis* and Morality: Marx's Species Being and Aristotle's Political Animal," in *Marx and Aristotle: Nineteenth-Century Social Theory and Classical Antiquity*, ed. George McCarthy (Totowa, N.J.: Rowman and Littlefield, 1992).

22. See, for instance, Karl R. Popper, "Of Clouds and Clocks," in *Objective Knowledge: An Evolutionary Approach* (Oxford: Clarendon, 1972).

23. See Peirce, *Collected Papers*, 5.436. Peirce is a perceptive critic of Hegel as well.

24. Imre Lakatos, "Popper on Demarcation and Induction," in *Philosophical Papers*, vol. 1 (Cambridge: Cambridge University Press), 161.

25. Lakatos, "Popper on Demarcation and Induction," 155. See Karl R. Popper, *The Logic of Discovery*, 2d ed. rev. (New York: Harper and Row, 1965).

26. Karl R. Popper, "Two Dogmas of Common Sense: An Argument for Commonsense Realism and Against the Commonsense Theory of Knowledge," in *Objective Knowledge*, 32.

27. Karl R. Popper, "The Aims of Science," in *Objective Knowledge*, 196.

28. Popper, "The Aims of Science," 196; italics added.

29. Karl R. Popper, *Realism and the Aim of Science*, from *Postscript to the Logic of Scientific Discovery*, ed. W. W. Bartley, III (Totowa, N.J.: Rowman and Littlefield, 1938), xxxv, 57–58.

30. Karl R. Popper, *The Poverty of Historicism*, 3d ed. (New York: Harper and Row, 1964), v.

31. Popper, *The Poverty of Historicism*, vii.

32. Popper, *Realism and the Aim of Science*, 58. The issue is clearly central already to *The Logic of Scientific Discovery*; see, for instance, Preface (1958) and §82.

33. Popper, *The Poverty of Historicism*, viii. See, also, Popper, "Of Clouds and Clocks"; and Karl R. Popper, *The Open Universe: An Argument for Indeterminism*, from *Postscript to the Logic of Scientific Discovery*, ed. W. W. Bartley, III (Totowa, N.J.: Rowman and Littlefield, 1982).

34. Popper, *The Poverty of Historicism*, vi–vii.

35. Popper, *The Poverty of Historicism*, vi; italics added.

36. Popper, "Two Faces of Common Sense," 84; cf. 65–68.

37. Popper, *The Poverty of Historicism*, 41.

38. Popper, *The Poverty of Historicism*, 28.

39. Two specimen views may be offered in evidence from the most recent work in the philosophy of physics. Nancy Cartwright explicitly holds that the exceptionless laws of theoretical physics distort and falsify the phenomenological laws of the same domain, in order to conform with the covering-law model of explanation; see Nancy Cartwright, *How the Laws of Physics Lie* (Oxford:

Clarendon, 1983). Bas van Fraassen explicitly holds that there simply are no nomologically invariant laws of nature; they may be denied, he holds, without any loss of rigor in the advanced sciences. See Bas C. van Fraassen, *Laws and Symmetry* (Oxford: Clarendon, 1989). In different ways, both accounts are concerned to determine just what sort of realism the physical sciences can justifiably be said to require and support.

40. See Ernst Mayr, *The Growth of Biological Thought: Diversity, Evolution, and Inheritence* (Cambridge: Harvard University Press, 1982), ch. 2; and J. J. C. Smart, *Philosophy and Scientific Realism* (London: Routledge and Kegan Paul, 1963), ch. 3.

41. Popper, *The Poverty of Historicism*, 36.

42. Popper, "Two Faces of Common Sense," 103. See, also, Karl R. Popper, *Conjectures and Refutations; The Growth of Scientific Knowledge* (New York: Harper and Row, 1968), 234f.

43. Thomas S. Kuhn, "The Relations between the History and the Philosophy of Science," in *The Essential Tension: Selected Studies in Scientific Tradition and Change* (Chicago: University of Chicago Press, 1977), 15–16.

44. Kuhn, "The Relations between the History and the Philosophy of Science," 15–16.

45. Kuhn, "The Relations between the History and the Philosophy of Science," 16.

46. It is ironic (though it also betrays Kuhn's equivocal tendencies) that *The Structure of Scientific Revolutions* was first published in the *International Encyclopedia of Unified Science*. Actually, the expansion of the intended *Encyclopedia* came to be titled *Foundations of the Unity of Science* and subtitled *International Encyclopedia of Unified Science*.

47. Kuhn, "The Relations between the History and the Philosophy of Science," 17–18.

48. Kuhn, *The Essential Tension*, xiii; also, xv.

49. Kuhn, "The Relations between the History and the Philosophy of Science," 19.

50. See Popper, *Conjectures and Refutations*, ch. 10, particularly 216.

51. Kuhn, "Logic of Discovery or Psychology of Research," *The Essential Tension*, 280.

52. Popper, *Conjectures and Refutations*, 216.

53. Thomas S. Kuhn, *The Structure of Scientific Revolutions*, 2d ed. enl. (Chicago: University of Chicago Press, 1970), postscript—1964.

54. For an impression of rather different views on this matter, see Cartwright, *How the Laws of Physics Lie*; and Wilfrid Sellars, "The Language of Theories," in *Science, Perception and Reality* (London: Routledge and Kegan Paul, 1963).

55. Kuhn, "The Relations between the History and the Philosophy of Science," 19–20.

56. Kuhn, "The Relations between the History and the Philosophy of Science," 20.

57. Kuhn, "The Relations between the History and the Philosophy of Science," 18, 20.

58. Kuhn, *The Structure of Scientific Revolutions*, 2.

59. Kuhn, *The Structure of Scientific Revolutions*, 2–3.
60. Kuhn, *The Structure of Scientific Revolutions*, 3.
61. Kuhn, *The Structure of Scientific Revolutions*, 169; italics added.
62. Kuhn, *The Structure of Scientific Revolutions*, 166, 170; italics added. See, also, Larry Lauden, *Progress and its Problems: Towards a Theory of Scientific Growth* (Berkeley, Los Angeles, London: University of California Press, 1977).
63. Kuhn, *The Structure of Scientific Revolutions*, 200; see also 193.
64. See Kuhn, *The Structure of Scientific Revolutions*, 189.
65. Kuhn, *The Structure of Scientific Revolutions*, 201; see 187.
66. Kuhn, *The Structure of Scientific Revolutions*, 201.
67. Kuhn, *The Structure of Scientific Revolutions*, 206.

CHAPTER 4

1. See E. H. Gombrich, "Experiment and Experience in the Arts," in *The Image and the Eye: Further Studies in the Art of Pictorial Representation* (Oxford: Phaidon, 1982), 215.
2. Hans Reichenbach, *Laws, Modalities, and Counterfactuals* (previously published as *Nomological Statements and Admissible Operations*, 1954), now with a Foreword by Wesley C. Salmon (Berkeley, Los Angeles, London: University of California Press, 1976), 1.
3. Reichenbach, *Laws, Modalities, and Counterfactuals*, 126. See Hans Reichenbach, *The Direction of Time*, ed. Maria Reichenbach (Berkeley: University of California Press, 1956).
4. Wesley C. Salmon, *Scientific Explanation and the Causal Structure of the World* (Princeton: Princeton University Press, 1984), 17; see 276–279.
5. See Bas C. van Fraassen, *Laws and Symmetry* (Oxford: Clarendon, 1989), parts I–II.
6. For a brief discussion, see Joseph Margolis, "Métaphysique radicale," *Archives de Philosophie* LIV (1991).
7. See Maria Reichenbach, "Introduction to the English Edition," in Hans Reichenbach, *The Theory of Relativity and A Priori Knowledge*, trans. Maria Reichenbach (Berkeley, Los Angeles: University of California Press, 1965).
8. Salmon, *Scientific Explanation and the Causal Structure of the World*, 18; see 135–139.
9. Salmon, *Scientific Explanation and the Causal Structure of the World*, 137–139, 277–278. See, also, Wolfgang Stegmüller, "Toward a Rational Reconstruction of Kant's Metaphysics of Experience," in *Collected Papers on Epistemology, Philosophy of Science and History of Philosophy*, vol. 1, trans. in part by B. Martini, partly rev. by W. Wohlheuter (Dordrecht: D. Reidel, 1977), particularly 129–131; and "The Problem of Induction: Hume's Challenge and the Contemporary Answer," vol. 2, particularly 68–69.
10. See Rudolf Carnap, "Intellectual Autobiography," in *The Philosophy of Rudolf Carnap*, ed. Paul Arthur Schilpp (La Salle: Open Court, 1963), 71–77; also "Replies and Systematic Expositions," in *Philosophy of Rudolf Carnap*, 966–988.

11. Edmund Husserl, *The Crisis of European Sciences and Transcendental Phenomenology: An Introduction to Phenomenological Philosophy*, trans. David Carr (Evanston: Northwestern University Press, 1970), 5.

12. Gail Soffer, *Husserl and the Question of Relativism* (Dordrecht: Kluwer, 1991), 147, 148; compare the whole of ch. 5. In the same spirit, Soffer shows that the question of relativism occupied Husserl through the whole of his work. The difficulty is that Husserl never satisfactorily justified the bifurcation of the "natural" and "phenomenological" *methods* in the context in which the *existence* of the inquiring subject remains (must remain) one and the same (although there are temptations on Husserl's part to avoid the full import of the admission).

13. See Edmund Husserl, *The Phenomeneology of Internal Time-Consciousness*, trans. J. S. Churchill (Bloomington: Indiana University Press, 1950).

14. See Edmund Husserl, *The Crisis of European Sciences and Transcendental Phenomenology*, part II, particularly §14.

15. Maurice Merleau-Ponty, *Phenomenology of Perception*, trans. Colin Smith (London: Routledge and Kegan Paul, 1962), 170.

16. For a hint of such a conception, see Robert Sokolowski, *Husserlian Meditations: How Words Project Things* (Evanston: Northwestern University Press, 1974), ch. 3.

17. See Maurice Merleau-Ponty, *The Visible and the Invisible*, ed. Claude Lefort, trans. Alphonso Lingis (Evanston: Northwestern University Press, 1968).

18. Husserl, *The Crisis of European Sciences and Transcendental Phenomenology*, 17–18.

19. Husserl, *The Crisis of European Sciences and Transcendental Phenomenology*, 18.

20. See Michel Foucault, *The Order of Things: An Archaeology of the Human Sciences*, in translation (New York: Random House, 1970), ch. 10.

21. See, for instance, Michel Foucault, *Discipline and Punishment: The Birth of the Prison*, trans. Alan Sheridan (New York: Pantheon, 1978).

22. Jürgen Habermas, "A Review of Gadamer's *Truth and Method*," in *Understanding and Social Inquiry*, ed. Fred R. Dallmayr and Thomas A. McCarthy (Notre Dame: Notre Dame University Press, 1977); incorporated in Jürgen Habermas, *On the Logic of the Social Sciences*, trans. Shierry Weber Nicholsen and Jerry A. Stark (Cambridge: MIT Press, 1988). (Further references are to the *Logic of the Social Sciences* volume.)

23. See Habermas, *On the Logic of the Social Sciences*, 118–119.

24. Habermas, *On the Logic of the Social Sciences*, 171–172. See Hans-Georg Gadamer, *Truth and Method*, trans. from 2d ed. Garrett Barden and John Cumming (New York: Seabury Press, 1975), 420 (cited by Habermas).

25. Habermas, *On the Logic of the Social Sciences*, 153–154.

26. Habermas, *On the Logic of the Social Sciences*, 172.

27. See Gadamer, *Truth and Method*, 153–214.

28. Hans-Georg Gadamer, "The Universality of the Hermeneutical Problem," in *Philosophical Hermeneutics*, trans. and ed. David E. Linge (Berkeley, Los Angeles, London: University of California Press, 1976), 3.

29. Gadamer, "The Universality of the Hermeneutic Problem," 7–8.

30. Gadamer, "The Universality of the Hermeneutic Problem," 9.

31. Gadamer, "The Universality of the Hermeneutic Problem," 8.

32. Habermas, *On the Logic of the Social Sciences*, 173.

33. Habermas, *On the Logic of the Social Sciences*, 174.

34. Gadamer, *Truth and Method*, 115, 264.

35. Hans-Georg Gadamer, "On the Scope and Function of Hermeneutical Reflection," in *Philosophical Hermeneutics*, ed. David E. Linge, 26, 28, 30.

36. Perhaps the most perspicuous discussion by Habermas appears in Jürgen Habermas, "Discourse Ethics: Notes on a Program of Philosophical Justification," in *Moral Consciousness and Communicative Action*, trans. Christian Lenhardt and Shierry Weber Nicholsen (Cambridge: MIT Press, 1990), particularly 76–94. See, also, Karl-Otto Apel, "The A Priori of the Communication Community and the Foundations of Ethics," in *Towards a Transformation of Philosophy*, trans. Glyn Adey and David Frisby (London: Routledge and Kegan Paul, 1980).

37. Gadamer, *Truth and Method*, 254.

38. Gadamer, *Truth and Method*, 254, 256, 257.

39. Gadamer, *Truth and Method*, 247–253.

40. It is possible that Gadamer believes that *any* normative vision is "classical" if it is only species-wide, inclusive of mankind, in a historically pertinent sense. This would bring Gadamer close to Marx's line of argument (though not to Marx's values). See, for instance, Karl Marx, "On the Jewish Question," in *Karl Marx: Early Writings*, trans. and ed. Tom Bottomore (New York: McGraw-Hill, 1964). Gadamer never pursues such a strategy. It would be too teleological for him. It might also permit (or require) norms that, in his own opinion, were incompatible with the humane values of Greece. There is no obvious resolution to Gadamer's difficulty. (Many, in fact, would deny that there is a difficulty.)

41. Edmund Husserl, *The Crisis of European Sciences and Transcendental Phenomenology*, trans. David Carr (Evanston: Northwestern University Press, 1970), 143.

42. See Joseph Margolis, "Les trois sortes d'universalité dans hermeneutique de H. G. Gadamer," *Archives de Philosophie* LIII (1990).

43. See Alasdair MacIntyre, *Beyond Virtue: A Study in Moral Theory*, 2d ed. (Notre Dame: University of Notre Dame Press, 1984) and *Three Rival Models of Moral Enquiry* (Notre Dame: University of Notre Dame Press, 1990).

CHAPTER 5

1. See W. V. Quine, *Word and Object* (Cambridge: MIT Press, 1960), §§15–16.

2. Quine, *Word and Object*, 73.

3. Quine, *Word and Object*, 220–221.

4. Michel Foucault, *The Order of Things*, in translation (New York: Vintage, 1973), 344.

5. Foucault, *The Order of Things*, 371.

6. See Joseph Margolis, *The Truth about Relativism* (Oxford: Basil Blackwell, 1991).

7. Quine, *Word and Object*, 195–200. See, also, C. I. Lewis, *A Survey of Symbolic Logic* (Berkeley: University of California Press, 1918); and W. V. Quine, "Two Dogmas of Empiricism," in *From a Logical Point of View* (Cambridge: Harvard University Press, 1953).

8. Aristotle, *Metaphysics*, trans. W. D. Ross, in *The Basic Works of Aristotle*, ed. Richard McKeon (New York: Random House, 1941), bk. III, ch. 4, 999b.

9. Aristotle, *Metaphysics*, bk. IV, ch. 4, 1007b; italics added.

10. Aristotle, *Metaphysics*, bk. IV, ch. 4, 1011a.

11. Aristotle, *Metaphysics*, bk. IV, ch. 4, 1007a–b.

12. See Joseph Margolis, "Métaphysique radicale," *Archives de Philosophie* XIV (1991).

13. Aristotle, *Metaphysics*, bk. IV, ch. 3, 1005b.

14. See Margolis, *The Truth about Relativism*.

15. From a letter of 1846 to P. V. Annenkov, translated (and excerpted) in *Karl Marx: Selected Writings*, ed. David McLellan (Oxford: Oxford University Press, 1977), 193–194. The letter appears also (but is also cut) in *Karl Marx and Friedrich Engels: Selected Works in Two Volumes*, vol. 2 (Moscow: Foreign Languages Publishing House, 1951), 400–410.

16. See, further, Joseph Margolis, "*Praxis* and Morality: Marx's Species Being and Aristotle's Political Animal," in *Marx and Aristotle: Nineteenth-century Social Theory and Classical Antiquity*, ed. George McCarthy (Totowa, N.J.: Rowman and Littlefield, 1992).

17. The most important and sustained account of history in general sympathy with the unity vision (though it is not intended in a reductionist spirit) is offered in Arthur C. Danto, *Narration and Knowledge* (New York: Columbia University Press, 1985).

18. Robert C. Stalnaker, *Inquiry* (Cambridge: MIT Press, 1984), 2.

19. Hilary Putnam, "The Logic of Quantum Mechanics," in *Philosophical Papers*, vol. 1 (Cambridge: Cambridge University Press, 1975), 174.

20. Putnam, "The Logic of Quantum Mechanics," 188.

21. Further, on the distinction between first- and second-order questions, see Joseph Margolis, *Pragmatism without Foundations: Reconciling Realism and Relativism* (Oxford: Basil Blackwell, 1986), ch. 11; and *Texts without Referents: Reconciling Science and Narrative* (Oxford: Basil Blackwell, 1989), 3–38.

22. See, further, John Stachel, "Comments on 'Some Logical Problems Suggested by Emergent Theories' by Professor Dalla Chiara," in *Language, Logic, and Method*, ed. Robert S. Cohen and Marx Wartofsky (Dordrecht: D. Reidel, 1983), 92. The classic location of all modern notions of the a priori necessity of mathematics as affecting the conditions of knowledge but not dependent on any prior metaphysics appears in Kant: "Hitherto it has been assumed that all our knowledge must conform to objects. But all attempts to extend our knowledge of objects by establishing something in regard to them *a priori*, by means of concepts, have, on this assumption, ended in failure. We must therefore make trial whether we may not have more success in the tasks of metaphysics, if we suppose that objects must conform to our knowledge. This would agree better with what is desired, namely, that it should be possible to have knowledge of

objects *a priori*, determining something in regard to them prior to their being given." This appears in *Immanuel Kant's Critique of Pure Reason*, trans. corr. Norman Kemp Smith (London: Macmillan, 1953), Bxvi. In a fair sense, it is Kant's thesis that Stachel neatly subverts.

23. See, further, Margolis, *The Truth about Relativism*.

24. Michael Dummett, *The Logical Basis of Metaphysics* (Cambridge: Harvard University Press, 1991), 12; italics added.

25. Dummett, *The Logical Basis of Metaphysics*, 12.

26. Dummett, *The Logical Basis of Metaphysics*, 12.

27. Dummett, *The Logical Basis of Metaphysics*, 305; italics added. See, further, ch. 15.

28. See Michael Dummett, *Truth and Other Enigmas* (Cambridge: Harvard University Press, 1978), Preface.

29. Dummett, *The Logical Basis of Metaphysics*, 7–8.

30. Dummett, *The Logical Basis of Metaphysics*, 338–339.

31. See P. F. Strawson, "On Referring," *Mind* LIX (1950); and Bertrand Russell, "On Denoting," *Mind* IXV (1905).

32. Quine, *Word and Object*, 90f.

33. Quine, *Word and Object*, 179.

34. See Russell, "On Denoting." For an account of Russell's optimism about "knowledge by acquaintance," see D. F. Pears, *Bertrand Russell and the British Tradition in Philosophy* (London: Fontana, 1967), chs. 6, 7, 11.

35. See J. J. C. Smart, *Philosophy and Scientific Realism* (London: Routledge and Kegan Paul, 1963), ch. 3.

36. See P. F. Strawson, *Individuals: An Essay in Descriptive Metaphysics* (London: Methuen, 1959).

37. See, for instance, W. V. Quine, *The Roots of Reference* (La Salle, Ill.: Open Court, 1973), 81–84.

38. Jerrold J. Katz, *The Philosophy of Language* (New York: Harper and Row, 1966), 247–248; italics added. See, also, 269. See G. W. Leibniz, *New Essays Concerning Human Understanding*, ed. and trans. A. C. Langley (La Salle, Ill.: Open Court, 1949), cited by Katz.

39. Katz, *The Philosophy of Language*, 272f. See, also, Jerrold J. Katz, *The Underlying Reality of Language and Its Philosophical Import* (New York: Harper and Row, 1971).

40. Jerry A. Fodor, "On the Impossibility of Acquiring 'More Powerful' Structures," in *Language and Learning: The Debate between Jean Piaget and Noam Chomsky*, ed. Massimo Piatelli-Palmarini (Cambridge: Harvard University Press, 1980), 143–146.

41. Jerry A. Fodor, *Representations: Philosophical Essays on the Foundations of Cognitive Science* (Cambridge: MIT Press, 1981), 273–214. See, also, Jerry A. Fodor, *The Language of Thought* (New York: Thomas Y. Crowell, 1975), ch. 1.

42. Noam Chomsky, *Knowledge of Language: Its Nature, Origin, and Use* (New York: Praeger, 1986), 43; italics added. See, also, Noam Chomsky, *Rules and Representations* (New York: Columbia University Press, 1980).

43. See Chomsky, *Rules and Representations*, ch. 5, particularly 185.

44. See, for instance, N. Tinbergen, *The Study of Instinct* (New York: Oxford University Press, 1969).

45. Nelson Goodman, "Seven Strictures on Similarity," in *Experience & Theory*, ed. Lawrence Foster and J. W. Swanson (Amherst: University of Massachusetts Press, 1970), 29.

46. Eleanor Rosch, "Principles of Categorization," in *Cognition and Categorization*, ed. Eleanor Rosch and Barbara B. Lloyd (Hillsdale, N.J.: Lawrence Erlbaum Associates, 1978), 32.

47. Rosch, "Principles of Categorization," 30.

48. Rosch, "Principles of Categorization," 30.

49. Rosch, "Principles of Categorization," 28. See, also, Amos Tversky and Itamar Gatl, "Studies of Similarity," in *Cognition and Categorization*, ed E. Rosch and B. Lloyd.

50. It may be helpful to mention that Ronald Giere has recently begun to accommodate the general line of Rosch's approach to the analysis of concepts in a theory of the natural sciences billed as at once "cognitive," "realist," and "naturalistic." See Ronald N. Giere, *Explaining Science: A Cognitive Approach* (Chicago: University of Chicago Press, 1988). Giere's discussion of Rosch seems to be later than the work that led to this volume. It was noticeably salient in a paper Giere presented in a symposium in the philosophy of science, at the Greater Philadelphia Philosophy Consortium Conference: "Symmetry and Variance in the Sciences," 10 October 1992, at St. Joseph's University, Philadelphia. I cannot endorse the "naturalizing" of knowledge (*à la* Quine), though that is not to oppose the rigorous testing of cognitive claims. The issue also affects Rosch's account.

51. Dummett, *The Logical Basis of Metaphysics*, 73.

52. Charles Sanders Peirce, *Collected Papers of Charles Sanders Peirce*, ed. Charles Hartshorne and Paul Weiss (Cambridge: Harvard University Press, 1960), 5.402.

53. Peirce, *Collected Papers*, 5.314–316.

54. Peirce, *Collected Papers*, 5.289.

55. See Margolis, *Texts without Referents*, ch. 9. See, further, Pierre Bourdieu, *An Outline of a Theory of Practice*, trans. Richard Nice (Cambridge: Cambridge University Press, 1977).

56. See, further, Margolis, *Texts without Referents*, ch. 4.

57. See Gadamer, *Truth and Method, passim*.

CHAPTER 6

1. Hans-Georg Gadamer, *Truth and Method*, trans. from 2d ed. Garrett Barden and John Cumming (New York: Seabury Press, 1975), 245: "In fact history does not belong to us, but we belong to it." This is Gadamer's formula for subverting the "romantic" conception of historical understanding in Dilthey.

2. See Gadamer, *Truth and Method*, 5–10, 192–225. See John Stuart Mill, *Logic*, ed. J. M. Robson (Toronto: University of Toronto Press, 1973); and Rudolf A. Makkreel, *Dilthey: Philosopher of the Human Studies* (Princeton: Princeton University Press, 1973).

3. Adolf Grünbaum, *The Foundations of Psychoanalysis; A Philosophical Critique* (Berkeley, Los Angeles, London: University of California Press, 1984), 47.

4. See Grünbaum, *The Foundations of Psychoanalysis*, ch. 1.

5. See, for instance, Freud's much disputed "Scientific Project" ["Project for a Scientific Psychology"], in *Standard Edition of the Complete Psychological Works of Sigmund Freud*, vol. 1, trans J. Strachey et al. (London: The Hogarth Press and the Institute of Psycho-analysis, 1966); and Grünbaum, *The Foundations of Psychoanalysis*, 83–94.

6. Grünbaum, *The Foundations of Psychoanalysis*, 69–70. The best-known discussion of this general matter (reasons and causes) appears in Donald Davidson, "Reasons, Causes, and Actions," in *Essays on Actions and Events* (Oxford: Clarendon Press, 1980).

7. See Donald Davidson, "Causal Relations," in *Essays on Actions and Events*.

8. See Donald Davidson, "Mental Events," in *Essays on Actions and Events*.

9. Grünbaum, *The Foundations of Psychoanalysis*, 77–83, 89–90.

10. See, for instance, Davidson, "Mental Events."

11. See Paul Ricoeur, *Hermeneutics and the Human Sciences*, ed. and trans. J. B. Thompson (Cambridge: Cambridge University Press, 1981).

12. See Jerry A. Fodor, *The Language of Thought* (New York: Thomas Y. Crowell, 1975), ch. 1. It is odd that, having remarked on the widespread use of contingent "cross-category" predicates, Fodor should have remained so sanguine about the "rationalist" view of predication. The point applies as well, of course, to Rosch's taxonomic treatment of common predicates (discussed in the preceding chapter).

13. I have explored the question of interpretation in an as yet unpublished manuscript, *Reinterpreting Interpretation: The New Puzzle of the Arts and History* (forthcoming).

14. I have heard Feigl discuss the question but have been unable to find a written account of it. It clearly lies behind his well-known monograph. See Herbert Feigl, *The "Mental" and the "Physical": The Essay and a Postscript* (Minneapolis: University of Minnesota Press, 1967).

15. See, for instance, Fred I. Dretske, *Knowledge and the Flow of Information* (Chicago: University of Chicago Press, 1981).

16. This is also the valid point of Peter Winch's *The Idea of a Social Science* (London: Routledge and Kegan Paul, 1958), which was so unfairly ridiculed when it first appeared.

17. Gadamer, *Truth and Method*, 6.

18. Gadamer, *Truth and Method*, 5, 6.

19. See, for instance, Ricoeur, "What is a Text? Explanation and Understanding," in *Hermeneutics and the Human Sciences*; also, Wilhelm Dilthey, "The Development of Hermeneutics," in *Selected Writings*, ed. and trans. H. P. Rickman (Cambridge: Cambridge University Press, 1976).

20. For a sense of Dilthey's treatment of issues bearing on the second matter, see Makkreel, *Dilthey*.

21. Gadamer, *Truth and Method*, 267.

22. This is the central theme in Hans-Georg Gadamer, "On the Scope and Function of Hermeneutical Reflection," trans. G. B. Hess and R. E. Palmer, in *Philosophical Hermeneutics*, trans. and ed. David E. Linge (Berkeley: University of California Press, 1976).

23. Gadamer, "On the Scope and Function of Hermeneutical Reflection."

24. Leopold von Ranke, "The Role of the Particular and the General in the Study of Universal History," trans. Wilma A. Iggers, in *The Theory and Practice of History*, ed. Georg G. Iggers and Konrad von Moltke (New York: Irvington, 1983), 57.

25. Leopold von Ranke, "On the Character of Historical Science," trans. Wilma A. Iggers, in *The Theory and Practice of History*, 44. There is a very close convergence between Ranke and Humboldt here. See Wilhelm von Humboldt, "On the Historian's Task," published together with Ranke's essays, in *The Theory and Practice of History*.

26. Gadamer, *Truth and Method*, 266f.

27. See Grünbaum, *The Foundations of Psychoanalysis*, 83–94. (There are two brief mentions of Dilthey but no discussion of the hermeneutic issue.)

28. Martin Heidegger, *Being and Time*, trans. from 7th ed., John Macquarrie and Edward Robinson (New York: Harper and Row, 1962), 6 (p. 1 in the German pagination).

29. Heidegger, *Being and Time*, 486 (435–436 in the German pagination).

30. Heidegger, *Being and Time*, 269 (226 in the German pagination).

31. See, for instance, Heidegger, *Being and Time*, 43 (21–22 in the German pagination). Heidegger's running analysis of Hegel is given largely in §82.

32. Heidegger, *Being and Time*, 484–485 (433–434 in the German pagination).

33. See, for instance, G. W. F. Hegel, *Phenomenology of Spirit*, trans. A. V. Miller (Oxford: Oxford University Press, 1977), ch. VIII, §§804–805.

34. Alexandre Kojève, *Introduction to the Reading of Hegel: Lectures on the "Phenomenology of Spirit,"* assembled by Raymond Quesneau, ed. Allan Bloom, trans. James H. Nichols, Jr. (Ithaca: Cornell University Press, 1980), 101–103. See the whole of ch. 8; also, Hegel, *Phenomenology of Spirit*, §801 and §§46–97.

35. Grünbaum, *The Foundations of Psychoanalysis*, 17.

36. Grünbaum, *The Foundations of Psychoanalysis*, 17–18.

37. Thus, Grünbaum accuses Habermas of "trading on . . . stone age physics," in *The Foundations of Psychoanalysis*, 20. See, further, the whole of pp. 15–21; also, Jürgen Habermas, *Knowledge and Human Interests*, trans. J. J. Shapiro (Boston: Beacon, 1971).

38. Paul Horwich, *Asymmetries in Time: Problems in the Philosophy of Science* (Cambridge: MIT Press, 1987), 42.

39. Adolf Grünbaum, *Philosophical Problems of Space and Time*, 2d ed. enl. (Dordrecht: D. Reidel, 1973), 211; cited by Horwich.

40. Horwich, *Asymmetries of Time*, 45–47.

41. Grünbaum, *Philosophical Problems of Space and Time*, 646 in the context of ch. 19; also, 236–264. The reference to Jaynes is to E. T. Jaynes, "Gibbs vs. Boltzmann Entropies," *American Journal of Physics* XXXIII (1965). See,

also, Ilya Prigogine, "Irreversibility and Space-Time Structure," in *Physics and the Ultimate Significance of Time*, ed. David Ray Griffin (Albany: SUNY Press, 1986).

42. See Kurt Gödel, "A Remark about the Relationship between Relativity Theory and Idealistic Philosophy," in *Albert Einstein: Philosopher-Scientist*, ed. Paul Arthur Schilpp (La Salle, Ill.: Open Court, 1949); and Einstein's brief response in the same volume.

43. There is a splendid, fresh account of this enormous puzzle in Irwin C. Lieb, *Past, Present, and Future: A Philosophical Essay About Time* (Urbana: University of Illinois Press, 1991), particularly ch. 4.

44. See Arthur C. Danto, *Narration and Knowledge* (New York: Columbia University Press, 1985).

45. See, for instance, Davidson, "Mental Events."

46. For a pertinent overview, see Joseph Margolis, *Texts without Referents: Reconciling Science and Narrative* (Oxford: Basil Blackwell, 1989), ch. 6.

47. For a discussion of Danto's theory of history, see Joseph Margolis, *Reinterpreting Interpretation*, forthcoming.

48. This is illuminatingly developed in Lieb, *Past, Present, and Future.*

49. See Thomas S. Kuhn, *The Structures of Scientific Revolutions*, 2d ed. enlarged (Chicago: University of Chicago Press, 1970).

50. I owe an appreciation of this extraordinary truth to a reading of Lieb's *Past, Present, and Future.*

CHAPTER 7

1. Hans-Georg Gadamer, *Truth and Method*, trans. from 2d ed. Garrett Barden and John Cumming (New York: Seabury Press, 1975), 274.

2. Gadamer, *Truth and Method*, 267–274.

3. Gadamer, *Truth and Method*, 268.

4. See Hans-Georg Gadamer, "The Universality of the Hermeneutical Problem," in *Philosophical Hermeneutics*, trans. G. B. Hess and R. E. Palmer (Berkeley, Los Angeles, London: University of California Press, 1976), 7.

5. Gadamer, *Truth and Method*, 271.

6. Gadamer, *Truth and Method*, 256; see, further, the whole of 253–258.

7. See for instance, Gadamer, *Truth and Method*, 259.

8. See, for a hint of the problem, Michel Foucault, *The Order of Things: An Archaeology of the Human Sciences*, in translation (New York: Random House, 1970), ch. 10; Jürgen Habermas, "Reconstruction and Interpretation in the Social Sciences" and "Moral Consciousness and Communicative Action," in *Moral Consciousness and Communcative Action*, trans. Christian Lenhardt and Shierry Weber Nicholsen (Cambridge: MIT Press, 1990); and Hans Kellner, *Language and Historical Representation: Getting the Story Crooked* (Wisconsin: University of Wisconsin Press, 1989), ch. 2.

9. See, for instance, Hans-Georg Gadamer, *The Idea of the Good in Platonic-Aristotelian Philosophy*, trans. P. Christopher Smith (New Haven: Yale University Press, 1986), ch. 6. Furthermore, in clarifying Aristotle's debt to Plato, notably anchored in the text of the *Republic*, Gadamer specifically remarks:

"This 'one' [the idea of the good] is certainly not Plotinus's 'One,' the sole existent and 'trans-existent' entity. Rather, it is that which on any given occasion provides what is multiple with the unity of whatever consists in itself. As the unity of what is unitary, the idea of the good would seem to be presupposed by anything ordered, enduring, and consistent. That means, however, that it is presupposed as the unity of the many. . . . for the Greeks 'one' was not an arithmos, that is, not a sum, not a unity of many. Rather, it was the constitutive element of the numbers" (32–33). It certainly seems reasonable to construe this reading as informing Gadamer's own account of the classical. That he undoubtedly means to avoid anything like the Forms merely confirms the problematic standing of his appeal to the classical.

The appeal to this and similar texts is here intended only dialectically. See, for example, the deliberately unguarded use of expressions like "common spirit" (of humanity) in articles like "Are the Poets Falling Silent?" (1970), in *Hans-Georg Gadamer on Education, Poetry, and History: Applied Hermeneutics*, ed. Dieter Misgeld and Graeme Nicholson, trans. Lawrence Schmidt and Monica Reuss (Albany: SUNY Press, 1992). Reflecting on a poem by Paul Celan, Gadamer says, in answer to the implied question, "The I of the poet?": "In a composition belonging to the lyric genre, it would not be the I of a poet, if it were not to become the I of everyone" (p. 75). How strenuously Gadamer intends his remark is difficult to say, but it lends support to the "traditionalist" theme.

10. See Gadamer, *Truth and Method*, 10–39, particularly 13.

11. Foucault, *The Order of Things*, 344–348.

12. See, particularly, Robert Sokolowski, *Husserlian Meditations: How Words Present Things* (Evanston: Northwestern University Press, 1974), 170–171.

13. See Karl Marx, "On the Jewish Question," in *Karl Marx: Early Writings*, trans. and ed. Tom Bottomore (New York: McGraw-Hill, 1964); also "Marginal Notes on the Program of the German Workers' Party," *Critique of the Gotha Program*, in Karl Marx and Frederick Engels, *Selected Works*, 2 vols, (London: Lawrence and Wishart, 1950); and Joseph Margolis, "*Praxis* and Meaning: Marx's 'Species-Being' and Aristotle's 'Political Animal'," in *Marx and Greek Philosophy*, ed. George McCarthy (Totowa, N.J.: Rowman and Littlefield, 1991).

14. On bivalence and related options, see Joseph Margolis, *The Truth about Relativism* (Oxford: Basil Blackwell, 1991).

15. Compare Friedrich Nietzsche, *The Gay Science*, trans. Walter Kaufmann (New York: Random House, 1974), §374. I owe the reference to my colleague Tom Rockmore. See, also, Nietzsche's provocative remark, "an excess of history is harmful to the living man," in "On the Uses and Disadvantages of History for Life," in *Untimely Meditations*, trans. R. J. Hollingdale (Cambridge: Cambridge University Press, 1983), 67.

16. Thomas S. Kuhn, *The Structure of Scientific Revolutions*, 2d ed. enl. (Chicago: University of Chicago Press, 1970), 111.

17. Kuhn, *The Structure of Scientific Revolutions*, 118.

18. See, for instance, Ian Hacking, *Representing and Intervening; Introductory Topics in the Philosophy of Natural Science* (Cambridge: Cambridge University Press, 1983).

19. See Kuhn, *The Structure of Scientific Revolution*, ch. 13.

20. For a convenient summary of the entire issue as it bears on the metaphysics of human culture, see Joseph Margolis, *Texts without Referents: Reconciling Science and Narrative* (Oxford: Basil Blackwell, 1989), ch. 6. This may also serve to elucidate the distinction of the cultural world.

21. For a specimen view of this sort, see John F. Post, *The Faces of Existence: An Essay in Nonreductive Metaphysics* (Ithaca: Cornell University Press, 1987).

22. On the meaning of "emergent," see Joseph Margolis, *Science without Unity: Reconciling the Human and Natural Sciences* (Oxford: Basil Blackwell, 1987), ch. 10.

23. D. C. Dennett, *Content and Consciousness* (London: Routledge and Kegan Paul, 1969), 28–29.

24. Dennett, *Content and Consciousness*, 189–190. These are in fact the closing pages of the book. Dennett has never "recanted." See Daniel C. Dennett, *The Intentional Stance* (Cambridge: MIT Press, 1987); and *Consciousness Explained* (Boston: Little, Brown, 1991). For a fuller sense of various other forms of impoverished views of persons in the analytic literature, see P. F. Strawson, *Individuals: An Essay in Descriptive Metaphysics* (London: Methuen, 1959); Bernard Williams, *Problems of the Self* (Cambridge: Cambridge University Press, 1973); Derek Parfit, *Reasons and Persons* (Oxford: Clarendon, 1984).

25. I first introduced the distinction between the *real!* and the *reall* in *Texts without Referents*, ch. 8.

26. See Ludwig Wittgenstein, *Philosophical Investigations*, trans. G. E. M. Anscombe (New York: Macmillan, 1954), pt. I, §§240–241, for instance. See, also, Pierre Bourdieu, *Outline of a Theory of Practice*, trans. Richard Nice (Cambridge: Cambridge University Press, 1977).

27. This, of course, is a way of coopting Strawton's *Individuals*.

28. See W. V. Quine, "Naturalizing Epistemology," in *Ontological Relativity and Other Essays* (New York: Columbia University Press, 1969); Alvin I. Goldman, *Epistemology and Cognition* (Cambridge: Harvard University Press, 1986), particularly Introduction. It is a non sequitur, it should be noted, to suppose that the avoidance of an a priori epistemology entails "naturalizing" epistemology or strengthens the sense in which epistemology is "autonomous" or "prior" to the special sciences. This is actually Goldman's view, but it is nowhere defended.

29. Michael Dummett, *The Logical Basis of Metaphysics* (Cambridge: Harvard University Press, 1991), 305; italics added (apart, of course, from the use of the variable "n").

30. Dummett, *The Logical Basis of Metaphysics*, 305; see, also, 12–13.

31. See W. V. Quine, *Word and Object* (Cambridge: MIT Press, 1960).

32. See Margolis, *The Truth about Relativism*.

33. See Charles Sanders Peirce, *Collected Papers of Charles Sanders Peirce*, ed. Charles Hartshorne and Paul Weiss (Cambridge: Harvard University Press, 1960), 5.505.

34. Peirce, *Collected Papers*, 5.289, 5448nl.

35. Gadamer, *Truth and Method*, 261.

36. Gadamer, *Truth and Method*, 273; italics added.

37. Gadamer, *Truth and Method*, 273.

38. The most compelling recent discussion of the conceptual difficulties involved in denying the reality of the past appears in Irwin C. Lieb, *Past, Present and Future: A Philosophical Essay About Time* (Urbana: University of Illinois Press, 1991).

39. See Paul Ricoeur, *The Rule of Metaphor: Multi-disciplinary Studies of the Creation of Meaning in Language*, trans. Robert Czerny, with Kathleen McLaughlin and John Costello, S.J. (Toronto: University of Toronto Press, 1981), study 8. It is also true that Ricoeur sees a very strong connection between history and literature (even fiction)—in particular, an imaginative and paideutic function—which leads him to treat narrative structure as falling within a twilight zone between the real and the fictional. See, for instance, *Time and Narrative*, vol. 3, trans. Kathleen Blamey and David Pellauer (Chicago: University of Chicago Press, 1988), Conclusions, particularly 261–274.

40. See Hayden White, *Tropics of Discourse: Essays in Cultural Criticism* (Baltimore: John Hopkins University Press, 1978).

41. See Aristotle, *Poetics*; and Ricoeur, *The Rule of Metaphor*, study 8.

42. Ricoeur, *Time and Narrative*, 3: 192.

43. Ricoeur, *Time and Narrative*, 3: 81–82.

44. Ricoeur, *Time and Narrative*, 3: 191.

45. Hayden White, *The Content of the Form: Narrative Discourse and Historical Representation* (Baltimore: Johns Hopkins University Press, 1987), ch. 7, particularly 177.

46. See White, *The Content of the Form*, 147; also, 180–182.

47. White, *The Content of the Form*, 178.

48. White, *The Content of the Form*, 46–47.

49. White, *The Content of the Form*, 45; italics added. White relies here on Louis O. Mink, "Narrative Forms as a Cognitive Instrument," in *The Writing of History: Literary Form and Historical Understanding*, ed. Robert H. Canary and Henry Kozicki (Madison: University of Wisconsin Press, 1978). He claims the same thesis appears in Marx's account of the 18th Brumaire (47). Our realist emphasis converges in a general way (but not more) with that in William Dray, "Narrative and Historical Realism," in *On History and Philosophers of History* (Leiden: E. J. Brill, 1989). Dray terms both Mink and White "antirealists" or "skeptics" about historical narrative. He himself insists on the objectivity of recovering the historical past; but, apart from a very strong opposition to Hempel's model, an insistence on the autonomy of history as a cognitive discipline, and a certain (quite limited) tolerance for a "perspectivism" or objective relativism of perspectives (which he draws from a suggestion made by Ernest Nagel), Dray has rather little to say about the metaphysics of history. See, further, "Point of View in History," also in *On History and Philosophers of History*; and Ernest Nagel, "The Logic of Historical Analysis," in Hans Mayerhoff, *The Philosophy of History in Our Time* (Garden City: Doubleday, 1969). On the quarrel about the compatibility of views of the historical past as both "constructed" and "real" (*real!*) and its bearing on uniquely correct or alternative ("incongruent") interpretations of the past, see also Leon J. Goldstein, *Historical Knowing* (Austin: University of Texas Press, 1976); and Michael Krausz, "Ide-

ality and Ontology in the Practice of History," in *Objectivity, Method and Point of View*, ed. W. J. van der Dussen and Lionel Rubinoff (Leiden: E. J. Brill, 1991).

In a curious way, the theme developed in Ricoeur and White is very close, structurally, to the dampened "theological" theme of Walter Benjamin's intriguing notion of "now-times" (*Jetztzeiten*). Benjamin's notion similarly bifurcates time and the historical meaning of temporal events. See Walter Benjamin, "Theses on the Philosophy of History," in *Illuminations*, trans. Harry Zohn (New York: Schocken, 1969). Benjamin's essay, unlike Ricoeur's and White's accounts, however, treats history "existentially." In this sense it is related to a literature that includes Nietzsche's "On the Uses and Disadvantages of History for Life," Kierkegaard's *Repetition*, and Heidegger's *Being and Time*. For a perspicuous reading of Kierkegaard and Heidegger along these lines, see Joan Stambaugh, "Existential Time in Kierkegaard and Heidegger," in *Religion and Time*, ed. Anindita Niyogi Balslev and J. N. Mohanty (Leiden: E. J. Brill, 1993). There is a strong analogy between Benjamin's "*Jetztzeit*" and Heidegger's "*Augenblick*" and between Heidegger's term and Kierkegaard's Danish cognate.

50. Lieb, *Past, Present, and Future*, 134.

EPILOGUE

1. Hilary Putnam, "Beyond Historicism," in *Philosophical Papers*, vol. 3 (Cambridge: Cambridge University Press, 1983), 287.

2. Putnam, "Beyond Historicism," 287–288.

3. For a sustained discussion of the matter, see Joseph Margolis, *The Truth about Relativism* (Oxford: Basil Blackwell, 1991).

4. Putnam, "Beyond Historicism," 290.

5. W. V. Quine, "Naturalizing Epistemology," in *Ontological Relativity and Other Essays* (New York: Columbia University Press, 1969).

6. See, further, Joseph Margolis. "The Novelty of Marx's Theory of Praxis," *Journal of the Theory of Social Behavior* XIX (1989).

7. See Peter Winch, *The Idea of a Social Science* (London: Routledge and Kegan Paul, 1958).

8. Michel Foucault, "Two Lectures" (Lecture 2: 14 January 1976), in *Power/Knowledge: Selected Interviews and Other Writings 1972–1977*, ed. Colin Gordon, trans. Colin Gordon, Leo Marshall, John Mepham, Kate Soper (New York: Pantheon Books, 1980), 93.

9. See Joseph Margolis, *Pragmatism without Foundations: Reconciling Realism and Relativism* (Oxford: Basil Blackwell, 1986), ch. 2. I may say that I have had occasion to confront Habermas on the issue. Habermas had delivered a talk at the Greater Philadelphia Philosophy Consortium, at Bryn Mawr College (1982–1983), and had used the expression "all possible worlds" in developing his thesis. I suggested later that, as a philosopher committed to the thesis of praxis in a spirit akin to Marx's and the Frankfurt Critical position, he was not "entitled" to generalizations of that sort. After a bit, he said that he did not know much about formal semantics and had not meant the expression in a technical way. I replied that the example merely served as an instance of the general *aporia*

of his undertaking—the reconciliation of universalism and historicism. His only response at that time—nearly ten years ago—was: "Perhaps we could discuss this in Germany sometime." I confess I have not heard from Habermas further.

10. Jürgen Habermas, "Some Questions Concerning the Theory of Power: Foucault Again," in *The Philosophical Discourse of Modernity: Twelve Lectures*, trans. Frederick Lawrence (Cambridge: MIT Press, 1987), 274.

11. See Jürgen Habermas, "What is Universal Pragmatics?" in *Communication and the Evolution of Society*, trans. Thomas McCarthy (Boston: Beacon, 1979).

12. Foucault, "Truth and Power," in *Power/Knowledge*, 117.

13. See Karl-Otto Apel, *Towards a Transformation of Philosophy*, trans. Glyn Adey and David Frisby (London: Routledge and Kegan Paul, 1980), ch. 7. I note that Rudolf A. Makkreel has made a valient attempt to reconcile Kant's philosophy (through the Third Critique) and hermeneutics. But, as he himself says: "Although Kant does not thematize the problem of history in the *Critique of Judgement*, his discussion there of teleology and culture provides a basis for a reflective interpretation of history. If aesthetic ideas point to the possibility that nature may be in harmony with morality, teleological ideas in reflective interpretation provide the means for conceptualizing how nature and morality can be reconciled in human history"; in *Imagination and Interpretation in Kant: The Hermeneutical Import of the Critique of Judgment* (Chicago: University of Chicago Press, 1990), 131. See, in this connection, Makkreel's brief linking of Kant to Hegel and Dilthey, 12, n. 5. The matter may be construed, also obliquely, in terms of the dispute between Gadamer and Habermas.

14. Habermas, "Questions concerning the Theory of Power: Foucault Again," 276.

15. Habermas, "The Undermining of Western Rationalism through the Critique of Metaphysics: Martin Heidegger," in *The Philosophical Discourse of Modernity*, 154. Habermas relies here on Tugendhat; see Ernst Tugendhat, "Heideggers Idee von Wahrheit," in *Heidegger; Perspektiven zur Deutung seines Werks*, ed. Otto Pöggeler (Cologne: Kiepenheuer and Witsch, 1969).

16. See, also, Habermas, "The Entwinement of Myth and Enlightenment: Max Horkheimer and Theodor Adorno," in *The Philosophical Discourse of Modernity*.

17. Michel Foucault, "Nietzsche, Genealogy, History," in *Language, Counter-memory, Practice: Selected Essays and Interviews*, ed. Donald F. Bouchard, trans. Donald F. Bouchard and Sherry Simon (Ithaca: Cornell University Press, 1977), 140.

18. Michel Foucault, *The Order of Things: An Archaeology of the Human Sciences*, in translation (New York: Random House, 1979), 318–319; see the whole of ch. 9.

19. Foucault, *The Order of Things*, 308.

20. Foucault, *The Order of Things*, 144.

21. Michel Foucault, "What Is Enlightenment?" trans. Catherine Porter, in *The Foucault Reader*, ed. Paul Rabinow (New York: Pantheon, 1984), 32.

22. Jürgen Habermas, "Modernity's Consciousness of Time and Its Need for Self-Reassurance," in *The Philosophical Discourse of Modernity*, 8; cited from Charles Baudelaire's "The Painter of Modern Life."

23. Foucault, "What Is Enlightenment?" 40.

24. A penetrating analysis of the differences between Foucault and Habermas is forthcoming in the papers Michael Kelly has contributed to his own collection. See Michael Kelly, "A Critique of Habermas's Interpretation of Foucault," in *Power and Critique: Recasting the Foucault-Habermas Debate*, ed. Michael Kelly forthcoming.

25. Foucault, "What Is Enlightenment?" 38.

26. Foucault, "What Is Enlightenment?" 46.

27. Foucault, "What Is Enlightenment?" 36.

28. Foucault, "What Is Enlightenment?" 46.

29. Foucault, "What Is Enlightenment?" 45, 47.

30. Look, once again, at the elegantly simple suggestion in John Stachel, "Comments on 'Some Logical Problems Suggested by Emergent Theories' by Professor Dalla Chiara," in *Language, Logic, and Method*, ed. Robert S. Cohen and Marx Wartofsky (Dordrecht: D. Reidel, 1983), 92.

Index

235